A Walden Two Experiment

A Walden Two Experiment

The First Five Years of Twin Oaks Community

Kathleen Kinkade

Foreword by B. F. Skinner

William Morrow & Company, Inc.
New York   1973

335.9
KSSw
1973

Kinkade, Kathleen.
    A Walden Two experiment.

    1. Twin Oaks Community. I. Title.
HX656.T9K5   335′.9   72-8090
ISBN 0-688-00020-7
ISBN 0-688-05020-4 (pbk)

Foreword

by B. F. Skinner

What should a person do when he does not like his way of life? The Utopian answer is clear: Build a better one. But of course it is easier said than done. Even the great Utopists showed a certain lack of confidence when they placed their better worlds in faraway places or distant times in order to make them seem plausible. Someday, somewhere, there will be a better life, but probably not here and now. And to most people the word "Utopian" still means impossible.

New ways of life have nevertheless been explicitly designed and built. The blueprints of workable religious communities are to be found, for example, in the Rule of Augustine and the Rule of Benedict. The *vita monastica* was not so much a better way of life here on earth as a step toward that greatest of all Utopias, the Christian heaven. But in the sixteenth and seventeenth centuries glowing reports of life in the South Seas suggested the possibility of heaven on earth, and a century or two of idyllic Utopian speculation led to many practical tests. Étienne Cabet's *Voyage en Icarie,* in the idyllic vein, seemed so promising that Cabet and a group of followers left France in the 1850's to build Icaria—not in the Mediterranean or the South Seas but on the Red River in Texas. Cabet died on the way but his followers set up several Icarias in the Midwest. They attracted no particular attention because many similar communities were being founded in the United States at that time.

Conditions were unusually favorable for such ventures in the nineteenth century. The successful design of the United States as a nation had lent support to the perfectionistic enterprises of the Enlightenment, and in that vast fertile land which lay to the west groups of people could be left alone to do as they pleased. A new life did not need to be luxurious, because most Americans were accustomed to what we should today regard as a rather spartan standard of living. Moreover, members of most of those communities brought with them well-established ethical and religious practices, which solved some of the problems of government. Many of the communities of the nineteenth century were in fact religious, either as offshoots of various Protestant sects like the Rappites or Hutterites or as newly founded sects like the Shakers or Mormons. Secular communities, such as Robert Owen's New Harmony, tended to be, perhaps significantly, shorter-lived.

Contrary to popular belief, most nineteenth-century communities were economically successful. If Utopia continued to mean impossible, it was because there were other problems to be solved. The important ones concerned personal relations—relations among the members of a community or with its neighbors. The Oneida community in central New York State was an imaginative social experiment, but its sexual practices, designed to further a well-planned eugenics program, could not be tolerated by the surrounding countryside. As John Humphrey Noyes, the founder of Oneida, pointed out, the sense of possession associated with sex is in conflict with the very idea of communal ownership, and it caused trouble for most of the nineteenth-century experiments.

It is not only in experimental communities that relations among people are troublesome. No matter where people live, a great deal depends on whether or not they live together peacefully, happily, and productively. A failure to do so is often obscured by apparent successes in other fields. The American way of life in the last third of the twentieth century does not seem so very bad. No one need starve or go without shelter or clothing, and education is, up to a point, free. Reasonable medical services are available, and an inexpensive device, a television set, provides almost continuous entertainment. Social security takes care of old age, and with a little extra effort all of these amenities can be greatly improved. Why, then, should anyone try to build a better way of life today?

The answer is that we have achieved all this at a terrible cost in personal relations. And we are beginning to see why. We have chosen the wrong behavioral processes in the design of cultural practices. Young people today sum it up in their slogan, "Make love, not war!" but they are easily misunderstood. Love and war are extreme forms of personal intercourse, and the slogan tends to conceal the basic issue: our present culture is in trouble because of its prodigious use of punitive control. Our international stance sets the pattern: when a nation displeases us, we bomb it, and we refuse to relinquish the power to do so in order to move toward an effective world government. Order in the streets is now treated almost entirely as a matter of police power. Children are still severely beaten in some of our public schools. Economic incentives seem at first glance to use rewards rather than punishments, but a worker does not come to work on Monday morning because he receives a week's pay on Friday afternoon; he comes because he will be discharged and cut off from that pay if he does not.

Certain characteristics of the genetic endowment of the human species explain why we so readily turn to punitive control and why it has taken us so long to see the potential of positive reinforcement and to design more effective social structures with its help. But we are beginning to learn. *Walden Two* was not by any means the first Utopia to minimize punitive control, but it was, I believe, the first to offer substantial scientific evidence of the feasibility of alternative methods. It was not only a plea for love against war, it offered concrete suggestions about how a way of life might be made to work without punishment.

In a chapter near the end of *Walden Two*—a chapter which has puzzled many readers—Frazier, the protagonist, plays God. He and the narrator, Burris, are sitting on a ledge of rock far above the community, and Frazier has taken out a small telescope and is surveying his handiwork. Burris goads him into comparing himself with God.

> "There's another point of similarity," [Frazier] said at last when he saw that I was not going to speak. "I don't know whether you'll understand this, Burris. I expect you'll laugh. But try to forget your professional cynicism."
>
> He dropped the telescope and hesitated for a moment. Then he flung his hand loosely in a sweeping gesture which embraced all of Walden Two.
>
> "These are my children, Burris," he said, almost in a whisper. "I love them."
>
> He got to his feet and started back along the ledge. I followed carefully. He turned into the underbrush and waited for me to catch up. He was embarrassed and rather confused.
>
> "What is love," he said, with a shrug, "except another name for the use of positive reinforcement?"
>
> "Or vice versa," I said.

When I wrote *Walden Two* (in 1945), only seven years— and war years at that—had passed since I had published the *Behavior of Organisms*, in which I reported research on the principles used in the design of the community. Nothing had actually been done to put those principles to a practical test, and I was obviously guessing. I had no way of knowing what a ten-year-old experimental community founded on those principles would be like. But I should not have to guess today. We have learned a great deal in the intervening years, and what has come to be called behavior modification is now widely practiced in many different kinds of "communities"—homes for retardates, schools for juvenile delinquents, hospitals for psychotics, classrooms in public schools, and so on. The members of these communities are not representative of the population at large, but what has been done could be regarded as a kind of flank attack on the design of an intentional community suitable for everyone.

Whether or not the kind of life I described in *Walden Two* was feasible and worthwhile nevertheless remained to be shown, and this book is the story of a practical test. Kat Kinkade and her associates founded Twin Oaks, in Louisa, Virginia, in 1967 on the model of Walden Two. What happened to them is told here with delightful and disarming candor. Many mistakes were made, but it was possible to correct them in time. Disagreements were often vigorous if not violent. Money was always in short supply, and many of the amenities of life had to be neglected. People with children came and went, and the community remained childless.

There were many other problems to be faced, often disheartening but some of them in retrospect amusing. What do you do when, having gone back to the land to raise your own food, you discover that the farmers in the neighborhood are buying dressed chickens at the supermarket? You agree that all labor shall be voluntary, but what do you do when people join the community who voluntarily do nothing? You want the goodwill and understanding of your neighbors, but does that mean that your menfolk should cut off their long hair and that you must give up nude bathing in the river? You have left the crowded city behind, but what do you do about the streams of visitors who begin to pour in? You believe that government is best when it governs least, but decisions must be made, and who is to make them, and why should they be accepted? What do you do when you decide to practice open criticism and nobody comes to the meetings? You know that people are more relaxed and friendly when they are not in competition, but what about sports and games?

These are some of the questions that arose, and were for the most part answered, during the first five years of the Twin Oaks experiment. Is the result a Walden Two? Not yet, says Kat, and she is right. Is it a Walden Two experiment? Certainly it is not much like the experiment described in the book. The life portrayed in *Walden Two* was the goal of Twin Oaks, but it was not approached through the application of scientific principles. Kat and her friends simply muddled through. But the important point is that they got through. And if Twin Oaks is now on its way to something close to Walden Two—and I think it is—it is because certain principles have stood the test. There is much more in an experimental analysis of behavior that is useful, and I shall be surprised if it is not eventually used. One great source of wisdom is now about to be tapped: Twin Oaks is ready to raise children. If the lives of those children are properly managed, lessons will be learned of extraordinary value to the community and to us all.

It is easy to dismiss the problems faced by the founders of Twin Oaks as of local interest only, but we are all trying to solve problems like them all the time. We are all engaged in the design of cultural practices. Twin Oaks is simply the world in miniature. The problems it faces and the solutions it tries are those of a world community. While Kat and her friends seek solutions to their problems, the rest of the world must do something about *its* food supplies, *its* educational systems, *its* sanitation and health, *its* "interpersonal" relations, *its* cultural activities, and *its* Olympic games.

Non-competitive volleyball, anyone?

Contents

xii

Contents

A Walden Two Experiment

I

Why Would Anyone Want to Live in a Commune?

The biggest single misconception in the public mind about communes is that they are an escape from reality.

"Oh, yes," sighs a businessman, "I would like to forget the whole thing and just go join a commune. But unfortunately I have things to do in the real world."

"I don't see how you can justify escaping to this idyllic farm life, when there is so much work to be done," says a socially conscious visitor.

"I'm just like you," drawls an inebriated local youth who has dropped by to check us out. "All I really want is a motor-cycle and my freedom."

We answer patiently that, far from running away from life or our social responsibilities, we are trying to make a new and better society, that farm life isn't idyllic, that we had to prohibit motorcycles because they are too dangerous for general use, and that this world is as real as they come. But people don't believe us. They aren't even listening. It is more fun to categorize us as a kind of dream world and admire or reject us accordingly. The importance of the commune to the average intellectual or student is that it gives substance to his fantasies. If he dreams of rural living, of throwing off responsibility, or even of freedom and a motorcycle, he conveniently believes that communes have achieved these aims.

That fact, more than any other, accounts for the instability of the average commune. Dreamers drift into them and out again when they find their dreams unfulfilled. It is the people who want to escape who are unable to deal with the realities of commune living. For there is no escape in a commune! Responsibility is a fact of human society. Communes face it in a grimmer form than ordinary citizens do, in that they accept even the responsibility for holding their very society together against odds.

Escapist fantasies are bad for communities, but dreams are fundamental to their existence. To be successful at community living, you have to keep adjusting your dreams to reality without ever quite giving them up.

The communal idea is big enough to stimulate a lot of different dreams. Some are noble visions of a brighter future for mankind; some deal with the inner reaches of the soul; many people seek a place to work out experiments in fundamental cultural change, particularly in traditional sex and family roles. But commonest of all is the personal dream, the dream of no longer being lonely. Whatever else brings people to community, the hope of a compatible mate or a close, warm group of friends is usually just underneath the surface, and the success or failure of a person to be content with community often depends on his success or failure in finding love.

This rough division into different kinds of idealism provides a working key to the kinds of communes now being tried. There are the political communes (usually in cities) whose focus is on political work in the neighborhood and whose communal pattern may not be seen by its members as permanent or important but simply as an economic convenience and a congenial atmosphere. There are the communities in the classic utopian tradition, self-consciously working out structures that they believe will someday be patterns for larger society. There are the religious groups, drawn together by a strong leader or teacher, interested primarily in the state of their souls or consciousness—and in this category I include the mystical groups with their Eastern rituals, disciplines, and sometimes drugs. There are the groups that get together simply because they are seeking a close-knit "family" that they believe will make them comfortable. These latter generally do not think of themselves as a pattern for society but simply as dropouts from an America of which they do not approve, trying to keep morally clean hands by getting back to the land, growing their own food, and minding their own business. And of course there are groups that combine these aims in different ways.

There are vast areas of experience and feeling in common among all types of communes, and we have noticed that, in spite of philosophical differences, communes are sympathetic to each other and will lend each other a hand when they can. But actually we know little about each other. That's why this isn't a book on "communes" but a book about Twin Oaks. True, there are hundreds of groups, but no honest person can write anything significant about more than one of them. I can write about Twin Oaks because I was one of the people who founded it in 1967 and because I have lived here for all of its five years and expect to be here for the rest of my life.

Our group is of the classic utopian type, thinking always in terms of what society ought to be like and trying to approximate it within the limits of our resources. Our dreams are far-reaching, but our means are small. As we farm our hundred acres and get along on $1,200 a year per capita gross income, we do not miss the humor of the contrast between our goals and our accomplishments. Commenting on our low standard of living, a college girl who visited us once said, "I don't see that you've proved anything except that a bunch of dropouts can run a farm." Maybe not. But it isn't only what we have proved that makes our life worth living. It's also what we mean to prove. Once beyond the simple level of sufficient food, shelter, and a friend or two, dreams are much more important than reality. Man really does not live by bread alone.

Our Community was founded in the summer of 1967 by a group of eight people. We came from the States of Michigan, Wisconsin, California, New York, and Georgia. Most of us did not know each other before we started the group, but we had been in correspondence with each other about our ideas and plans. I was the oldest of the group, thirty-six; my thirteen-year-old daughter, Jenny,* was the youngest. The others were in their twenties. Brian and Carrie had been married only a few months.

Hal, a community enthusiast who had not yet joined the group, had given us a free, six-year lease on a farm. We settled on the land in the middle of June, but we had already managed to plant a garden on the premises and put in a tobacco crop. Also, the former owner had put in his usual hay before he sold to Hal. So we moved onto an operating farm.

The buildings on the premises when we took possession were one small farmhouse, several medium-sized barns, and some outbuildings (smokehouse, woodshed, chicken coop). We put up a large building to serve both as living quarters and as workshop, and were living in it when the coldest part of the winter arrived.

Five years have passed. Our population has risen from eight to forty. We have built two large dormitory buildings, a root cellar, and a walk-in freezer. We produce and process our own vegetables, meat, and milk, and do all our own mechanical work. All the work is divided equally among the membership, and everyone does work of his own choosing as far as is reasonably possible. We live either singly or

---

* Names have been changed for this book.

two to a room, and we all eat our meals communally in the Community dining rooms in the original farmhouse.

When we first came here we knew nothing of farming or any other way of making a living, other than working for wages in the city. Some of us had never even done that. What we did know was what kind of a world we wanted to live in.

Of the eight people who started this Community, only two are still here. But the central idea of the Community has not changed. We are still after the big dream—a better world, here and now, for as many people as we can manage to support. More, a new kind of human to live in that world: happy, productive, open-minded people who understand that in the long run, human good is a cooperative and not a competitive sort of thing. One man's gain must not, if we are to survive, be another man's loss.

Where do such dream-driven people come from? Who peoples the utopian community?

A large part of our group were dropouts from universities and colleges. Brian was a student at a large Southern university. He marched in civil rights protests and was rebuked by his parents and the school administration for taking part. He continued to march and to identify with the disadvantaged, but after a while he lost faith in the efficacy of demonstrations. He looked around for groups to which he could in good faith devote his energies, but found all existing political groups lacking in what he called "post-revolutionary thinking." Everybody knew that the "system" was wrong, but even the most serious groups seemed to give little attention to the kinds of structure that would replace it to advantage.

Brian had some ideas along these lines. He had read socialist literature, including the utopian novels that report visions of small communities living in peace and harmony. He began to be fascinated with the idea of experimenting with social beliefs in a small, malleable group. He wrote:

The major question to which most organizations for social
change have no answer is this: How do you set up a society
that guarantees these basic things we all talk about being
in favor of? What is an economic system that insures
equitable distribution without mass inefficiency? What
system of government has checks against power and cor-
ruption but still doesn't sacrifice decision-making by competent people? These are the sort of questions a small
community would have to consider every day, and the
answers would have to be practical. No time would be
lost in long-winded theoretical papers which present un-
testable propositions. Proposals would be put to the test
immediately. No time would be lost waiting for those in
power in the United States to be convinced that an experiment is worth making.

This kind of thinking was and is far from the mainstream
of radical action, and Brian found it necessary to start his
own group in order to realize his dream. He started a mimeo-
graphed newspaper and began to get in touch with other
people who might be interested in the experimental-society
approach to social change.

Dwight, like Brian, joined the Community almost purely
for idealistic reasons. He was a talented graduate student
studying philosophy at a large Midwestern university. Philosophy really interested him, but as the United States got
more and more deeply involved in the Vietnam war, Dwight
began to feel that he would have to set philosophy aside
and devote his energies to doing something positive about
the world. By thought processes similar to Brian's, and from
reading some of the same books, he concluded that the Good
Society ought to be set up in miniature, and then, as its
appeal became obvious to people, it would simply grow.
Unlike Brian, he never thought of the community as being
experimental. "It is asinine," he would say, "to say that we
ought to experiment to find out what makes people happy.
We already know that people can be happy under almost
any conditions. But that doesn't make those conditions right.

What we want to set up is a model community based on the best social theory we have, stick to the plan, and solicit membership on that basis." Dwight's dogmatism made trouble later on, mostly because he would imply in public that anyone who didn't agree with the central theoretical thrust of the Community hadn't been invited to join and wasn't welcome. But in the beginning his habit of being sure of the right answers was a help. For he chose as his social theory the ideas expresed in B. F. Skinner's *Walden Two*. Brian had arrived at more or less the same conclusion, and so had I. The three of us agreed on every central issue, and we became the solid core that saw the Community through its first shaky year.

For my part, it was more than political ideology that brought me to turn my energies to community. The long-range goals that are so much a part of my thinking now were mostly communicated to me by Brian and Dwight. In the beginning I had more immediate and personal satisfactions in mind. At the time I read *Walden Two* I was thirty-four years old, divorced, raising a child, and making a living working at office jobs. I disliked office work very much, finding it boring and meaningless, and I wanted to get into an environment where I could find more interesting people to talk to. Though I lacked a college education, I thought I might be able to get a degree slowly by taking night classes, and with a B.A. might qualify to teach in a junior college—maybe English, maybe philosophy. It was in an extension course in philosophy that I ran into *Walden Two*, recommended by the professor as "sinister" and "dangerous." *Walden Two* for me was a brilliant flash of light. I cannot exaggerate the excitement I felt as I read it. The community it depicted was everything I had ever wanted, everything I had ever believed in, everything I needed to be happy. It was impossible to believe that there was no such place in real life. I could not squarely face that fact, and I haven't faced it yet. There has *got* to be such a place.

In a few months I had made contact with other interested people, and two years later we began on the land. Though our Community is still a long way from the Walden Two of the book or of my dreams, I have not personally been disappointed in my hopes. The building of the dream has turned out to be as satisfying as moving into it could possibly have been.

Another member who was turned on by the book was Leif. The son of missionaries who hoped to see him go "into the Lord's work," Leif was studying in college and ran into the drug scene. He spent about three months experimenting with marijuana and LSD, and realized during this period that he didn't really need a college degree to do what he wanted to do. He dropped out of school, lost interest in drugs, and began to read heavily. Because of his romance with Thoreau, he was attracted by the title of *Walden Two* and read it. He was immensely excited by the book and persuaded his friend, Barbara, to read it. She became equally interested. Leif wrote to Skinner ("but I didn't expect anything to come of it—it was like writing to the President of the United States or something"). Dr. Skinner answered in a brief, friendly note, referring him to us.

In Pete's case, there were years of thought behind the decision to join Twin Oaks. Too old to fall into commune living easily, he nevertheless dreamed about it and tried to contact other people who might have similar dreams. He wrote us:

> I am an agricultural extension agent in charge of dairy education in two counties here. I did some graduate work and obtained a Master's degree. I grew up on a farm and so did my wife. We both prefer to live in the country where we can grow much of our own food and have more freedom.
>
> I have had some experience with the lots and lots of people that want to talk and talk, and that is as far as it goes. Then others are ready for action, but think that they

[...]e answers—that is, preconceived ideas as to how
[...] done if at all. Fortunately the Walden Two pro-
[...]xperimental and flexible.

I [...] just about given up hope of ever meeting up with
people who were not blindly chained to the past. We are
looking for people who have tolerance and openminded-
ness which permit a free flow and exchange of ideas and
who are willing to stand behind what they believe by their
practice.

Hilda was a college girl at Oberlin. She got Twin Oaks's
address from an office in the Student Union that gave out
information on communes. But why, I asked her, did she
originally want to go to a commune at all? "I don't know,"
says Hilda. "I can't remember. I just thought it was a neat
idea." After she had visited for a month, she decided to
go back to college and give it another try, "because I could
get into art there, and Twin Oaks doesn't have the money
or facilities for art yet." But a month in the college routine with its red tape, competition, and role playing con-
trasted so strongly with the atmosphere that she had just
left that she dropped out again and scurried back to Twin
Oaks.

Amos is not a dropout. He came to Twin Oaks originally
between his freshman and sophomore year of high school,
and he got his diploma before joining. He says, "So there
I was, a freshman in high school, and I read *Walden Two*
and got very excited about it. Then one day on my way
home from New York City, where I had been on a heavy
drug trip, I picked up a copy of an underground newspaper
and saw an article about Twin Oaks. I came to visit that
summer, brought my tent and spent several weeks. Then I
went back to school, as you know. And got sicker and sicker,
as you maybe don't know. More and more drugs. Every once
in a while during a vacation period I would come and visit
Twin Oaks for a few days. I noticed that after each visit

I was in better shape emotionally than I was before I came. I was using it as a mental health resort. In my senior year of high school I started going to a psychiatrist, and that helped. I got saner during this period and cut down on the drugs. Then last summer I visited Twin Oaks one more time, and I made up my mind. I said to myself 'What in the world is drawing me back out there? There's nothing out there. Why don't I just join?'"

"What did you find here?" I asked Amos.

"Something definite to do. I canned beans. It was a very concrete thing, canning beans. It was useful, and it wasn't difficult."

"But," I interrupted, "if all you wanted was manual labor, you could have got a job washing dishes in a restaurant."

"But that would have been for somebody else," said Amos. "Everything I do here is for myself. Even these dishes I'm washing are basically for myself—because the dishes have to be washed, and because I have to do my share. I understand that, and it's basically a selfish motivation behind my doing them. I'm not here because I want to create a better world. I mean, I'd like to create a better world, and if my being here helps, I'm glad about it, but even if this weren't the way to create a better world, I'd still be here. For one thing, it's a very real place. The size of the group is limited, and the number of things to do is limited. There's no escape. I have to deal with problems as they come up. If I didn't get along with somebody today, I may as well face it, because tomorrow I'm going to have to get along with them. There's just no burying myself in drugs or crowds, forgetting the whole thing.

"And it's a healthy place. People give a shit. I hear a lot of talk about how we're not a close, loving, caring kind of group, but what I say is, we're the closest, most loving, most caring group I ever had anything to do with without being ridiculous about it."

A few people are here who never intended to stay at all. Naomi was nearly sixteen years old in the summer of 1968 when her parents sent her to us for the summer. Naomi had been having trouble with the local juvenile authorities. She had been brought to juvenile court on a drug charge and put on probation. Naomi was never one to take obedience to authority very seriously, and her parents feared that she would do one more foolish and illegal thing and end up in juvenile detention for two years. It seemed a good idea to get Naomi out of her home state and into a permissive environment where there would be less authority to defy. So she came to Twin Oaks simply as a place for the summer. Naomi was not fundamentally a behavior problem but just a high-strung girl with a great deal of energy. Twin Oaks gave her plenty to do and some new things to believe in. The rules are minimal, and she has no trouble with the work. Both parents have visited and approve of us. She is now our Food Manager and our Budget Manager, overseeing both the menus and the accounts. Both skills she learned here.

Another very young member is Felix. I recall the day he arrived. We had just had a visit from the County Sheriff, who had been looking for a runaway named Richard Epstein. He described him—thin, dark, wears glasses, wearing a blue jacket. He had left word with one of his friends back home in Pennsylvania that he might come to Twin Oaks, and the parents had been trying to trace him by telephone. We told the Sheriff that we had not seen the boy but would get in touch if he should arrive. Half an hour later a thin, dark boy with glasses and a blue jacket walked up our driveway and announced that his name was Felix. "No, it isn't," we told him. "It's Richard Epstein. Call your parents."

Felix did call his parents, and his mother took the next plane down here to talk to him. He talked to his mother, but he wouldn't go back. His mother went home, and his father drove down in the family car. ("That really shows the difference between my mother and my father," says Felix. "She would have to take a plane.") Mr. Epstein stayed the whole weekend, enjoying the atmosphere of the farm. He brought with him the news that Felix had won a merit scholarship to go to the college of his choice. Wouldn't he please go back and finish high school? He had only one more year to go. But Felix wanted to stay in the Community. His father gave the necessary permission, and Felix is still with us.

Jeremiah and Katherine found us because they were looking for a commune. They had been working together with some friends in Illinois toward the formation of a commune in West Virginia. But the other members of that group felt that Jere and Katherine did not fit into their group, and voted them out. That left the two looking for a communal home. They were hitchhiking into New Mexico to investigate the possibilities in Drop City or New Buffalo when they ran across an article about Twin Oaks in an underground magazine. As soon as they read it, they headed straight here. "It made so much sense," says Jere, "embracing technology instead of rejecting it. Everybody else is involved in this back-to-the-land horseshit." The main thing that attracted him about Twin Oaks, though, was the sheer fact that it existed and had been going on for two years. They had seen just enough of the hippie commune movement to know that stability in a commune is a rare thing, and just going out into the country to do your own thing with faith that you will all naturally love one another was a project doomed to a short life. Katherine left Twin Oaks a year later to do Women's Liberation work in the city, but Jere is here and in charge of Fences, Pets, and Bees.

Sometimes people come not because of their own interest but because of their mates'. Such was Emily's case. "I originally visited just because my husband was interested.

I had never thought about communes at all. But when I got here, I realized that I could relax here. It is small enough that I can spend most of my time with people I can get to know well. I don't like being tense, and I was always tense on the Outside—having always to deal with people I didn't like much or didn't agree with. But here I live and work in the same place, and I have friends. I feel comfortable. This is my home."

A few people come here "because I have to go somewhere." Severely damaged psyches have found refuge here from time to time. Usually, however, the same problems that blew them here blow them away again. A commune is not free of tension, especially one in its first years of struggle for survival.

The average Community member, according to some statistics we took, is 23.5 years old and has two years of college. I would also add that he is likely to be quite intelligent, pleasant mannered, easygoing, familiar with counter-culture values and definitely not interested in the jobs that he could get working for the corporations.

Communal life is for everyone. That's an article of faith. Somewhere in the community of the future there is room for everything worthwhile and good. Everyone who lives there will be happy, and everyone will want to live there. The same cannot be said of Twin Oaks. Our current conditions unquestionably select for a fairly homogeneous population, and our commitment to this Community is made quite deliberately, knowing that there are other choices open to us, and that some of those choices are in themselves good. Those of us who are committed to the Walden Two idea, though we reap pleasure from our day-to-day lives, are essentially future-oriented. To us, a new sink in the kitchen is not merely a better way to wash dishes; it is a step toward Walden Two. Inventing a new kind of charades is not just a pleasant way to pass the evening; it is a tentative experiment in a new culture. This view makes dull tasks bearable and lends a luster to the ordinary. We are making a new world according to our own specifications. We are living out our utopian dream.

II

Other Communes

There was once a group of students in one of the Midwest universities that used a computer to match up individuals with communes. It was supposed to work something like a computer-date service. The communes would tell what kind of people they wanted; the people would tell what kind of commune they wanted; and the service would help them find each other. It was a good idea, but ahead of its time. The fact is that there are thousands of people who would join a commune if they could find one suited to their needs, but there are virtually no communes actively seeking members and prepared to accept them.

Even getting data from the communes is extremely difficult. Student after hopeful student has worked up questionnaires and sent them around to all the groups with known addresses. The results are discouraging. Most groups do not reply at all. Among those who do reply are groups that will have vanished before the data can be published, groups of such extreme religious views that most people do not consider them serious alternatives, or even communities that exist only in the fantasies of the correspondent. The person compiling the data has no way of telling truth from falsehood, and simply publishes what he can get. Thus one hears vaguely that there are hundreds, or even thousands, of communes. We have heard fantastic rumors about the States of California, Oregon, West Virginia, and Vermont, in particular, saying that the commune movement is widespread and that lots of these groups have existed for several years, still with the original people. We would like to believe these rumors, but we have no way of substantiating them. For most groups do not publish.

It is very understandable why a lot of groups do not spread word about themselves through the news media. For one thing, newspaper coverage has damaged more than one commune because of its aftermath of tourists. For another, the groups may not be interested in a larger population and have no wish to advertise. Word of mouth keeps most communes full to overflowing. A more fundamental reason yet was expressed by a girl in a young commune in Tennessee. Writing to a magazine, she asked them to print nothing more about her group:

> We really don't need the visitors. We are trying to get our heads together out here. When I am in the middle of washing some clothes or fixing a meal, here comes a carful of people who want to look at us because they've read about us in a magazine. I may not feel like talking to strangers right then.
>
> The mail is getting us down, too. We don't have a typewriter, and if we did, I don't know where we'd put it in our overcrowded house. People ask so many questions and expect nice letters. In the daytime I don't have time to sit and write those letters by hand. At night there isn't any light, since we don't have electricity yet . . .

The picture I get from this letter—a group living without electricity, without organization enough even to keep a table cleared, and without any interest whatever in prospective members—may and may not be typical. I think it probably is. I once visited a commune at about that level of subsistence.

One fall morning in 1969, when Twin Oaks was already

two years old and beginning to gain a measure of stability, five young people drove up our driveway and introduced themselves as members of High Top Commune, a new group only fifty miles away from us. We were overjoyed to talk to them and listened eagerly to their tale. It went something like this:

"The five of us are the sort of central people out of a group of thirteen. We live on fifty acres of land at the top of a mountain. The owner of the land is letting us live there for nothing. Another commune used to live there, but it was burned out. Now there are skeletons of buildings there that we might try to rebuild. And there is one small house that we are all living in now.

"We met in Richmond. One of us knew the owner of the land and put an ad in the paper to attract people interested in living on a commune. A lot of people answered the ad, and we tried living together in Richmond before actually settling on the land. That was pretty successful. We learned a lot about group living. So we figured we could make it all right. We moved out here a month ago, and things are not going well at all.

"The problem is labor. There are just a lot of people in our commune who don't want to do any work. I mean it is really bad, to the point where they will lie there and ask one of us to go get them a cigarette. The five of us do almost all the work. Making the fire and keeping it going, cooking the meals, and trying to get some construction started. The others are so young. They've never had to work before. They can't get it through their heads that there are things that have to be done if we are going to survive on the place over the winter. Last night it just got to be too much. We were having our evening meeting, and I suggested that we all commit ourselves to some task for the following day—just agree to work on something in particular, so that we would all be sure that things were being done. But a lot of people didn't like the idea at all. They said it was like the

outside world. They said they didn't want to be 'structured.'
But man, I didn't want to structure them. I just wanted
them to do something. So we five said to each other, let
them build their own fire one day. Let's go down and visit
Twin Oaks and ask them what they do about labor problems. So here we are."

We gave the group what advice we could, but unfortunately they were unable to accept much of it, because it
cut across their sense of what freedom ought to be like. The
only thing that came out of the meeting was a mutual invitation to visit. We accepted immediately. Some of us followed them back to their own property that same day.

They lived on a beautiful spot on the summit of a mountain. A shabby wooden structure perhaps 12 by 25 feet
housed them all. Their sleeping bags were neatly rolled up
against the wall during the daytime and evidently were un-
rolled on the floor around the fireplace at night. It was already cold in October. Nothing had been done to make the
commune comfortable during the weeks they had been
there, except a little winterizing of their cabin. There was
no latrine of any kind, or any way to dispose of garbage.
They cooked over the open fire. It was virtually impossible
to reach the buildings by road, and groceries had to be
carried by hand a full mile after parking one's car at the
dead end of an old fire road.

Pioneers might have made the place work. Some of the
group worked in town at the foot of the mountain, and with
the small amount of money this brought in, it might have
been possible to finish one of the burnt-out buildings, build
an outhouse, purchase a vehicle that would take the rutted
mountain roads. But the money went for medicine and dope
and grocery store goodies and traffic fines and auto repair,
and High Top was gone before it was four months old. Yet
the five people who visited us that day were good people,
idealists, workers, happy with each other and with the communal idea.

I know better than to comment on the reasons for the demise of any community, no matter how shakily founded, on the basis of a visit of one afternoon. It could have failed for any one of a dozen reasons. I still think it could have succeeded, too, in spite of them. But that is their story, and they are the only ones who can say anything conclusive about it.

One thing I learned from our contact with High Top was that Twin Oaks lacks appeal for the members of the looser-structured communes. We urged them to visit, to take advantage of our swimming hole, hot showers, washing machines. We invited them to use us to help them get on their feet, particularly offering to have a member-exchange for the purpose of digging each other's life styles. Several Twin Oaks members, including me, were interested in experiencing a week or so of primitive communal life. What would it really feel like, I asked myself, to get up in the morning and have no place to wash my face, find something to wear from a sack or box, and start to work building a wood fire, trying to cooperate with a group of people who have not agreed on the division of work? Further, what would it feel like to be a newcomer in a group that already has its norms established? I was impatient to make the experiment. But the High Top people, to my surprise, did not want to spend as much as a week at Twin Oaks. They were uncomfortable as they explained their reasons. They said they hadn't yet had time to get themselves together as a group, and they couldn't spare anybody. This was obviously not the real reason, for some of their members took off for the city any time they wanted to. It seemed that High Top members did not think they could feel at home at Twin Oaks, because we were not their kind of people. We somehow resembled the Establishment too much. It was partly, they admitted, that they would miss the marijuana and other drugs that were common at High Top and prohibited at Twin Oaks. But it was mostly that they did not want their time structured by a labor credit system. Just the word "system" turned them off.

Indeed, there is a language barrier between Twin Oaks and the average commune. When we say "efficiency," we mean a way of getting the work done better and faster, so that we can have more time for swimming, listening to music, making love, or doing yoga. To others, "efficiency" conjures up visions of grim-jawed, glittery-eyed robots that have forgotten (if they ever knew) how to live joyfully. There have even been visitors to Twin Oaks who have imagined that they could see our dedication to science, technology, and efficiency in our faces. Fortunately or unfortunately, none of us who actually live here notice the prevalence of efficiency. If anything, we are more inclined to criticize ourselves for the same faults that the Establishment sees in us—namely, laziness, slovenliness, and a trifle too leisurely a pace toward our goals.

There are a lot of people who want to join communes, who are not poor and do not want to become poor. One glance at the High Tops of this country tells them that they aren't interested in that level of existence. They are people with good jobs or even professions that they do not find satisfying. I have talked to a lot of such people. The message that comes across to me is something like this: "Please tell me where there is a nice, middle-class commune that will offer me a better life without my having to give up any security to get it. I am so lonely. I feel that my present life style is pointless and stale. There has got to be a better way. But I can't go so far as the garbage-ridden hippie crash pad. Tell me about *your* commune."

I tell them about my commune, but most of them go away sorrowful after hearing about it, either because of our stringent property rules or because we are not far enough from the bare subsistence level to make them feel secure and comfortable about the future.

These people mystify me. Our group started with a hand-

ful of extremely naïve people and a piece of land, with
enough capital for a single, inexpensive building. The wist-
ful, would-be communitarians I am talking about could
among a small group accumulate much more than that and
start at a much higher standard of living then we did. They
could pool their business know-how and make a very comfortable life for themselves. Why don't they do it? They reject us because of our radical property rules, which threaten
their inheritances and accumulated property. Why don't
they make a commune with more lenient laws? They smile
at our naïveté and stumbling incompetence. They are a
hundred times more competent. There are community-
minded lawyers out there, businessmen, doctors, architects,
people who know how to get grants. They could make a
dozen communes better off financially than we are. Why
don't they do it?

Perhaps they will, and just haven't got around to it yet.

Or perhaps the very hesitation to take chances with their
accrued property will prevent them from trusting each other
enough to try it. Maybe there is something about being well
off financially that makes one conservative, makes one stop
and plan and consider too long.

If these professional and business people don't make a
commune within the next few years, Twin Oaks will have
caught up to their economic level, and they will be joining
us. We will be glad to accept them when the time comes,
if we have room.

I didn't mean to imply that there are no communities better off than Twin Oaks. On the contrary, there are established
groups that are very comfortable. All the ones I know about
have a deeply religious base. Some of them, as well, are
engaged in important social services and accept as members
only fellow workers in their social field.

Generally speaking, Twin Oaks shares with the established
religious communes a similar structure, or belief in structure

—a definite government, a clear labor system, formal membership contracts—but parts with them philosophically. The religious groups often have a good life, but that is not their aim. With the hippie communes we share a common belief in the importance of the good life, but differ sharply on the necessity and desirability of structure.

Taking as we do a middle road between respectable established communities on the one hand and "anarchist" communes on the other, we are continually in a position to disappoint and frustrate would-be members. The anarchists see our long hair and note our sexual freedom and are tempted to join, but are put off by our organization; the middle class are attracted by our common-sense organization combined with our relaxed life style, but in their turn are repelled by our restrictions on private property, by our minimal living standard, and perhaps by our long hair and sexual freedom. We hope this problem will cure itself by the formation of more communes, each along slightly different lines. If there were more choice, there would be less internal trouble in each group. It would be perfectly reasonable to say, "If you don't like it here, why don't you go join another commune." It is not reasonable to say that now. Though there have been lists of communes that run into the hundreds of names, and rumors place the figure even higher, most of these groups are not able to support themselves well. Such luxuries as a clean room with a bed and dresser, electric light and a toilet that flushes are not available in many rural communes.

We look with favor upon communes in general—religious, anarchist, or whatever. But we are most excited about groups of our own type—structured, experimental, and frankly interested in the good life. Most people can accept the label "experimental" without difficulty, because they can make it mean anything they want. And everybody except the most ascetic will admit to an interest in the good life. Our difficulty comes with the word "structure." The word is pure poison to nine-tenths of the commune movement, so our defense of it demands some explanation.

Carefully analyzed, there is no such thing as an unstructured commune. Human beings (as well as other animals) naturally do structure their relations with each other. Most obvious is the dominance hierarchy. Every group has some kind of leadership and some kind of status order. You can label it or not, as you choose, but it is there all the same.

A group that chooses to have no government is not thereby going to go without one. It is merely going to deliver government into the hands of the head of the dominance hierarchy—to those people who just naturally rise to the top. There, without guidelines or rules of any kind, the natural leader will exercise his power for good or bad, and recognize or not recognize his responsibility to the other people, depending on his ideas and conditioning.

Furthermore, there is no such thing as unstructured division of labor. If a commune survives at all, the work is divided somehow. Somebody does it. An "unstructured" situation will quickly evolve into a structured one where certain people accept a role as workers and do the bulk of the work, while others do very little or avoid it entirely. This is not only obvious on the face of it; it has been painfully demonstrated in commune after commune.

What the structured commune does is make a decision to do its structuring deliberately. It is true that in the process it is necessary to ask people to do work that they would not choose to do, but this is a better alternative than either leaving it undone or assuming that volunteers just naturally love working. Deliberate structure causes a commune to have to name its decision-makers, too. But in naming them, it makes them responsible.

That is why, in a movement dominated by a cry for freedom, we invent systems and use them with enthusiasm, meanwhile crying Freedom as loud as anybody. Freedom is doing what you want to do. What we want to do is build a solid community as fast as is reasonably possible, and at the same time have a lot of leisure time and a good conscience. We manage that.

III

The First Two Years— A Calendar of Events

The original eight people were actually two small groups and some unaffiliated individuals. Brian, Carrie and Sandy were all from Atlanta. Brian and Sandy had worked together putting out a community-oriented newspaper called *Walden Pool*.

Fred and I had been cooperating in an effort to set up and run in Washington, D.C., an urban forerunner of Twin Oaks, called Walden House. We had not been at all successful at this and were heavily encumbered financially because of mortgages on the city house itself. Jenny lived with me at Walden House, though she was pretty much a child at the time and was not ideologically involved in the project. To Walden House also came Quincy, then as now a stranger to us, a man of very odd behavior, alternately friendly and hostile, a person with overwhelming social needs that we never sought to satisfy. In fact we avoided him. His presence in the group was simply the result of our open membership policy, which refused no one.

Walden House had put out a newsletter, and through it attracted the attention of Dwight, a Michigan graduate student who was devoted to radical social change, and Hal, who had a little bit of inherited money and a passion to do something good with it. Neither Dwight nor Hal ever lived at Walden House, but they had visited and corresponded and had a lot of sympathy with our effort to start a Walden Two community.

Walden House was a dismal failure in every way. The only good thing it ever did was attract the attention of Dwight and Hal. Fred and I poured two years of work and money into it and lost it all because the house was not worth what we had paid for it. That, plus problems we had with boarders and would-be members, convinced Fred and me to get out of the city and onto rural property by whatever means might become available to us, even if we had to rent land. Fred developed an intense interest in farming. Hal's offer of money to buy a farm came just in time.

In the fall of 1966 a conference was organized near Ann Arbor, Michigan, with the purported intent of trying to set up a real, rural Walden Two community. The Atlanta group attended, and so did the ·Walden House people. There we met each other and got acquainted with Dwight. Hal had gone to the conference to find out if a movement arising out of it might be a more promising place to put his money than betting on Fred and me, whom he had already met. We were all hoping that someone at the conference might have the skills—especially the financial skills, to get a Walden Two community started.

The conference did not come off well, because the people who had called it didn't have the necessary commitment to the ideas of community. They were all intrigued by Walden Two, but they wanted a large Ford Foundation grant to start it with and a cadre of Ph.D.'s to plan the future community's behavior patterns before they even considered dedicating their own energy. The conference did serve, however, as a meeting place for those of us who were already emotionally committed to community. Sandy and Brian, Dwight and Hal, Fred and I—we wanted community and we wanted it right then, money or no money, psychologists or no psychologists, planning or no planning. Hal talked to a lot of people at the conference, discovered he was the only one there with readily available capital for community purposes, and decided to put his money at the disposal of the small group of dedicated fanatics (us) rather than search any further. "You kids want to farm?" he asked in his soft Carolina drawl. "Well, I'll buy you a farm." I have never heard, nor do I expect to hear, words as golden as those.

I want in this chapter to set down a rough chronological outline of events in Twin Oaks's history during its first two and a half years. The rest of the book isn't told in chronological order but takes examples and illustrations from various periods. Any reader who is specifically interested in the history of Twin Oaks can use this chapter as a frame to hang those stories on, each in its proper place in time.

The conference was in the fall of 1966. By January of 1967 Hal had definitely committed himself to purchasing land for us, though he would not be able to join us at first, because his wife was opposed to community. We began looking for a suitable location in early spring and purchased the farm in April. Our scheduled date for formally settling on the land and beginning community living officially was June 16, 1967.

June. We moved onto the land. We had purchased an old school bus with joint funds. Fred and Hal helped Brian, Carrie and Sandy move their belongings here from Atlanta. The bus and a rented trailer between them brought all their furniture, a printing press, two motorcycles, and a pet skunk in a cage. The first few days were used mostly to unpack and store things, but other things happened, too. There were meetings, and our first clumsy efforts at government and labor distribution. We went swimming every day. We kept up the garden. And we talked a lot. We got our bylaws writen during this period, put out a newsletter, chose the name Twin Oaks, appointed managers. Our well ran dry, and we drilled a new well with money donated by Hal.

July. We settled into a routine with our new labor credit system. Long-term visitors increased the size of our group. A lot of our time went into canning and freezing berries and

vegetables, and into caring for the tobacco crop. Our meetings were concerned with ideas for making money and with
the relative merits of agriculture and industry.

August. Hal proposed we try making rope hammocks for
a living. He had already analyzed the techniques of making
them and had made one sale. He felt confident he could sell
more, and he volunteered to be our salesman. We accepted
his leadership in this field gratefully. We set up the hammock factory on the front porch of the farmhouse and made
hammocks while talking or listening to music.

We talked a lot about our need for additional buildings,
especially for a winter hammock workshop and for housing.
But we didn't have any money to build anything.

We harvested the tobacco and put it up in the barn.

September. Hal offered to cash in an insurance policy in
order to get money for a new building. We accepted with
relief, and Hal began to draw plans.

Interpersonal difficulties began to arise. Fred and Sandy
did not get along well. Everybody found it hard to live with
Quincy. Quincy worked at a snail's pace, and this, in addition to his acute personality problems, was more than either
Carrie or I could stand. Between us we put pressure on the
others to agree to ask Quincy to leave. The men cooperated,
but with some misgivings.

We sent off our first hammock order, but no further orders
came in that year. We talked of stockpiling hammocks for
spring sales, but did not have the money for the inventory
of rope.

October. Hal's money arrived, and construction began on
the building we now call Harmony. Hal now moved onto
the farm full time and devoted himself to construction. All
of the rest of us worked on it, too, but not hard enough to
please Hal, who wanted to see more dedication and less
leisure. Sandy often slept until noon. Fred was still in Wash-

ington except on weekends. Dwight worked hard, but he had fallen in love with a new member, and his mind was occupied with personal things.

Two new members joined, Charlie and Marie: Neither of them got along at all well with Hal. We began having meetings to try to straighten out the problems. Marie brought her child to live in the Community, and little Timothy became a major part of everybody's life.

November. Fred quit his Washington job and came to live full time on the farm. He carried on the farm and maintenance work while the rest of us did the housework and construction. Sandy began to think about religious ideas, drugs, and the hippie movement, and decided to leave Twin Oaks and go to Haight-Ashbury. His departure was frightening to us, because he was the first of the original members to leave, and only one of the new people had turned out to be a good member. Charlie was eased out because of his reluctance to work. Marie left shortly afterwards because of loneliness and because she did not get along well with Carrie. Jenny followed Sandy to California. Visitors kept pouring through, as they have before and since.

December. We completed the Harmony Building sufficiently to move people out of the barns and into partially finished bedrooms.

We butchered and cut up our first hogs, with the help of our neighbors. Most of the month was devoted to the tobacco crop, which had to be sorted and tied into bundles for market. The low return on this labor gave rise to a lot of anti-agriculture conversation, which Fred resented. Relations between Fred and the other men of the Community were not good. Morale was generally low, except for high spots like completing the building, or giving a lecture to a group of visiting students. Telling them about the advantages of communal living seemed to make us more confident about our chosen life style.

I was probably the only happy member at this point. Carrie went into deep depressions. Brian, Dwight, Hal, and Fred, each in his own way, were all impatient with the Community's progress.

January. Hal got a divorce and joined the Community as a member. Another new member was Mary, a thoughtless and mixed-up teen-ager who was an emotional drain on the Community. We became discouraged at the quality of new members that were attracted to Twin Oaks. Mary recruited another hippie, and he brought hepatitis with him. The disease went no further, but we had to care for him in isolation for several weeks.

Pete, an agricultural agent, and his wife Rosa, with their two children, visited the Community and decided to join. They scheduled their arrival for June, and we had meetings to discuss the physical details of their move.

Carrie set aside her doubts about the Community, accepted the communal life style for herself, and happily became pregnant.

February. Money was very low. Carrie and I both went to work in town. The people on the farm completed the interior of Harmony.

March. Dwight and Brian became enthusiastic about the idea of having a summer camp on our premises and began to look into it. It seemed we might make quite a bit of money if we could pull it off. We put out some advertising and got two responses, but that was all. We gave up the idea.

April. Our expenses exceeded our income. Everybody got an outside job except Fred, Hal, and the two hippies. Hal became deeply dissatisfied with the lack of progress and attempted a coup on our government. We dissolved the government. Feeling against Hal was intense. The rest of us were united in our indignation at Hal's behavior. It was Hal against everybody—except the hippies, who didn't even know what was happening and didn't care. Dwight and Brian worked out a new plan for a government. Hal invented one of his own.

Gwen, a divorced woman with two children, visited us and decided to join the Community when summer came. Since we would be crowded, she agreed to bring her house trailer with her. While here she met Hal, and they were attracted to each other.

May. We had a meeting and discussed the two rival plans for government. Hal's plan had no backers. He finally admitted defeat. We reelected the original planners. Hal was upset by the election and left the Community.

Five more people came and joined the Community, none of them destined to stay very long.

Fred put in a huge garden and corn crop.

June. We wrote to Gwen, suspecting that Hal might be with her, and relaying a message through her that Hal was welcome to return to the Community, that we recognized his value and would like to set the past aside and start over. Hal got the message, accepted our proffered peace overture, and returned with Gwen and the house trailer in June.

Pete and Rosa arrived with their children and belongings. Jenny, bored with Sandy and California, returned to Twin Oaks more mature and ready to take a greater interest in the Community. She found new love interests among the new members who had joined in the interim.

Naomi and Marjorie, teen-agers who originally had wanted to come to our summer camp, came for the summer anyway when our camp plans fell through. Naomi and Jenny became close companions. Marjorie fell in love with Brian, and vice versa.

July and August. A great deal of action going on at once. Hal once more was making trouble on the political front, challenging the board of planners to make him do an outside work shift, defending Gwen's right to the private use of her house trailer and authority over her children, and agitating to mortgage the farm in order to go into the toy business.

Pete and Rosa were trying to get adjusted to community living, especially profane language, sexual freedom, and a general atmosphere of chaos. Their baby, Maxine, was taking a great deal of our time and attention.

The presence of a whole group of very young people made the social scene very lively. Half the members did not fully realize the deadly political struggles that were going on, and thoroughly enjoyed that summer, swimming, falling in love, generally growing up.

There were a number of interpersonal hassles, open dislikes, accusations of various kinds. Several people urged that we try encounter groups, and we finally did.

Dwight became disillusioned because of Hal and the internal political situation, and left the Community. Brian and Carrie's marriage was threatened by Marjorie's presence and Brian's theories about nonpossessiveness.

September and October. Hal and Gwen finally got tired of fighting the rest of the Community and decided to leave, though their final departure was delayed until late November. We kept putting out shakily optimistic newsletters, telling people about the cheerful things that were happening, leaving the problems unaired.

Naomi got her parents' permission to stay on at Twin Oaks through the winter. Marjorie left.

October. Carrie's baby, Bonnie, was born.

November. Fred left the Community, dissatisfied with our continued poverty. Hal, Gwen, and Gwen's two children left also. We settled down to try to hold Pete and Rosa. Four of the people who had joined in the spring left about this time.

January, 1969. We bought ten cows and started our ill-fated veal-calf program.

Dwight, hearing that the most bourgeois elements of the Community had left, decided to return. We could already sense that Pete and Rosa would not stay much longer. There were also doubts about Carrie. The rest of us were united in a determination to keep the Community from going under. Most of the men were working on a highway crew to bring in money.

Spring, 1969. Pete and Rosa finally gave up trying and went away. In their places came a series of people with lower ideals, who just wanted a good place to live. Simon was among these. At first a help, later a drain, Simon kept the board of planners busy all spring and summer with questions of basic equality versus special privilege.

Carrie left in May and took the baby.

Summer, 1969. Henry occupied our time and attention. He was extremely obnoxious but finally left after beating up two members. This was also a summer with a lot of sickness. Mysterious fevers came and went, and everybody had typhoid shots. We put in a big septic tank and drain field.

We got a morale boost in this period from visitors who later joined as members. They stayed for months and made us feel good about the Community we were building, in spite of the problems we were having, because they were attracted to it and planned to join.

We had Utopia Class once a week, and this led to the Mutual Criticism sessions, which were quite productive and exciting at first.

We also started construction of the Oneida Building, a dormitory which we were trying to build with almost no money, on Dwight's faith that our membership would always expand to fill the available living space.

We sold quite a few hammocks and took all outside workers off their jobs for the summer in order to work on hammock production.

September. We expelled Simon for attempted theft and general underhanded financial dealings. Outside workers had to return to work as the hammock-buying season came to an end. Jenny and Naomi left the Community on an adventure trip across country.

October. Dwight became increasingly conscious of worldwide revolution and longed to take a more active part in it. He began agitating for Community activism. He and Brian talked external politics a lot. Most of the members were openly opposed to getting the Community involved in anything that even looked illegal. A number of them were just not concerned about the larger issues, anyway. The apolitical people began having nightly readings of *Winnie the Pooh* as a counter influence.

November. Dwight left the Community to join a more active revolutionary group. Brian was extremely upset and left also. There were very few members at this time, and most of them were less than dedicated to building the Community. I did not feel I could carry on without either Dwight, Brian, or some other strong person to help, and I began to think Twin Oaks might have reached its end. The few of us that remained kept working and pretending we still had a community, hoping that Brian would come back, or that some new members would come to take his place, or both. Brian returned on Thanksgiving Day, and the Community went crazy with joy.

December 1969 and January 1970. A lot of our physical difficulties piled up at this point. Most of our cars stopped functioning. Our cattle began to sicken of malnutrition. We were about a thousand dollars in debt for building materials that had gone into Oneida, which was still unfinished.

But psychologically this was a good period. This is the time I think of as Breakthrough. New members began to pour in, and this time they weren't mixed-up people looking for shelter but normal people looking for something significant to do with themselves.

Since then it's been mostly ups. Brian finally left a year later, when we were strong enough to survive without him. We got out of debt, got our cars on the road, planted the fields, finished Oneida, started selling hammocks. Jenny and Naomi returned.

Not that we haven't had any problems since. We have had some terrible hassles and been through periods of low morale and high turnover. But since early 1970 nothing that has happened has threatened the existence of the Community. We have the people we need, and we keep attracting more of them. These days Twin Oaks isn't afraid of anything short of a nationwide depression, and we might even make it through that.

IV

Shaping Equality Behavior

You drive to Twin Oaks through farm country. It is red and gray clay, poor land, worn out by tobacco crops long ago. Most of it grows grass now, for the small herds of Angus and Hereford cattle that look up at you as you drive past. There are no large farms here, just small ones of about a hundred acres. Twin Oaks is one of these. As you turn in the driveway marked by a mailbox with the Community's name, you notice a typical white farmhouse and a row of weathered oak barns. Different from the rest of the countryside are two large buildings, one black and green, one stained brown. They could be anything—factories, barns, warehouses. They are dormitories and workshops, you find out later.

Five dogs rush out to greet your car as you pull up beside the other parked vehicles. You see several people working or sitting around talking. They glance at you but continue their conversation. Someone yells, "Hey, Maggie—visitor!" A girl in a red and white striped turtleneck and patched jeans comes out of the farmhouse and approaches you. She introduces herself, asks how long you are staying, and shows you around.

The farmhouse has been converted into three dining rooms and a kitchen. A closet contains a stereo turntable, which is playing. There are two large speakers in one of the dining rooms. Several people are sitting quietly around the table in that room, listening. The other dining rooms are empty, except for a man sweeping the floor. There is a speaker in the kitchen, too, and two girls and a man are singing along with the record while they prepare the next meal. They smile at you as you pass through but do not stop singing. Maggie shows you the Community's only bathroom, and you ask leave to use it. There are two towels on the floor, slightly wet, and three more towels thrown carelessly over a towel rack. The bathroom does not look as clean as you would like. Perhaps the man with the broom hasn't got to it yet. Later you will notice that some parts of the buildings are freshly cleaned and organized, others gathering dust, cobwebs, and dirty laundry. The longer you stay, the more you will notice this—the clean, sparkling areas getting dirtier, and the messy spots being cleaned up, giving the overall effect of a household caught in mid-spring cleaning and not at all prepared for visitors.

The big green-and-black building contains an auto shop, wood shop, print shop, and hammock-weaving shop, as well as several private rooms and the community clothes area. The community clothes are housed in a large room and are evidently much used. You see boxes marked "good turtleneck shirts," and "grubby turtleneck shirts," "black socks," "white socks," "matched socks." Rack upon rack of blouses, shirts, and dresses present a variety of clothing for the members. Your guide tells you that you are welcome to use community clothes if you like.

Your room is in the brown building. It contains four bunks, evidently made on the premises by the members. Two of the bunks are already taken by other visitors. You put your sleeping bag on a lower bunk and follow Maggie out into the hall for a look at the library. The Community's books line the walls of the two hallways and the living room. This building contains the bedrooms of the members.

Maggie tells you a little about the Community's history and institutions and then leaves you to do as you please. You step outside and look around. The fields are a pleasing bright green. A man is clearing away piles of mulch from what he tells you is a strawberry bed. Two others are making some rows for the spring planting of peas. Three or four people are lounging in hammocks which have been hung in a group underneath the apple trees. The man who was sweeping comes out of the farmhouse, his arm around a girl. They stop and kiss each other without self-consciousness, then continue their walk.

Someone steps out of the farmhouse and strikes a large metal disc with a horseshoe. The resultant clanging is evidently the lunch bell. You follow the others back into the farmhouse and stand in line. There is a blackboard with the menu for the meal printed on it. Today's offering says "Onion soup; toasted cheese sandwiches; various yummy leftovers; lemon pudding." Someone turns off the record player for the meal, and members and visitors carry their full plates to one of the dining tables. You seat yourself and are tasting the leftovers (not too yummy, but edible) when you are spotted by a young girl with a sheaf of papers. "Aha!" she says. "A visitor. How would you like to help with lunch dishes?" You say you would be glad to, and she beams at you with satisfaction. "I knew there must be a visitor around here someplace," she says.

Thus you begin your first job on Twin Oaks's labor credit system. If you stay as long as a week, you may wash dishes several times. You will probably also do some gardening, learn to weave a hammock, and perhaps help to put up the hay. Visitors' work assignments are fairly predictable, since there are many jobs they cannot do without training. The same is not true for members.

There is no such thing as a typical day at Twin Oaks. I will have to describe several people's days in order to give a realistic picture.

My day today, for example, is set aside entirely for writing this book. In fact, I am taking several consecutive weeks for that purpose, being interrupted only occasionally to do a little manual labor that the labor people found hard to fit into somebody else's schedule.

That doesn't make me a special person. Any member who has demonstrated the ability to interest a publisher in his writing could do the same. I get paid a standard one credit an hour for my actual writing time. If the book doesn't sell or isn't ultimately accepted, it is the Community that has taken the risk—I don't have to make up the lost labor. On the other hand, if it sells well and brings in a fat check, I still get only one credit an hour. The profit, if any, goes to the Community.

Gideon's day is quite different. He put in a 9:30–11:00 typing shift (one of our little businesses, addressing envelopes for a local concern), then drove the tractor over to a neighbor's farm to borrow their scraper-blade attachment. By the time he returned, it was lunch time. This afternoon he will probably scrape the cow yard and level the new volleyball court with the borrowed scraper. He might take time out for a bath before supper, and quite possibly work in the automobile shop for a while afterward, unless there is a meeting of some kind. The only part of the day which is actually scheduled for Gideon by the labor people is the morning typing shift. The rest is simply written "20 hours auto maintenance during the week" and "level cow yard." Gideon prefers a loose schedule of this kind. He works out his own hours, and he generally gets everything done, sometimes doing unscheduled things that come up midweek.

Naomi, on the other hand, is likely to have a tight schedule with precise hours. This is because she likes cooking and kitchen work, and this work must be done at specific times. Today, for instance, she did "Morning Kitchen Clean," fixed supper, and will do the late night dishes shift. In addition, Naomi is signed up for several "during the week" jobs like food inventory and cleaning out the freezer. Since she is also our bookkeeper, she is scheduled to spend one afternoon paying the bills and balancing the checkbook, as well as overseeing the bookkeeping, which is being done by other members, recently trained.

Phil takes a daily shopping trip to nearby Louisa as part of his labor quota, and makes up most of the rest of it in dishwashing or hammock weaving. He is Library Manager, so he schedules some managerial time for himself each week to keep the library in usable shape.

Rod spends almost his full time in farm and garden work. Yesterday he supervised the planting of 150 fruit trees; this afternoon he is disking up some land for the garden. Farming is his specialty. Other than an occasional shift of dishwashing, he virtually lives out-of-doors.

Members of Twin Oaks are required to do a full, equal share of the necessary work. Within that limit, they are free to choose whatever work they like. The system makes that freedom possible and practical.

Community members work about forty hours a week, usually spread over the full seven days. This work includes all the farming, housework, cooking, shopping, businesses and industries, office work, and anything else that is necessary for the group's survival and progress.

In the book *Walden Two* there is a labor system hinted at but not described. The basic theme of it is that, while all work is equally honorable, not all is equally desirable, and that those who do the nastiest jobs should get the shortest hours. We were gung-ho Walden Twoers even from the beginning, but we did not invent a labor system until we had been on the land for three weeks. I think that we wanted to have a free, unstructured time of just doing what we pleased. So we did as we pleased, and there were some gross inequalities, but it didn't matter a lot in those first days of excitement.

Carrie did almost all the cooking and housework. Perhaps once a day someone would help wash the dishes at one of the meals, but she carried the brunt of it. I was still in the city, trying to untangle myself from some financial problems, and went to the land only on weekends for the first two months of the Community's existence. So the only other female on the premises was my daughter, Jenny, aged fourteen, who wasn't interested in housework. The men worked at projects that appealed to them. They built a work table and put up some shelves in a storage barn. They experimented with rammed earth. They built a swimming dock.

The first request for a labor structure came from Carrie, who simply wanted to know why Jenny didn't help out with the housework. Jenny, who has understood women's liberation from her crib, replied that she would rather help build shelves and experiment with rammed earth. The men backed her up but also agreed with Carrie that if the housework had become a chore, it was time to share it. It was evidently time to begin the intriguing task of structuring the distribution of labor. The initially difficult problem was defining work. Everybody agreed that there were tasks which, though useful to the group, were so much fun to do that they couldn't really compare to housework. Finally it was settled that the group would divide that work which the members did not enjoy doing but leave creative work off the system to be done when we felt like it.

The line between creative and unpleasant moved steadily toward the unpleasant as the weeks progressed. At first there was nothing on the system except housework. Then hoeing the garden lost its savor and was added. Tending the tobacco crop quickly became part of the system, then blackberry picking. Within a month we were going by the concept that every kind of work that was useful to the group (except thinking, talking, reading, and research) belonged on the labor credit system. This served two purposes—making sure everyone did a fair share of the work, and making sure that everyone got a chance to do the more interesting parts of it.

Deciding who worked at what was a more complicated task. The first system was a card game. On 3″ x 5″ cards we wrote the names of the jobs and the lengths of time estimated

to complete them. One card said, "Tuesday fix lunch, ½ hour,"
and another said, "Blackberry picking Wednesday, 1 hour."
Then we sat in a circle and dealt out the hand. Each of us
examined the hand we had been dealt and determined which
jobs we might like to keep and which to pass on. Then we
started passing cards to the right, each discarding jobs which
seemed to us most disagreeable. The person on my left passed
cards to me, and I selected one or two of them and passed
the rest on. When I had acquired by this means a full hand
(my fair share of hours, previously calculated and announced), my part of the game was over, and the others
continued until each person was satisfied that he had done
as well for himself as he could. Everybody got stuck with
something he didn't like, and everybody got something he
preferred, and all of us got a lot of things in the middle range
of desirability. From there we made out our own schedules.

This system was fun, but it took too long. Brian kept saying that we couldn't seriously think of a community of one
thousand people (our theoretical goal) sitting in a circle
and passing cards every week.

After a few weeks we moved on to a signup system,
whereby the jobs were all described on cards in a file box,
and we each took turns placing our initials on the job cards
of our choice. Then a clerical person took the data, tossed
coins to determine who among competitors got a desirable
job, and assigned the losers to jobs that nobody wanted. We
adjusted the credit value of the jobs at this time. If you com-
peted for a job, the credit value went down (and stayed
down for succeeding weeks); if it had to be assigned to someone who didn't want it, the credit value went up. We used
the increment of 10 percent per week, an arbitrary figure
that controlled inflation. The average credit is always worth
one hour.

A further variant on this system, called simultaneous
signup, allowed each person to sign up on a separate sheet,
not knowing who else was signing up for what. This elimi-
nated some logrolling and general manipulation.

The clerical part of the labor credit system rapidly became systematized. Two people working together complete it each week, using the better part of two days to do the work. This may seem a high clerical cost, but we don't find it too high. From it come (1) individual labor schedules—every member has his own sheet to refer to at any time; (2) general schedules posted where everyone can find out who is scheduled for what; and (3) bookkeeping in which members' surplus credits or deficits are recorded. All jobs are covered with assigned workers; all members have a fair share of the work.

We are willing to pay the price in clerical labor, because the alternative is role assignment. No serious community of our size and complexity (forty members plus about ten working visitors) can just let the work go from day to day on the assumption that someone will do it. Meals must be fixed on time and the kitchen cleaned. The cows have to be milked. The garden does not thrive on haphazard labor, and nobody would even propose trying to run a business or industry without a labor system of some kind. The anarchistic commune may be therapeutic, but it is not serious about proposing an alternative societal structure.

Since the work must be done, it must either be assigned (as we do it) in a carefully worked-out jigsaw of moving pieces, or it must be handled by professional workers—the kitchen people always doing kitchen work, the cow people always doing cow work, and the hammock workers making all the hammocks, etc. This is the way it is handled in every other serious commune that we know of or have read about. We are willing to conduct our work lives by role assignment if it turns out to be necessary. But our members do not want it. They want not only to choose their work but to choose it anew from week to week or even from day to day. This fiercely defended desire to try everything has created and maintains our complex labor system. A lot of visitors shake their heads over it and tell us it isn't worth the bother of the clerical work and weekly signup. But the critics are not members, and the members are not the critics. We like it.

We like it so much, in fact, that at one time it was difficult to make any changes in it. After the development of simultaneous signup, we worked for two years with no changes in the system. It worked smoothly, and minor complaints were handled by saying, "Well, somebody has to do it, and you were assigned by a random-number table," which was true.

In 1970 a combination of sudden population growth and fresh minds applying themselves to old problems brought about another revolution in the labor credit system. The new people could see what some of us longer-term people had overlooked—that with forty people on the system it is possible to do away with random assignment of aversive tasks. The chances are that in a group as large as this, we can almost always find somebody who doesn't mind a particular job as much as somebody else. It might literally be possible for us all to work just at those things we like—or at least didn't hate. With this exciting possibility in mind, it became important to know the degree of desirability each job had for each person.

Our current system asks each member to take a list of all the available jobs and place them in the order of his personal preference. After that, he doesn't have to sign up at all. The labor clerical people take over and work for two days filling out everyone's schedule as close to their personal preferences as possible. These days one gets high credits for doing work which one finds *personally* disagreeable. Two people might be shoveling manure side by side, and the person who enjoys the work is getting less credit for it than the person who doesn't. Most of us these days don't have to do a lot of unpleasant work. One dishwashing shift a week perhaps, or a shift of hay baling, might fall to each member. This system works even better than the one we had for two years.

But this is not the end. There are still problems to be worked out, and we will undoubtedly find that fundamental changes in the labor system will be necessary from time to time. We may even lose our resistance to specialization and find some of our members preferring and requesting role-assignment jobs. There is already some evidence of this. What will probably not change is the basic idea of the labor credit—all work is equally honorable. But the less pleasant the work, the less time one should have to put into it.

Since early in our history we have had to adjust the labor credit system to make it possible for members to take vacations. We do that by working longer hours than we are assigned and accumulating a surplus of credits. Most members have fairly large surpluses and can take a vacation whenever they choose. Money for traveling is provided by the Community in very small amounts, and members are allowed to accept travel money from their parents or to work for their own spending money on their own vacation time.

"What would you do if a member didn't do his work?" asked Burris of Frazier in *Walden Two*. "I can't imagine it," said Frazier. "We'd think of something." We are often asked the same question, but our answer is a little more definite, probably because our techniques of behavioral engineering aren't worked out quite so well as they were in the book. "We would ask him to leave," is what we reply. The problem of laziness and willingness to sponge off the labor of others is not a serious one here at Twin Oaks. We try to make it obvious that leaving one's work undone is equivalent to asking other members to do it for you, and not many people are so lacking in conscience that they are willing to do that on a regular basis. All of us goof off from time to time, and minor infractions of work equality are largely ignored by the group. There have been very few occasions when we have had to implement our rule that allows us to expel members who don't do their share. There are a lot of things we can try before resorting to such extremes.

The first step would be for the Labor Manager to talk to the member who is getting behind. The chances are pretty good that the member will be worried about it, anyway, and it will be a relief to him to have the problem in the open. Together the two will look at the kinds of work that the member has been signing up for (but not doing) and talk about ways of overcoming the specific behavior problems that get in his way. Perhaps he has trouble getting up in the morning. The Community can, at his request, have someone wake him. Changing to scheduled work, like cooking, milking, or dishwashing, might solve the problem, or at least help him catch up. The Labor Manager will arrange a schedule with the member whereby he makes up his labor deficit a little at a time. The group would never expel a member who made a real effort to change his behavior, no matter how lazy he might have been or how many credits he had to make up.

Occasionally there is a case of work undone that is not caused by bad habits or carelessness but is a deliberate attempt to avoid work entirely. It is rare, but it happens. It has happened twice in our history.

The first one was Charlie, in the fall of 1967. Charlie didn't say to himself, "I don't like work much, but I'm going to have to do my share here, so I may as well face it." If he had admitted that much to himself, he might have been able to adjust to Twin Oaks. What he said to himself was that he was a philosopher and a poet. He spent a good deal of time practicing his guitar, and he said that a decent society ought to be able to support its philosophers, poets, and musicians. He was aware, of course, that society at large had not arrived at that utopian stage. Charlie had spent most of his adult life (he was twenty-eight) being supported by women who fell in love with him, including a wife who had borne several children by him. He had never in his life faced and solved the problem of doing something for which society was willing to support him in return. Even the women in his life left him after a while. Charlie's view of all this was that society was all messed up and that he had

won a spiritual independence of the system by not depending on money. "I don't use money," he told us with pride.

It turned out that he didn't use labor credits either. He
did, however, use other people. Marie, a woman who joined
the Community about the same time Charlie did, fell in
love with him immediately and understood his need to be
free to devote himself to poetry. She made out his labor
sheet for him (he refused to touch it) and kept track of
what he was supposed to be doing. She signed both of them
up for cooking or washing dishes together, quietly did the
work alone, and awarded the credits to him. We were only
twelve people then, and we could not help noticing that
Charlie had a great deal more free time than the rest of us.
Brian, as Labor Manager, intervened. It was then that we
made the policy which is still fundamental to our system:
"The person who does the work gets the credit," Brian told
Charlie. "Regardless of who signs up for the job, the credit
goes to the worker." This made it impossible for Marie to
make a gift of her labor to her lover. Marie was as angry
and frustrated as Charlie. "Why can't I work for him?" she
asked. "That's what I want to do. He needs to be free of
work, and I can carry his share. The group isn't losing anything. What business is it of yours if I do his work? I love
him." It was difficult to answer this question, coming from
Marie. When someone demands the right to be exploited,
the designers of an equalitarian society feel muddled, to
say the least. But we stuck to our principles, and insisted
that Charlie support himself with his own labor. We felt
that our society could not stand a precedent that would
permit work to be laid on the altar of love.

Charlie next circumvented the system by signing up for
long hours of hammock weaving at no special hour. That
gave him time to procrastinate. He did do some work, when
he felt inspired, so it was four weeks before the group became sufficiently annoyed to take any action. We had a brief
meeting at which we decided that the principle was more

important than the member in this case, and that Charlie
should be faced with a clear alternative—work or leave.
Dwight was appointed to bear the message. All Dwight
said to Charlie was, "You are seventy-five credits in deficit,
and the group feels that you should be making some progress
toward making that up." He was going to go on to suggest
a program whereby Charlie could do this a little at a time,
but Charlie did not care to listen to it. "Well, to be frank,"
he said, "I was thinking of leaving anyway. My only problem is getting enough money for a bus ticket back to Indiana.
If you people would be interested in buying my wrecked
VW in exchange for the bus ticket . . ." The bargain was
sealed in short order.

Two years later another member tried to live here without working. But Henry didn't mind dirtying his hands with
labor credit sheets. He was a college graduate and very
intelligent. He understood the system very well, and he
turned in all his sheets clearly marked with the credits he
claimed. Unfortunately, the truthfulness of these records
was less pronounced than their neatness. If Henry had done
fifteen hours of hammock weaving, no one, least of all the
Hammock Manager, had seen him. Yet the sheet was clearly
marked as if he had done the work. His sheet said he had
done four hours of food processing; the Kitchen Manager
remembered that he had worked for less than an hour, taken
off for a cigarette break, and not returned to the job.
Cheating of this magnitude went beyond our willingness
to overlook. The Labor Manager asked him to explain the
discrepancy. Henry replied with a barrage of verbal abuse
and ended by beating up the Labor Manager. There is more
to Henry's story than his laziness. In his case even being a
good worker would not have made it possible for him to
get along in community. In both his case and Charlie's, the
refusal to work was combined with an extreme hostility to the
Community, a continuous sarcastic commentary on our institutions and approaches to problems, and a sneering disdain

of the "power structure." Both members, before they left, thoroughly alienated not only the power structure but every individual in the Community. It may be the case that only people who feel such hostility would openly refuse to do their work in an equalitarian society. Certainly such attitudes have been very rare. Most members bog down in their work from time to time, but perk up again after a vacation or a fresh approach or a change of job. Occasional members have taken refuge in questionable "sick leave," but even this is uncommon.

Neither is there any truth in the classic assertion that there is no incentive to work without personal financial gain. We have members who have the same intense dedication to their work that characterizes happy professionals in the competitive outside world. Their involvement is with the work itself and with building the Community. The credits are beside the point, as the money would be beside the point if they were working for wages. They want to get a good hammock brochure printed, or an engine rebuilt, or a new labor system perfected, or an orchard properly planted, or the kitchen remodeled. The reinforcement comes from the finished product, the purr of the new engine, the neat rows of baby trees— and from the appreciation of the other members of the Community.

Equality in labor is a large step toward social justice, but it is not the only step Twin Oaks has taken toward equality. Our financial and property policies reflect our determination to avoid a privileged class. Members get no cash income except a very small allowance which has ranged between twenty-five cents and a dollar a week. Any money which they might have owned before joining simply stays in the bank for their first three years unless they want to donate it to the Community. In any case, Twin Oaks receives the interest on it, as well as dividends on any stocks and bonds, rents from any real property, or any continuing income of any kind. It is not common for incoming members to own much property beyond their clothing and a few records and books, and we have had scant experience with stocks and bonds. Nevertheless the principle is clear: no member should enjoy financial privileges that are denied the rest of us. The three-year delay in making all property communal is meant to be a protection for the individual member, in case he changes his mind about being a communitarian. We have yet to collect any money from this provision. The Community is only four years old, and members who have been here for that length of time have long ago donated what property they owned.

Twin Oaks's government, unlike the rest of its systems, is not left to rotation, coin tosses, or personal choice. It is one area where we feel it necessary to choose people for their ability.

The overall direction of the Community is in the hands of a three-person board of planners (a name derived from *Walden Two*). Their job is to appoint and replace managers, settle conflicts between managers, decide touchy questions having to do with ideology, and replace themselves when their eighteen-month terms expire. Most of the authority of the Community, most of the important decision-making that affects the daily lives of the members, belongs not to the planners but to a group of managers, members who are in charge of various areas of work. Managerial positions are continually being created, and are awarded on the basis of interest and work.

The Visitor Managership, when Maggie took it over, was simply a job of telling people whether they could visit or not. Maggie took a real interest in it and began to keep good records on the visitors. She also got a room in our newest building set aside for guests, saw to it that it was painted and furnished with sturdy bunks, and bought matching fitted sheets for them. She decides how many guests we can accept at one time, and which ones to turn down. She deals with visiting psychology classes, prospective members, and local drunks. On those rare occasions when a visitor's behavior is such that he isn't welcome here, it is Maggie's job to ask him to leave. Maggie is eighteen.

If someone else had been Visitor Manager, the job might have been entirely different. There might be six bunks in the room, or visitors might be sleeping on the floor on mattresses. The room decor would be different, and there might be more (or fewer) than ten at a time. Thus, Maggie has a great deal of authority in her area.

We pair authority with responsibility, and we are usually short of managers. There are more areas of community work to be expanded than there are people interested in getting involved in them.

We have been told from time to time that the word "manager" really turns people off. There is something about it that reminds one of the word "authority" or "boss." All I can say is that after you have lived a while at Twin Oaks, it loses those connotations. The actual job comes closer to "servant" than "boss," as in the commonly heard "Where's the Animal Manager—the cows are out again," or, "Nobody has showed up to wash supper dishes—where's the Labor Manager?" What the term means here is "person responsible." Anybody willing to take responsibility can get it. The more time and thought a member puts into his particular job, the bigger that job gets.

It seemed to us when we started the Community that eight people didn't need much government. On the first day of our communal lives, we called a meeting to discuss decision-making. Our first problem was that Carrie did not want to come to the meeting. She wanted to take a nap. Carrie was fond of country living, and she was willing to go along with communal principles up to a point, but at the beginning, at least, she didn't want to have to think about it any more than necessary, and meetings constituted more than necessary. So we gathered without her and talked about how to make decisions. Sandy proposed that we should meet each week as a group and make decisions by consensus. He explained that consensus procedure consisted of discussing problems and possible solutions until everybody agreed. I thought the idea absurd, but I did not want to break the harmony of the first afternoon by saying so. I just asked Sandy what we were supposed to do if someone remained unconvinced, and we still disagreed at the end of a meeting. He said it was an experiment, and that if it didn't work, we could change the government. Even a decision to change the government, I pointed out, would have to be made by consensus, and anyone who was benefiting by a breakdown of consensus procedure might not be willing to go along with a different system. But Sandy kept saying that it was an experiment and that he knew of groups that had made it work. Finally I shrugged my shoulders and went along with it. By consensus that first day we made decisions to have community of property and to open a group bank account. We drew straws to determine who would be signers on the account.

But most decisions were really made by individuals who just thought of doing something and did it. Sandy opened up a cash record book, and Carrie decorated a cash box, which was kept in a public room. Any member took money for whatever he deemed necessary but wrote it down, together with what it was spent on, in the cash book. Incoming money was entered in the same book. It wasn't an efficient system, but we do have records, of a sort, even from those early days.

Consensus government was sorely tested on the issue of buying cattle. It had been suggested to us by our neighbors that we purchase a few head of beef cattle and let them graze our pastures during the summer, then sell them in the fall. We were supposed to make a profit on their increased weight, and at the same time keep our pastures under control. I was in favor of this plan, and so was Fred. Sandy was dead set against it. He didn't approve of agriculture as a community activity. The more we talked about it, the angrier we got. I found myself shouting and shaking, and Sandy just talked slower and slower and got stubborner and stubborner. Unable to come to a "yes, buy the cows" decision by consensus, we were automatically left at the end of an exhausting meeting with a "no, we won't buy the cows" decision. It was clear to me that consensus was operating as a one-person veto. I was ready to go to a voting system, or anything else that would get a decision based on something besides one person's stubbornness. But Brian, outside of meeting time, talked to Sandy and persuaded him to go along with the cattle plan. Brian didn't really care one way or the other. He just wanted to keep peace. So we bought the cattle and kept consensus procedure for a while. But Carrie never would come to meetings, and Jenny to fewer than half of them. The decision-making group became defined as simply those people who were willing to put up with the slowness of consensus procedure. Arguments could go on for hours, and there were other things to do. We needed managers—people who would take responsibility for one area of work or another and make sure it was taken care of. A few managerships arose spontaneously, like Fred and auto maintenance. I found myself in charge of canning and freezing the garden produce, just because I had seen my mother do it years before and had confidence that I could follow a cookbook. Brian had already begun to invent labor systems, and that was the issue that caused the conflict that precipitated our getting a formal government after five weeks without one.

Quincy liked everything to be precise and carried out according to the rules. He could not deal with Norms, Understandings, or Assumptions. He could not function with gray areas. He liked precision and order. In addition, he had a hankering for leadership. So when Brian began inventing labor systems and the rest of us started referring to Brian as "Labor Manager," Quincy protested. "Who elected him?" he demanded. "Since when does a labor manager appoint himself?" I mumbled something about its being generally understood that Brian would be Labor Manager. Quincy said it wasn't understood by *him*. That I believed. I didn't want to argue against Quincy's position, because in theory I agreed with it. Formally designated leadership has advantages. For a group of eight it seemed superfluous. If Quincy had not been one of us, I believe we could have gone up to a group of ten or twelve without formal government. But not even a group of three could have functioned informally if Quincy was one of them. I talked the matter over with Dwight. I suggested that we could best deal with Quincy's absurdities and his ambitions by voting in a set of officers. Once the rules were set up, Quincy would obey them to the letter. Didn't we intend to have a system of government eventually? What would be the harm of starting now? Dwight was worried lest the wrong people be put into office. He thought Brian our most capable leader, and he didn't want to submit to a democratic election that might by some fluke omit Brian from the board. This worry sounded almost as silly to me as Quincy's protests. I told him there was no way in the world for the group not to have noticed Brian's talents, and that he would of course be elected. Dwight's distrust of democracy was deep, but he submitted to the election process. The others were not difficut to persuade. Sandy was disappointed to see consensus procedure abandoned after such a short trial, but he recognized that our particular group was not really interested in making it work, and he gave his consent to the election. Brian, Dwight, and I were elected planners. Our first task was to organize the community work into managerships. We immediately appointed Brian Labor Manager, and Quincy made no protest. The rest of the managerships were divided as best we could among the members, by asking all the members what areas they felt capable of directing.

Our bylaws leave us free to change our form of government any time two-thirds of the group wants it different. I personally think Twin Oaks would survive under a variety of governmental systems, including consensus or even democracy, as long as the managerial system was left intact. The important decisions are made at this level. It is the Construction Manager who researches sewage systems and building designs and presents them to the Community with his recommendations. The garden and food managers between them determine our diet. The Clothing Manager decides whether we buy new clothes or make do with old ones, and the Health Manager makes doctor's and dentist's appointments on the basis of need. Any of these people can be overruled by the board of planners, and the board in its turn can be overruled by the membership as a whole, but such occasions are exceptional. Managers use their best judgment in making decisions that benefit the group as a whole. They have nothing to gain by doing otherwise.

What keeps our system from turning into a tiresome bureaucracy is its simplicity—that decisions can be made swiftly by at most three people, and usually by a single manager, using his or her own judgment. What keeps it from being a dictatorship is that there is nothing to gain from being dictatorial. All decisions that are of interest to the group as a whole are discussed with the group as a whole. No legislation can be put across unless members are willing to go along with it. There is no police force here to carry out anybody's will. Our only technique is persuasion.

In spite of our hierarchical-sounding governmental setup, we are anti-authoritarian in both principle and practice. Bossiness quickly dies out as a personal trait, because the group does not reward it with obedience. Bossy people are simply avoided; bossy managers can't get people to work with them. We like having managers in charge of things, because we need to feel that someone has done some research and knows what should be done, but managers simply do not give orders. They point out things, make suggestions, define the job, and occasionally disqualify a sloppy worker. Once in a while we have as a group asked a manager to get tough in a troublesome area like kitchen cleanliness, in order to make sure that the dishwashers do a thorough job. All such requests have been refused. Managers may try it for a day, but no longer. "I would rather resign," they say, or, "I would rather leave the kitchen dirty. It isn't worth it."

I remember one summer we were having trouble getting stretcher work done. Stretchers are the wood part of our hammocks. Stretcher work is machine work, drilling holes with the drill press and sanding with an electric sander. It is boring and noisy. Also, the machinery kept breaking down, and the whole operation used to take place out-of-doors with no protection from the heat at certain hours of the day. The need for stretchers was great, and we had people scheduled for the machinery all during the daylight hours. The work was extremely unpopular, and the credit value skyrocketed without effect. Fewer than half the scheduled work hours were actually being done. People simply skipped their shifts and went swimming instead. As a possible solution, the hammock manager added the job of foreman to the system. It was to be the foreman's job to go around to all the people signed up for stretchers each day and ask them if they had done their work for the day, thus giving a small reminder and making it more difficult to skip out on the work. The job of foreman fell by lot (no one volunteered for it) to Naomi, seventeen years old. She tried to do her job, but the replies she got left her in tears. People were not accustomed to being reminded, did not want to be reminded, and also did not want to do stretcher work. The foreman idea was discarded.

Actually, we should have known better. In the end we solved the problem the Walden Two way. As soon as we got a little money, we brought the job indoors and bought a better drill press.

In general our approach to systems has been to take first

the ones proposed in *Walden Two* and stick to them as long as they work well. As we find fault with them, we then make changes to correct the faults and make the systems fit our situation better. Skinner's book has been of immense service to us in giving us a point of general agreement for a starting place. Because we have *Walden Two,* we do not need a leader or teacher. Cooperation is possible because we have all, before we even joined, agreed upon the general principles of the community described in that book. Enormous ground is covered in that general agreement—including such items as the scientific, experimental approach to problem solving, the community of property, the dissolution of the nuclear family, and the willingness to be deliberate about the molding of character and personality. The debt we owe Dr. Skinner is enormous, but there is nothing sacred about the institutions we derived from his book. All of our systems are subject to change, and most of them have changed even over the few years that we have been a community.

We are a long way from Walden Two, not only in our modest physical plant and substandard per capita income, but even in its fundamental goal of creating a society where every member does what he ought just because he wants to. We believe in that, but we don't know how to do it yet, and we still use some of the traditional props of government— rules, systems, pep-talks—as substitutes for more "natural" reinforcers. Part of the reason for this is sheer poverty. Just as we couldn't get good work behavior for making stretchers until we improved the working conditions, just so we can't really run our entire community on positive reinforcement until a higher degree of affluence makes it possible for us to get rid of some of the rules.

If it weren't for shortages, equality wouldn't be very important. Nobody worries about getting an equal plateful of food here. There is plenty of it, and we each eat according to our desires. It is perfectly reasonable to predict that machinery and automation will some day put desirable work in the same class as food. Not too far in the future we shouldn't have to do any work we don't like, because the machines will do it for us. With only a little money for construction, all our head-scratching over the distribution of living space will be a thing of the past. The principle has a very general application: first provide an adequate supply; then let everybody take what he wants. The need for rules and propaganda falls away by itself.

There is one other important factor, too. In order to make even an adequate supply of anything go around, it is necessary for everyone to have simple and modest tastes and desires. That means the creation of an entirely new culture—noncompetitive, nonconsumerist. Twin Oaks is tackling both these problems at once, and both of them are difficult. First there is the problem of making a decent supply of desirable things available. That's economics. Then there's the necessity of keeping people's desires within bounds, so that the economic problem doesn't keep multiplying. That's cultural planning. All of Twin Oaks's group activities fall under one or another of these goals. Until both of these states are achieved, it will be necessary for us to continue to legislate a rough equality, knowing full well that equality is just a halfway house on the road to the good life.

V

Back to the Land

The Walden Two idea is broad enough to include the industrial commune or even an urban group. Self-sufficiency, though traditionally a part of the commune idea, is not essential. In fact, complete self-sufficiency is not even practical. Nevertheless, for many of us, settling on farm land and doing farming was part of our basic assumption.

When he bought the land, Hal suggested that we try to make farming a business as well as subsistence endeavor, and we agreed. We found a suitable farm that had been growing wheat, hay, corn, and tobacco. It seemed reasonable for us to continue doing as the former owner had done, at least for the first year. By the time we agreed to purchase the farm in the spring of 1967, Mr. Edwards, the former owner of the farm, had already put in the tobacco seed bed. Realizing that he would not be on the land long enough to finish the project, he conferred with us prospective buyers about what we wanted to do. Fred and I, who were at the time negotiating for the group, were enchanted. Here was a real farm crop, raised on a real government allotment, with an automatic market and protected by price guarantees. Of course we would raise tobacco!

We offered Mr. Edwards one-third of the crop in exchange for the work he had already put in, his advice and help along the way in taking care of it, and his aid in marketing. He readily agreed to this figure and did indeed earn his share. We began working the tobacco crop right away, even before actually occupying the property, by coming to the farm on weekends after working in the city at regular jobs during the week. Hal drove three hundred miles each weekend from his home and helped us with the work. We brought friends from the city, too, and Mr. and Mrs. Edwards helped us transplant hundreds of seedlings. It did not seem hard work to us. There was too much excitement for that. We were tired at the end of the job, but it was a joyful fatigue.

By the time the Community actually occupied the property, and Mr. Edwards had moved away to town, the crop was doing well and needed to be suckered. To sucker a tobacco plant is to break off certain unwanted leaves, in order to improve the size and quality of the ones that are left. It must be done two or three times during the growing season. Sandy and Brian and Carrie and Dwight were not nearly so enthusiastic about the tobacco as Fred and I had been. The romance of farming failed to catch at their imaginations. To them it was just work, and unpleasant work at that. Added to the hot sun and the constant stooping was the sticky sap of the plant that stuck to our hands as we suckered. When we returned from the fields, we would try to scrub the black off our hands with everything we could find, including professional hand cleaner. But tobacco sap is tougher than cleansers. Eventually, after the suckering season, it wears off. In the meantime we had stained, sticky hands. Suckering soon became everybody's least favorite job. Unless it was tobacco hoeing.

When the romance died, I used to comfort myself with the thought of the amount of money we were going to make when we sold the crop. A government-supported price seemed a sure thing. After all, Fred and I assured each other, farmers do raise tobacco, and they have children and homes, and they aren't hungry. So there must be money in it.

These days we theorize that farmers raise their children and build their homes on something else. At any rate, after spending a week harvesting the tobacco crop in the heat of the day, then hanging it in the barn, we gave over a large room and a month's labor to sorting and tying it for market. Whether we made an error in the drying process or what we did, I don't know. I do know that we brought back a little over five hundred dollars from the tobacco auction, and a third of that belonged to Mr. Edwards. Subtracting what we had paid for fertilizer, we believe that we may possibly have earned twenty cents an hour on that crop.

It was only later that we discussed or seriously considered the moral implications of raising tobacco. Thinking back on it, it seems to show the difference in the public conscious-ness between the years 1967 and 1971. These days we would not raise tobacco even if it were profitable—the membership would not stand for it. I might exasperatedly point out that if we don't raise it, somebody else will, but it wouldn't do me any good. The members would just say, "We don't want to be involved in that sort of thing." It isn't profitable, how-ever, so the issue does not come up.

Every time we talk about raising chickens, we are up against the fact that we can buy fryers at the supermarket for twenty-seven cents a pound, and eggs by the case at thirty cents a dozen. Some members tell us that chickens raised on a farm taste better than the ones that are mass-produced by the chicken factories, but against this must be weighed the fact that the home-grown kind have to be killed, gutted, and plucked, all on top of the cost of raising them. We haven't actually tried to raise chickens, but every-body we've talked to tells us not to, unless we are awfully fond of them as a hobby. American efficiency and know-how has literally brought the price of ready-to-eat chicken below the price of chicken feed.

We did raise ducks, though. It was the Department of
Agriculture pamphlets that got us started. The pictures were
charming, and the text told us that ducks could be allowed
to wander freely during the day and would come to the
duckhouse at night to lay their eggs, thus feeding themselves
while being highly decorative, and giving us eggs into the
bargain. Fred loved the idea, and so did I. He sent away for
fifty day-old ducklings and some baby guinea hens.

The guineas were never anything but a nuisance. Their
mortality rate was discouraging. Though we followed the
instructions for their care, every day we would find another
one dead. Marie tried to nurse one back to health once by
carrying it around inside her bra. She thought it needed a
mother's warmth. But it died anyway. Those that did live
grew up to be the silliest animals we ever had. They never
got used to any human, not even Fred, who fed them
tenderly every day, and they would squawk and fly to the
highest part of the chicken coop at his arrival, bruising
themselves on the rafters. They never seemed to learn that
there was no place to fly to or perch on. We killed a few and
ate them, and we didn't notice anything particular about
their flavor, much touted by the farm sentimentalists. They
were tough, in fact. As to their being good watchdogs, we
tested them on several occasions, sneaking up at night. They
paid no more attention than our dogs did. I suspect their
reputation for being guardians arises from the fact that they
are noisy. I will certainly grant them that. They make awful
screaming noises at any time of the day or night. It was this
that led them eventually to the stew pot.

The ducks came a little closer to their promise. They were
indeed decorative. Furthermore, they ate gigantic quantities
of grasshoppers and weeds. Unfortunately, they also ate all
the baby cauliflower and broccoli plants that I had ordered
from Michigan and was trying to raise. Besides, their drop-
pings were extraordinarily messy, and they chose our side-
walks as a latrine. It became necessary to fence them in. I

mean to try to fence them in. The fact is, they liked the yard better than they did the pasture, and they did everything they could to get back over, under, around, or through that fence. I think now that if we had been smart, we would have immediately killed and eaten any duck that left its pasture and came into the yard. Thus, through a process of natural selection, we would have been breeding a race of ducks that stayed where it belonged. But we didn't think of that. We kept catching them and throwing them back into their enclosure, thus actually returning the revolutionary cadre back to the masses to teach the others their tricks.

We ate all the ducks, but we do not know for a fact that we will never again try to raise poultry. It seems to us now that farming, like other businesses, needs close management and attention. Fred had too many demands on his time, and so has every Farm Manager since that time. But as the population rises, and members look about for significant tasks to get involved in, it is probable that someone will try ducks, or chickens, or even guineas. Our experience cannot be classified as an experiment that failed. It wasn't a proper experiment at all. It was just a romance that lost its spark.

Back in 1967, when we first realized that we were really going to come to live on a farm, we were almost as excited about farming as we were about communal living and Walden Two. Our ignorance was boundless. I recall that I didn't know there was any difference in meaning between the words "tractor," "plow," and "cultivator," and I thought hay and straw were the same thing. I wanted to do everything there was to do on a farm. I thought we should grow every crop that would grow in our climate and construct a greenhouse to grow the things that wouldn't. I wanted a sample pair of every kind of farm animal. I grew ecstatic over ducklings and geese, delighted in feeding the pigs, grew personally acquainted with each calf. Most of the group felt somewhat the same way. The exception was Sandy, who wanted nothing whatever to do with farming.

Sandy opposed buying cows on the ground that "Once we get cows, we'll start spending time mending fences, and the next thing you know, we'll think of ourselves as a farm. We're not a farm. We are a community. There's no money in farming, and we ought to put our scarce resources into something industrial that will pay off quicker." Sandy may have been right, but the sentiment for farming overwhelmed his objections, and we went into it, head over heels, with very little planning or investigation.

Fred became our Farm Manager. Among the original eight of us, he was the only one who knew anything about keeping machinery running, and it was he who took the most avid interest in crops and animals. The responsibilities that are now divided into six managerships (Cows, Fences, Farm Crops, Garden, Automobile Maintenance, General Maintenance) were all in Fred's hands in 1967. Fred's basic gripe was that there were only about sixteen hours in a day that he could reasonably push himself to work, and there were still things left over to be done when he was finished. Related to this was his problem with the labor credit system and communal life.

The real problem was that there were two separate things going on at the same time. Fred was interested in farming and trying to make the Community's economics work from a practical point of view. Sandy, in his lonely corner, was working on getting us into industry. And the rest of us, especially Brian, Dwight, and I, were mostly concerned about working out our communal ideology. Ideology meant equality, and equality meant equality of opportunity. The opportunities at Twin Oaks consisted mostly of opportunities to learn different kinds of work. We devised the labor credit system that assured everyone an equal chance of getting any kind of work he signed up for—regardless of the skill he might have for it, or the lack of it. When Fred pointed out that he was more use on the tractor than in the kitchen, and that I was more use in the kitchen than on the tractor, our answer was that neither job was hard to learn, and that our ideology required that we sacrifice some efficiency in order to insure equality of opportunity. Fred accepted this, but grumpily.

Besides equality, our utopian aims demanded (and still demand) that we be able to arrange our work so as to enjoy it as much as possible. What that meant to us at the time was to spend only a short time doing any one thing. Most of us wanted a schedule, for example, that gave us an hour working in the garden, and then a couple of hours on hammock weaving, then some free time, and then perhaps some cooking or dishwashing. Few of us were prepared to spend all of our time making hammocks, or doing farm work, or, especially, working in the kitchen. We wanted variety, and in demanding it, we forced variety also on those who wanted to specialize. Fred wanted to spend all of his time in his own area of interest—the farm. Looking back on this now, it seems to me a most reasonable desire, and one which we can easily accommodate now that we have a community of forty people. But at the time it seemed like selfishness—a thinly disguised excuse to get out of washing dishes. We were, above all things, equalitarians, and the equalitarian way prevailed. Fred did some cooking and dishwashing, and other people got to drive the tractor.

Fred wasn't lazy, and it wasn't the kitchen work he minded. What bothered him was having incompetent people on "his" tractors. He complained bitterly to me, and I tried to act as liaison between him and the board of planners. "Fred says you need some training to be able to drive a tractor," I told them. But Brian said he didn't see what training it took, and Dwight said anybody could learn it in twenty minutes. So Fred's complaints never succeeded very far. What he usually did to circumvent the problem was to "forget" to requisition jobs on the labor credit system. Thus nobody could sign up for them, and he found time to do them himself.

The trouble with this conflict, as with most conflicts, was that both parties were right. It really was true that some inexperienced people were causing damage to our machinery. One short-term visitor, I recall, tried to plow up a rock the size of an office desk. The broken plow points cost twenty-six dollars to replace, plus the trip to Richmond and a two-day wait. But it was also true that Fred was impatient and intolerant, that his idea of a qualified tractor driver was mostly limited to himself, and that he really did want to do all the tractor work because he enjoyed it. Problems of this kind eventually caused Fred to leave, but that was a year later.

While Fred was here we farmed. We had tobacco and hay and a garden in 1967, and corn and sorghum and a huge garden in 1968. Before he left that fall, he was making plans for an ever-expanding farm operation that would have had us renting farm land all over the area. He liked to think big.

He certainly thought big when it came to beans and corn. I could not persuade him to sit down with paper and pencil and figure out how much of this food we could actually eat. He just thumbed through seed catalogs and bought a pound of every kind of string bean that appealed to him. A pound of seed goes a long way. I believe Fred planted nine pounds, nine different varieties, including the huge Kentucky Wonder.

The year 1968 was a pretty good one for beans. When the beans came in, we had bean picking on the labor system in shifts, starting early in the morning and progressing through the cooler part of the day. As for bean snapping and canning, it went on eighteen hours a day. Six people sat around huge tubs of beans in the back yard and snapped them. The pickers would come in with bushel baskets full, rinse them off with the garden hose, and pour them into our tubs. The job never ended. Late at night, members would still be putting two-quart jars of beans into the pressure cooker and taking them out some time later, reducing the pressure according to the directions. We canned 750 quarts of green beans that summer, a supply that lasted us two years, eating them almost every day. All those 750 quarts went through the pressure canner, six jars at a time.

The beans from the garden kept coming in until the people began to refuse to can any more. I spelled out to Fred what 750 quarts meant in terms of eating, explained that home-canned goods will not keep forever. Fred reluctantly called off the bean picking, and the remainder of that beautiful crop went dry on the vines. If we had not deliberately stopped, we would have had beans enough for a thousand quarts easily.

The corn was nearly as bad. Most of it went into the freezers, but scraping it from the cob was a messy and unpopular job. The pigs got a lot of that acre of corn. Even so, the frozen corn lasted us a year and a half.

The tomatoes were successful that year, too, as I recall, and we had a good apple crop. It was, in fact, the tremendous success of the 1968 garden that was responsible for the total failure of farming and gardening in 1969.

Part of it was that Fred left. And part can be blamed on the record floods that came in August and wiped out what little garden we did manage to plant and cultivate. But most of it was sheer reaction, rebellion, exhaustion. We have never collected really good figures, but it did seem to us that the cost of the vegetables we froze and canned could not possibly have justified the work that went into them. The jars alone cost twelve cents apiece. We noted that our neighboring farmers no longer feel it is worth their while to process a great deal of food, but simply buy it from the grocery store as they need it. They garden mostly for summer use. A neighbor of ours once told me, "I keep putting in the potatoes and raising my own beef, and I look at the supermarket prices and figure that by the time I've bought a freezer and all, I could afford to buy all my food preprocessed the way they do in the city. A lot of people around here do that. But I don't know. I would just hate not to have my own vegetables. I figure I break about even, if I don't count my labor. I don't save anything, but I know what I'm eating."

That year (1968) was marked by no new construction. All of our labor went into food processing. In 1969 we built a building instead, and the farm went to pieces. We plowed some of the land, with the intention of putting in a hay crop, but the machinery broke down before we could get the seed in, and we had no one who could fix it. The land went to the weeds. Other portions we did get seeded. We put in a crop of Sweet Sioux grass—a hay that must be harvested at just the right time to be good for the cows. Just the right time came and went, but our tractors, even when repaired, could not get into the fields to cut it because the ground was too muddy. Then the floods came and buried the whole fields, anyway.

In the spring of 1970 nothing had yet been done, and ragweed grew where nothing had been planted. That summer showed us the price we would have to pay if we literally let the farm go to weeds. Several members are highly allergic to ragweed. They spent the entire season sneezing and blowing their noses and taking various antihistamines to try to clear up their breathing enough to get some sleep.

But by this time we had recovered from the severe blows of the membership turnover of 1969, and once again we had people on the farm who could fix machinery and keep it running. This time our mechanics were people who cared both about farm machinery and about the equality principle. The tractors ran. The weeds were mowed down, the fields plowed and planted. Before winter hit, our fields were bright green with winter rye and barley. It was the prettiest sight around.

It is clear now that we must do some farming if we are to live on a farm. The fields and pastures must be kept under control. As to gardening, we are going through yet another experiment this summer, 1971, now with the mulched, organic approach.

Not all the romance is dead, either. In the midst of ordinary drudgery come days of excitement. There is a satisfaction in planting, and sometimes in harvesting. And it is a pleasure to look at acres of bright green rye, or deep gold winter wheat. Even putting up the hay, in spite of the heat, the stickery straws that get down your back, the sunburned neck, and the exhaustion, has a certain pleasure in it, especially riding back home from the fields on top of the bales.

The cows and calves are less adorable, perhaps, than when we first came from the city, but the cattle people still call them by name and speak to them with affection. One of our milk cows considerately gave birth to her latest calf in the cow yard, in full view of fifteen communitarians.

Sex education, if anybody should be lacking it, is a fringe benefit of farm life. When we first got here we were very curious about the process of artificial insemination of cows. When the man from the Breeders Association came out to inseminate one of our cows, the whole group of us gathered to watch him. The man didn't say a word about it to us, but later we heard that he had talked about us wherever he went: "And they all stood around and watched, even the pretty young girls. I was so embarrassed I didn't hardly know what to do."

Sandy was right when he said, "We aren't a farm; we're a community. There's no money in farming." We are first a community. Farming is just one of our activities. It does not bring in much cash, but it does produce food and also gives a certain amount of satisfaction. It would be very difficult for us not to farm. Hay fever is not the only deterrent to going entirely industrial. Every year our population changes a little, and almost all new members come from the city. They are as excited by a newborn calf and a packet of garden seed as I was in 1967, and it is their turn to live out their romance.

VI

Back to the City

We were very naïve about money when we started. In many ways I am sure we are still. But in the back of all our minds was one bit of knowledge that saved us from worrying about it too much. That was that, if we had to, we could and would get ordinary jobs in the city.

We hoped for a while that it might not be necessary. The tobacco crop we worked so hard on would bring in some money. We had a friend who was sending us two hundred dollars a month to get started on. There was the house in Washington that two of us owned some equity in. And we had some ideas for small industries that we hoped would put us on our feet.

As a matter of fact, the tobacco brought in about three hundred dollars, the friend eventually stopped sending the checks, the house could not be sold for even its equity, and our industrial ideas didn't do too well.

One of our ideas was to develop and manufacture a clever device that Brian had invented. It was a toilet trainer that would reward the child with bubble gum for urinating in the toilet. It was ingenious and it worked very well. We meant to change it from bubble gum to something else more appropriate for the age level, but we never got that far. The first thing we tried to do was advertise it.

Somewhere we had read that the big tabloid newspapers of New York were the best place to sell things through the mail. We sent in our ad. But they sent it back as unacceptable, because it contained the word "toilet." This was a newspaper that has headlines like "Doctor rapes patients under anesthetic." We were amused but also discouraged. The project was tabled and to this day remains undeveloped.

We brought in a little money by publishing a semimonthly newsletter about our activities and ideals. But we never tried to make a business out of it. The real purpose of the newsletter was to attract people to the Community.

Carrie wanted to sell Christmas-cookie tree decorations, which she had learned to make from a recipe of mostly cornstarch and salt. We sold a few through the mail, but it was never a satisfactory product, because the wet weather affected the material. Sandy spent a good bit of time trying to alter the recipe, using plaster of paris and various other materials, but we didn't produce anything that really looked very much like a cookie.

The original group wasn't very good at handcrafts, anyway. We played around with a lot of ideas. Hal wanted us to go into computer-dating, but the rest of us didn't think much of the idea. It was Hal, though, who got us into making the rope hammocks, the business we still engage in. Rope hammocks are a folk art of the Carolinas, Hal's home. He figured out how they were made, invented a wooden jig to weave them on, and taught the rest of us. The hammocks are a good product, and it is not bad work to make them. Our problem has always been sales. Until this year we had no experienced sales people, and everyone who tried sales work hated it. An occasional large contract kept the business afloat, and we have always sold a few of them through the mail and to visitors. In 1971 we acquired a member with the skill and determination to sell hammocks, and this business now accounts for about a third of our income.

But the fact is that in 1968 we did have to go out and get jobs, and we still have to. We will continue to do it as long

as necessary to keep the Community going. This is the main
reason Twin Oaks has continued where dozens of communes
with similar beginnings have failed. Our naïveté about
everything financial was counteracted by our willingness to
work for wages.

Carrie was the first to volunteer. She was a freshly graduated registered nurse, eager to work at her chosen profession, and it was not a hardship for her. Her income alone
was not sufficient, and I volunteered to work for the temporary clerical agencies. My first job was alphabetically
sorting checks, I recall, and I did it for eight hours a day for
three weeks. We were getting along all right on those two
incomes, we thought, until the day we discovered that we
had made a thousand-dollar mistake in the checkbook. Someone had made a subtraction error, and instead of having
$1,200 left in the bank, we had $200. It was at a planners'
meeting that we made this dismaying discovery, and the
other two planners immediately volunteered to go out and
get jobs. As soon as we announced it, two other people said
they wanted to go, too. We all got jobs right away, but the
financial outlook was fairly bleak for a while. I quote from
the planners' notes of March 7, 1968:

> Budget: We have $110 on hand. It is allocated as follows:
>
> | | |
> |---|---:|
> | To make token payments on outstanding bills | 54.00 |
> | Food for two weeks | 40.00 |
> | Gasoline for home and local use | 16.00 |
> | Work expenses for city workers | 15.00 |
> | Drivers' licenses for Dwight and Brian | 6.00 |
>
> To make this come out even we are figuring that we will
> take in $30 in newsletter subscriptions during this period.
> There is $9.00 left over. It is allocated as follows:
>
> | | |
> |---|---:|
> | Hal's departments | 3.00 |
> | Fred's departments | 3.00 |
> | Emergencies | 3.00 |

This probably sounds like some kind of joke. It is not. It is
really all the money we have.

We depended on volunteers for outside work for several months. Then it happened that several of us were laid off about the same time, and we felt that it was somebody else's turn to go. The obvious people were Hal and Fred, but neither volunteered. It was difficult to ask Fred, because his skills were so valuable on the farm. And it was even more difficult to ask Hal, because he was older and had been raised in an upper-class family and might have been humiliated by working at ordinary wage jobs. Besides, he knew and we knew that he had made the Community possible with his money. It wasn't supposed to make any difference (after all—from each according to his ability), but the fact was there and hung around, unspoken.

Getting a new set of outside workers turned out to be a problem. Those of us who had just been working felt that we ought to be exempt. Hal and Fred had their own reasons for feeling they ought not to go. A number of new people had joined the Community by this time, and we talked to them about it. Pete was not ready to go, because his wife, Rosa, would be too unhappy in his absence, and Rosa was not willing to go, because she didn't quite trust us with the baby. There were some other new people, and they professed willingness, but all of them said they had a special reason for preferring a later date. In desperation we drew lots. But the lot fell on Hal and Pete, and we were not brave enough to overrule their protests. Then we invented a bidding system, but the low bidders refused to go when they were tapped.

In the end we used volunteers again. Brian went back out, together with two new members who followed his example.

Brian tried teaching school for a while. It seemed senseless to be working for $1.60 an hour when he had a Master's degree and the Community needed the extra money he could make as a teacher. But it turned out that he could tolerate factory or construction work better than being, as he put it, a "warden" in a public school. He was supposed to be teaching algebra, but in his opinion the ninth-graders in his classes didn't need to learn algebra, and he was wasting his time and theirs. For the Community's sake he kept at the job for two months. But one day he just couldn't make himself go in.

The winter of 1968–69 was a low time for the Community as a whole. We lost a lot of members who were knowledgeable and did useful work. Fred left during this period. So did Hal and Pete. Their places were filled by much younger people who had few skills to contribute. But this same period was the time we established the equalitarian norm for outside work. None of the new people thought themselves too valuable to take their turn at the city jobs.

Brian felt guilty about quitting the high-paying teaching job, and he immediately got work with a bridge construction crew that did the steel work for the highway bridges. Two new members got themselves hired on the same crew, and so did Dwight. It was a dangerous job. The huge beams were swung into place by cranes, and once Ralph ducked barely in time to avoid being hit. The beams caught his hard hat and crushed it. Dwight once fell twenty feet from one of the bridges. Fortunately, he landed in a mud puddle, unhurt. The combination of bitter cold, physical danger, and long months on an unpleasant job persuaded us to take the men off this work in the early spring and send out some women. I went into office work once more, and so did Sheila, who had joined the Community in the interim. Brian, after a year and a half of outside work, could stay home at last.

It was then that we made up the rotation system we still use. Work two months, then quit, and somebody else goes out. Each member's turn comes up again when his ratio of days worked outside over days resident in the Community is the lowest in the group. New members' turns come up soon after they arrive, but they have at least thirty days to get adjusted to Community life before they have to go. Outside work is required of all members without exception.

Naomi and Jenny were still seventeen when they first tried their luck at getting outside work. Jenny found it easier than Naomi, partly because she looks older, but mostly because she can type. Naomi was determined, however. When the employment agencies showed no interest in her, she went from door to door on Main Street, trying to talk businessmen into giving her a chance. It wasn't easy. One day she realized that she had covered the entire town and was starting over again on the same places she had already asked. She would tell people that she was a cook and a bookkeeper and had had two years' experience. As a matter of fact, this was close to the truth. Few cooks can handle a kitchen as complex as Twin Oaks's, and Naomi is a genius at directing other people's labor efficiently. She can keep herself and four other people busy and engaged in conversation at the same time. The more labor there is available, the more dishes will be served at a meal. But Naomi was seventeen and looked even younger. Would-be employers thought she was cute, and they liked to talk to her, but they didn't have any jobs available for bookkeepers or cooks. Eventually Naomi got a clerical job for a soft-drink company and fulfilled her outside-work obligation.

By 1970 we needed eight outside-work incomes, and we began sending a carload of workers into the city together. It was a struggle just keeping a car in shape to make the daily trip to Richmond. I remember the day when the regular car broke down, and we had to send the workers in the old yellow Studebaker. It was raining, and the windshield wipers ceased working about half a mile from home. The brakes weren't in very good shape, either (but who needs brakes on the Interstate?) and one of the windows wouldn't close properly. It was just as well about the window, because the driver had to drive with it open, anyway, to see his way through the rain. Two members refused to go to work that day, on the grounds that the transportation was unfit for

human use, but the rest of the workers made it to Richmond
and back without incident.

After we got our van, life became a little easier for the
workers. We took the seats out of the van and lined it with
mattresses. The workers do not wear their costumes (good
clothes suitable for office jobs) in the van but carry them on
hangers. They wear their jeans or housecoats, wrap up in
blankets, and everyone except the driver can sleep through
the long trip to Richmond. The driver wakes them up in
time for them to change their clothes.

For some members getting a job is the hardest part of the
work shift. A few of us can work for the temporary place-
ment services. Some of these agencies are hiring both men
and women now. We have developed a very friendly relationship with two of the temporary agencies. They call us
and ask, "Do you have anybody out there who can work a
robotype? (or whatever)" This saves us the unpleasantness
of lying to employers about the length of time we expect to
work. Members who cannot do office work have to find work
on their own. They usually do construction work or similar
jobs in which high turnover is expected.

We have some members with degrees that enable them
to get professional positions if they want them. Very occasionally they do it. Most of them just do construction or office
work like the rest of us, because they do not want to commit
themselves to long-term work. One of our members, a
psychologist, decided to use his training to bring in a high
salary to the group's treasury. He got a job as a counselor
in a "Home" for delinquents. The school administrators were
suspicious of his big moustache and longish hair, and further suspicious that the delinquents liked and trusted him
intuitively. But they didn't actually fire him until the day
that they were explaining that homosexuality was a major
problem among the incarcerated boys. "But," questioned our
member, "why is that a problem?" When they digested his

meaning, they terminated his contract. Thus we were able to get the benefits of long-term employment without the bother of working for a long term.

You don't have to be a professional with outrageous opinions to get fired. One of our members was fired from a job as a hospital orderly because, while he was changing into his uniform, another orderly noticed that he wore no underwear. A whole group of members, who were planting trees on burned-over land, were fired simply for being members of Twin Oaks. "We don't want that kind of people," was the explanation.

A lot of us work in offices. Office work is not difficult. It has air-conditioning, carpets, and modern equipment to recommend it. But the degree of culture shock our office workers experience every day is greater than on other jobs. Offices are competitive and hypocritical places. The competition is not so much in the work as in the lunchtime conversations when the girls compare husbands, children, and possessions, vying for status as they pretend to sympathize with one another's problems. Coming home to Twin Oaks, where conversation is full of real sympathy and the old status symbols are meaningless, the workers find themselves less and less willing to go back to the office. Over and over we have heard outside workers say, "It isn't the job—it's the contrast."

At least two members have taken jobs as waitresses in preference to working in an office. It is exhausting work, but the hypocrisy level isn't as high. In its place is the nuisance of feeling oneself an object of lust to perfect strangers, day after day. Once when Martha was waiting table in a Holiday Inn, a man said to her, "Tell me where I can meet you— we'll discuss the terms later." Martha didn't understand him at first and asked him to repeat it. "When I finally got his meaning," she told us, "I couldn't help laughing. I didn't even answer him. I just laughed and laughed. He must have understood that I wasn't interested, so he didn't bother me anymore. He left me a nickel tip. From the size of the tip, I guess he wouldn't have been much of a customer even if I had been interested."

The men who do construction jobs also notice the general sexual frustration and consequent obsession in their fellow workers. Felix says, "Construction workers talk about two things. One is getting drunk on Saturday night. The other is pussy. When they see us longhairs, they get a new twist to their conversation. They want to know if we can arrange to get them any hippie pussy."

In desperation to avoid office work, a group of our female members once applied to the City of Richmond Department of Parks for a job raking leaves. The woman who took their application encouraged them. "I'm sure it is work you can easily do," she said. But her supervisor disagreed. He did worse. He laughed at them for applying. The women considered suing under the Equal Opportunities Act, but even if they won the suit, the leaves have long ago been raked up and burned.

Outside work was a real problem to a member named Ted. He got jobs without much difficulty but usually kept them only a few days. Occasionally he was fired. More often he quit. He explained his reasons for quitting. They were good reasons: the boss was rude; the work was too physically tiring; the fumes made him sick; the atmosphere was depressing. We believed the reasons, but we didn't believe they were any worse for Ted than they were for the rest of us, and we weren't willing to do his share for him just because he was extra sensitive. So every time he lost a job, the Labor Manager told him to go out and get another one. Under our system, members get labor credits for job-hunting as well as for working. We began to hear rumors that Ted was going into Richmond with the group of workers, making a few phone calls and checking with the State Employment Bureau, and then spending the rest of his days drinking coffee, or visiting friends in Richmond. In the

evening when he came home to the Community, Ted found
the members growing cold to him. No one said anything,
but he sensed that there was disapproval. The pressure
was so bad that Ted asked the board of planners in private session for a week's vacation to revive his spirits and
get in better shape to hunt for another job. He complained
that he had spent so much time away from the Community
that he hardly felt like a member any more. It was certainly
true. Six months had come and gone while Ted looked for
work, worked a few days, quit, and then looked for work
again—time enough for him to have done three shifts. And
still he lacked three weeks of completing his obligation. The
planners, however, refused his request and suggested that he
get a job and stick to it for the remaining three weeks and
get it over with.

Ted did get another job and he held it for nearly the
necessary three weeks. Then one day the Labor Manager was
figuring up the ratios of the members, to determine who
would be next to get a job. It turned out that Ted was among
the next four to be tapped. The reason: his ratio of days
worked to days spent on the premises was among the lowest
in the Community. He had taken his off days just miserably
looking for work. When Ted heard and digested this information, he left, taking his last paycheck with him to sweeten
his departure.

Ted's case became an issue, and one which is not settled
yet. Arguing "from each according to his ability," some
members feel that Ted should not have been required to do
an outside work shift. They say we had behavioral evidence
that city jobs were harder for Ted than they were for the
rest of us, and that the burden of supporting him would not
have been noticeable among so many members. The other
side says we cannot afford the precedent, or even that we
cannot afford people like Ted at all. I, like most of the Community, believe firmly in both sides. Forcing a member out
of the Community by the pressure of disapproval is not my

idea of creating a new society through positive reinforcement. But it is too easy to envision our precarious financial situation crumbling under too great a load of parasites. If this happened, not only Ted but the rest of us would be back in the city looking for jobs. We must not allow this to happen.

VII

Satisfying the Communal Appetite

If we were to try to start a community in 1971, it would be, I think, quite impossible to proceed without facing squarely the issue of Food. For this year's movement is full of vegetarians of various persuasions—natural-foods enthusiasts, yogurt eaters, raw-foods eaters, and macrobiotic people, in addition to just plain citizens who are disillusioned by the mercury in the tunafish and no longer trust the supermarkets, the FDA, or even the farmers not to poison them.

But in 1967 these issues were just small rumbles, and Twin Oaks proceeded blithely as if the question had no significance. When we talked about food, it was a battle of appetite versus economy. Carrie bought a jar of pickles to serve with our bologna sandwiches, and Dwight complained that we ought to do without the pickles and use the thirty-nine cents in the building fund.

We made bread sometimes. I made it myself, beautiful, crusty white loaves that were consumed as soon as they came out of the oven. Sandy did not approve of my making bread. He was impatient with the "back to the land" romance wherever he found it—in the kitchen as well as in the fields. He said I shouldn't get labor credits for baking bread. It was my recreation, and if I wanted to do it, I should do it on my own time. He shouldn't, he thought, have to put in any labor to match the labor I wasted on homemade bread. I said that good bread was part of the good life, and a part we could easily afford, and I thought we should always reward initiative on the part of members who did something for the group and not force them into making donations we would have to be grateful for. I quoted *Walden Two* at him. Sandy was never convinced, but he was defeated. The group liked the bread too much to relegate it to anybody's spare time and take a chance on not getting it. Or maybe I just argued him down. Sandy and I did not get along very well. In spite of all the correspondence we had engaged in before we actually moved onto the property, we soon discovered that we did not share the same vision.

We raised a large garden that first year, but we had to learn to eat the vegetables we produced. Carrie was suspicious of anything that didn't come in a can or a package with a neat label. The fact that heads of cabbage sometimes have worms in them that you have to wash off, and that the cabbage is still perfectly good to eat, was a new discovery to her. Nor had she ever eaten some of the vegetables that our garden produced, particularly summer squash and kohlrabi. My own knowledge was scant, but I had confidence in cookbooks and would tackle the preparation of any food we got our hands on. Carrie soon followed suit and rapidly became a versatile and competent cook, far better than I.

Cooking is a skill this Community has taught to dozens of people. Naomi, entering the Community at sixteen, had never been allowed in her mother's kitchen. She found herself with a free hand and a responsibility to feed twenty-two people, so she got a cookbook and followed directions. Without cooking experience of any kind, she didn't know the difference between an easy recipe and a hard one, so she cooked them all, one by one. It was thus that we established our tradition of having exotic things to eat. Egg Foo Yung or Chicken Timbales were no different from french fries and hamburgers to Naomi—except that we had eggs and we couldn't afford hamburger. Most Twin Oaks members find the food here more varied than what they have been accustomed to. Some of us are happy about it. Others grumble for meat and potatoes.

Our dining started out around a kitchen table, moved to a slightly larger dining table, and then went to cafeteria style. The original farmhouse is used for kitchen and dining. We pick up our plates and carry them to one of various dining rooms, or out-of-doors in good weather.

What you think of the quality of food at Twin Oaks depends on your point of view and particular dietary ideas. My own opinion is that suppers are almost always very good, and lunches have traditionally been terrible.

In the beginning it was sandwiches. Carrie believed that lunches should properly consist of sandwiches. Every day she set out bread, bologna, peanut butter and jam, pickles, and Kool-Aid and called us to lunch. When Carrie tired of the burden of preparing meals, others took her theory when they took her job. After about a month, some of us began to complain. I started signing up for lunch-making and serving soup or hash.

Hot lunches soon became traditional, and it is only occasionally now that we serve sandwiches. What we have never been able to get away from is the serving of leftovers. "Lunch is what you do with leftovers," says the Kitchen Manager flatly, and that is that. "Make lots of stew," she tells the supper cooks, "or we won't have anything much for lunch tomorrow." Leftovers sometimes don't go too far by themselves, and the cooks will combine them. There have been some minor tragedies. The sweet-and-sour pork doesn't really mix well with the barbequed hotdogs, and I almost cried the day somebody added gravy and string beans to the leftover paella.

Our budget has generally limited us to meat once a day, so lunch cooks have to struggle with the problem of putting out a palatable meal without having a meat base to start with. A standard dish, served at least once a week as long as I can remember, is corn fritters. Now corn fritters, as recommended in *The Joy of Cooking*, are delicate, crispy cakes of under-ripe corn, stripped from the cob, mixed with egg and just enough flour to hold them together, delicately flavored with salt and nutmeg. But we ran out of green corn long before we exhausted our need for cheap, easy dishes to prepare for lunch. So corn fritters at Twin Oaks are a heavy pancake about six inches across and half an inch thick, loaded with canned corn and weighing about a quarter of a pound each. For some reason people began calling them "groat cakes." Nobody knows what a groat is, but there is something about the word that suggests a solid, no-nonsense food that peasants eat every day because they are poor, and the term stuck. Groat cakes are a joke, but they are not bad food. They are a lot better, for example, than green spaghetti.

The excuse is generally that we are an experimental community. The reasons vary from boredom to sublimated parental disobedience. The behavior is putting food coloring in the supper. The Community comes to the meal, hungry and expectant, and finds there a giant potful of bright green spaghetti. The sauce on one occasion had been turned brown, the milk bright yellow. The fish batter was red, and there was a blue cake. It happens about twice a year, and the color-happy cook always believes himself quite original. It never fails to bring about an argument. Some people argue that nobody has a right to make the food unpalatable on purpose. The other side will say that to prohibit it would be interfering with the creative freedom of the cook. The disgruntled generally exercise their own freedom by leaving the food uneaten and are accused by the creative people of being unexperimental, poor, irrational slaves of conditioning. If we could really get free, they say, we could really dig green spaghetti. Look at it now. Objectively speaking, isn't it a gorgeous color? We admit that it is. Spaghetti takes food coloring very well. If it were frosting, it would lend appeal to a birthday cake; if it were yarn, it would make a beautiful rug. It is as spaghetti that it fails. Spaghetti, we point out, is an idea, and not an idea to be tampered with. It should not be overcooked, burned, underseasoned, or dyed green.

Once after such an episode I hid the food coloring in my room Brian was shocked at my behavior and demanded to know how I justified the high-handed act of removing the food coloring. "Well," I said, "it's like this: You and I both believe in Community government. We think society runs better if decisions are made carefully through channels. The cook, for example, should have checked with the Food Manager before making green spaghetti, but he didn't. For my part, I should go to the Food Manager and make my complaint. Matter of fact, I already did that. The Food Manager says, 'Don't yell at me—I don't like green spaghetti any better than you do.' Now channels are fine as long as they work. But there comes a point when government falls through, and each human being is left to work out his own destiny the best he can. If a baby falls down the well, I am not going to look for the Child Manager—I am going to pull out the baby. The same is true of the food coloring. Here is an abuse so outrageous that ordinary governmental procedures are powerless. So as an individual I feel called upon to do the simplest, most direct act. I remove the food coloring." Brian wasn't convinced.

The other day a visitor declared at the lunch table that we would all be dead within five years if we continued to pour junk into our stomachs. Probably a majority of our visitors are concerned about natural or organic foods, and they often take one or another of us aside for counseling in nutrition. The Community's nutrition may at times merit criticism, but it is usually not sound nutrition that is recommended by our visitors, but some version of the brown-rice-and-vegetables fad. When we visit other communes, we are often served what one member calls "gray soup," usually some grain cooked with vegetables and water.

The charge that we do not provide nutritious meals is not quite true. A visiting nutritionist did a study on our diet and reported that a fully balanced diet is available to our members, but not all of us get a balanced diet, because we do not all eat what is available. Any member who does not drink milk is probably short of protein, for instance.

It is perfectly true that we still lay a large emphasis on economy, and therefore serve casseroles in which small chunks of meat flavor large quantities of noodles, rice, or potatoes. What bothers the natural food people more than that, though, is our persistence in making available some of the plastic foods we learned to like before we got here—such as cocoa mix, Kool-Aid, and white bread.

Bread is a story by itself. A lot of members go through the same excitement that I did about baking bread. But it is so delicious that seven loaves of bread are eaten before four hours have passed. The amount of labor that would have to go into bread baking if we tried to supply all of our own bread from our own ovens would be enormous. We can't spare the ovens, kitchen space, or labor. So we bake once or twice a week for the pleasure of the members, and buy the rest of our bread from a thrift bakery outlet. Plastic it may be, but it is much cheaper than making our own.

The best the health foodists have ever been able to do with our diet is to add nutritious goodies to it—goodies that are gobbled up by the appreciative communitarians just as quickly as they eat the plastic goodies from the store. So once in a while we have whole wheat this or that, and we like it fine. But it remains a luxury until we can apply production techniques to it and make it feasible for daily consumption.

Our first food faddist was Sandy. He was convinced that we all paid too much attention to flavor and such trivia and could get along on a very simple diet. After arguing for spaghetti for a while, he switched to soybeans. In response to his grumblings, we tried to get hold of some soybeans to try them out. The local feed store had them—but they were treated for seed and therefore inedible. We would not go so far as to order from a health food store (too expensive). But somebody gave us some soy grits, and Sandy determined to eat them. He wanted us all to settle for soy grits as a diet, but we refused. So we continued to bake cinnamon rolls, and Sandy always ate his share of them. He said it wasn't fair for us to have all those delicious tempting dishes in front of him when he wanted to live the simple life, but he couldn't convince anybody. He abandoned the grits after a few trials, and we threw them away months later, together with the worms they had accumulated. When Sandy left the Community after a six-month trial period, it was partly for reasons like this disagreement. We put a lot of work into pleasing our palates and our other senses, and Sandy wanted neither the work nor the results of it. He yearned for the ascetic life. We were to learn that disagreements as basic as this always lead to separation.

Mary wanted to be vegetarian. This was not an attitude she brought with her but one she learned at Twin Oaks. Mary was an eighteen-year-old escaping from a middle-class family that didn't approve of her hippie behavior. She came to us, not out of interest in community, but in a search of a place to stay. She arrived in the dead of winter when we were low on members, and we accepted her. The day she arrived, we had just been killing and cutting up our first litter of hogs. We had finished with the hams and pork chops and were attempting to remove the jowls from the heads for lard. The sight that greeted Mary was four grinning, dead pigs' heads sitting on the kitchen table. Shortly after that, we decided to kill some of our ducks for meat, and Mary was asked to help pluck them. After that she refused to eat meat of any kind. The necessity of a living animal being killed just so humans could eat it revolted her morally as well as aesthetically.

Mary was welcome to live at Twin Oaks as a vegetarian, and some of us had sympathy for her point of view. What caused the trouble was that she was trying to learn to cook and would sign up for a lot of cooking. She carried her morals about meat into her work and we began to have vegetarian meals. A really good cook might have got away with it. Mary was a beginner, and her meals were often very bad. She didn't always read the recipes too carefully. I remember one time the recipe called for a teaspoon of cloves—it meant ground cloves, of course—but Mary found the whole cloves first and dumped a teaspoon of them into the cookies. They made lumpy eating.

We had a meeting on the subject of vegetarianism and decided that Mary would be allowed to cook only once or twice a week. That wasn't quite the end of the problem. After a while Mary realized that she didn't really like vegetables, either. What she liked to eat was fruits and nuts, and that touched on a delicate community problem. Who doesn't like fruits and nuts? Every member of the Community loves them. That was the winter that a friend from Koinonia Community in Georgia sent us thirty pounds of chopped pecans as a surprise. We kept the pecans in the basement and used them a little at a time for cookies, cakes, and salads. Mary didn't understand this niggardly philosophy. It seemed to her that there were a lot of pecans in that box, and she made them a staple of her diet. She would eat a cup of them for supper.

Both the pecans and Mary were gone before we had the big nutrition conflict in 1969. This time the argument was not a matter of faddism or blind selfishness. It was a genuine ideological conflict. Since then it has been termed generally the "standard of living versus expansion" argument. But at the time we just thought of it as the "meat on the table" problem.

What had happened was first of all a planning error. In trying to set up a budget for Community expenditures (something not theretofore attempted), the planners had taken the food cost figures for the preceding six months and asked the Food Manager to keep her buying within that figure. But in the meantime we ran out of frozen meat. The months from which the figures were taken were months in which we had bought no meat, because we had plenty in the freezer. Naomi had just been appointed Food Manager, a position of considerable responsibility for her seventeen years. She was anxious to make a good impression and not be called irresponsible. She took the planners at their word and kept the buying within the limit (two hundred dollars a month). There were twenty members at the time, plus half a dozen visitors. No matter how she figured it, she could not afford to buy meat. The problem could have been taken back to the board of planners, the error explained, and a new budget appropriated, but two personalities got in the way. One of them was Dwight, a planner at the time who had a tendency to asceticism. The other was Simon, a new member who didn't like the planners much at all, particularly didn't like Dwight, and emphatically *did* like meat.

From Simon's point of view, sacrificing at the table in order to put up a building, in order to take a larger membership, in order to build the Community, in order to present an example to the rest of the world, in order to do something about the mess the world was in, was simply too long-range a plan to deal with. He didn't think we needed a larger building. He didn't think we needed any more members. And he was quite certain that we needed meat on the table—large hunks of it, and every day.

Since Simon's time this same argument has been presented by people who are quite sincere in believing that a higher standard of living is really the best way to go about building the Community, and their arguments are listened to and respected. What weakened Simon's point was Simon himself. He was admittedly not a permanent member. He had joined for a short time only, he told us, to learn to milk and farm and other skills that might be useful to him later. Furthermore, he openly opposed the equalitarian ethic of Twin Oaks, and he often took special privileges for himself. Even people who agreed with him about having meat on the table were embarrassed about siding with him, because it was quite clear that he did not care whether the Community succeeded or failed. He watched out for Simon.

Dwight, on the other hand, took an extreme position in the other direction. He had been reading about conditions in China before and during the revolution there and was impressed by the amount which was accomplished on a starvation diet. Dwight was omnivorous, anyway, and thought Twin Oaks's food delicious. (We were eating mostly eggs, rice, corn, and string beans, with different seasonings and in different combinations.)

I found myself siding with Dwight, but not because I sincerely thought we couldn't afford to raise our food budget. It was simply uncomfortable to be on the same side of the argument as Simon. It amounted to saying, "I am in favor of self-indulgence, while half the world is starving to death." So we went without meat for about five months, and I hope the starving world benefited. When Simon went away in the fall, the pressure lessened, the budget slackened, and we began to taste hamburger once again amidst the rice.

There is, of course, no end to the argument. It once meant hamburger. As I write this, the same argument is raging over private rooms. When we get private rooms, we could bring up the same problem with private bathrooms or tennis courts. Shall we get bigger? Or richer? Will we get richer quicker if we get big first? Will we get bigger faster if we get rich first? At any rate, we didn't solve the problem in 1969.

VIII

Domes and Cubes—
Building Living Space

One of the reasons we were attracted to the particular farm
we bought is that it already had a number of buildings on it.
Five barns and a smokehouse, woodshed, outhouse, chicken
house, and pigpen, plus a nice snug white farmhouse with
four rooms, a half-cellar, and an unfinished attic. True, there
wasn't much room in the house itself, but we needed the
miscellaneous smaller shelters almost as much as we did
house space. Besides, we saw no other farms bordering on
rivers at anywhere near our price range. So we conceded
that we would have to build a dwelling very soon.

Very soon meant before winter. In the meantime the barns
were hospitable enough for sleeping. Sandy, Carrie and
Brian, Dwight, Jenny, and later others occupied the barn
lofts and decorated them as well as they could. There was
no way to make them insect-proof, so they had to share the
habitation with flies, wasps, and mosquitoes. Beds consisted
usually of hay bales stacked together and covered with a
mattress, on top of which sleeping bags were laid.

We talked a lot about what kind of building to put up.
Fred and Sandy, agreeing for once, favored rammed earth,
because it was almost free. Brian was interested in geodesic
domes. Dwight wanted not to build at all the first year but
to weatherproof one of the barns. I agreed with Dwight,

sharing with him a general lack of confidence in the group's ability to put up a real building. "The way I feel about weatherproofing a barn," said Dwight, "is that I think we could and would actually do it. We can afford that much money, and we have the simple skills. I'm not at all sure we have either the money or the skills for a new building."

We started most of these projects. Rammed earth was to be tried on a small scale for a print shop (we had a printing press that needed a heated space badly if we were to continue to put out a newsletter). We started digging the foundations for the print shop and sent away for a machine that uses leverage to make earth blocks. The blocks were not difficult to make, but we would like to talk to the person who advertised that the machine would make 600 blocks in an hour. The fact is that the dirt has to be dug, then sifted, then mixed with a little cement, and then and only then pressed into the mold to be made into a block. This process took so much labor that, poor as we were, we abandoned it after only a few days. Perhaps if we had had a heavy tractor with a front-end loader, the process would have made sense. We sold the brick-maker and abandoned rammed earth for the time being.

Geodesic domes, too, got a brief flicker of our attention. Brian, who wanted to try one out but did not want to spend much Community money on it, tried to construct one out of tobacco sticks, which we had in plentiful supply. Tobacco sticks are just sticks, ax-cut from lengths of oak, about three feet long and as thick as a broom handle. Their original purpose was to support drying tobacco plants in the barns. For that they were excellent. As framework for the dome they were not so successful. In fact, Brian did not make any kind of connectors for the struts of the dome and just hoped they would stay together with staples. They didn't. The dome, about fifteen feet across, which he constructed "following" instructions from a *Popular Mechanics* magazine plan, sagged in several places and threw the geodesic principle into question. We propped it up with some long poles and used it to sit in and sometimes take naps in on coolish days. It was covered with polyethylene and was warm inside. It acted as a greenhouse, and the grass inside was a rich color that the outside grass, in the fall, was beginning to lose.

We tried to weatherproof a barn, too, but that was later, for a workshop. It was never very successful. We didn't want to put a lot of good two-by-fours into it, for it began to look as if the price of converting a barn into living quarters was almost as high as the price of a new building.

For a day or so Sandy even considered making a sleeping shelter out of the bales of straw that we had outside. (We couldn't put the straw in the barn that was built for that purpose, because we needed the barn lofts for people to sleep in.) We joked about the house of straw, house of sticks, and house of bricks, referring to Sandy's, Brian's, and Fred's pet projects. But underneath the joking was a real concern about the wolf at the door. The wolf's name was winter, and our calendar already said September before we had done anything real about housing.

Hal supplied the missing ingredients—money, skill, and confidence. Neither Hal's financial contribution for the house ($3,000), nor his skill (mechanical engineering background), valuable as they were, seem so remarkable to me now as the calm confidence that he brought to us. Hal was the only one among us who believed that he could build a house. He drew up a plan and presented it to us for our approval. It looked fine to us, though we would have accepted any plan at all. The building was originally intended as a hammock workshop. Carrie said we wanted some bedrooms in it, and Hal said, "All right, you shall have some bedrooms," and drew them in. It was a good thing. Those bedrooms served to make the Community possible for the next two years.

Through working with Hal to build our first building, we

did away with the major obstacle that had bothered us—
namely, the Building Expert Mystique. Any of us who
worked on that building could, if we had to, build another
one more or less like it. Things that were mysterious then
are now just straightforward problems to be worked out.
We recognize that there is such a thing as building expertise,
and that none of us had it, not even Hal. Certainly experience counts, and some people can build better buildings
than other people. But if all you're looking for is reasonable
shelter, anybody with common sense can build one.

Putting up the building was our first clear and obvious
demonstration of our stand on equality for women. None of
us women had any experience with construction—not so
much even as being able to pound a nail without bending
it. Nevertheless, we helped level the ground with shovels,
helped smooth the concrete after it came out of the cement-
mixer, were part of the crew that nailed the plywood, the
tarpaper, and finally the shingles to the roof. Women put
together heating ducts and cut holes in them with tinsnips
for the registers. We nailed together the partitions between
the rooms and helped lift them into place. We installed windows and hung doors. We didn't think it particularly remarkable, either. Our labor was badly needed, and if we had
not done construction work, we would have had to do all
the kitchen and housework, which I, in particular, did not
care for.

The hammock building, later called Harmony, went up
in three months, starting in October. In the meantime, the
weather grew colder. The people who slept in barns dreaded
going to bed at night and getting out from the covers in the
morning. Sometimes the cold would wake them up at night,
in spite of the dozens of blankets they had heaped on themselves. Fred had, however, wired the barns, so there was
electric power available. We decided against the risk of
electric heaters in the flammable barns, but Brian and Carrie

took along Carrie's hair-dryer when they went to bed. When it became too cold, they would turn on the hair-dryer, putting the hose between the covers, and let the bed warm up, then turn it off again until later at night, when the cold demanded a repeat operation. This is the only use, by the way, that a hair-dryer has ever had at Twin Oaks.

On December 1 we moved people in from the barns and gave them partially completed rooms in the new building. The floor was not even fully poured in the center workshop area, but there was no time to be fastidious. Those of us who slept in the farmhouse delayed our move until the last rooms were finished.

Building number one was up and paid for. Hal did not ask for or expect the return of the building donation. Where would we get the money for the next building? To a certain degree we could take the money out of our regular budget. By now we had a steady income from outside work. Harmony, started with Hal's $3,000, had eventually cost $5,500, the Community paying the rest from its outside work labor.

Building number two was done the same way. Two members turned over their savings accounts for a base to start with—a total once again of $3,000, and Community labor paid the rest. This building cost us a total of $8,000, plus a diversion of $1,600 that during the same period had to be put into septic tank and drain field. But this time it took us a year and a half to build it. Months would go by in which no work could be done on the building, either because of lack of money or lack of labor or both. Hal was gone before we put up this building, which was named Oneida. We decided to use the same general plan as Harmony, because we felt some confidence that we could do again what we had accomplished successfully once. Oneida was never as good as Harmony, whether because of Hal's absence or not I do not know. Probably it is because we tried to cut too many corners and ended up with a badly functioning heating system and several leaks. Nevertheless it is a very large dormitory, housing eighteen members, plus a living room, office, small meeting room, and craft room. It made it possible to expand our membership to our current forty members. If we had spent more per square foot on Oneida, we would have had to make it much smaller, and that would have meant that some of the people who are with us now would not have been admitted for lack of space. Both of the buildings were built for a little over two dollars a square foot.

Every time we set out to build anything, there is always a slight controversy on the question of domes. To some people the word "commune" and the words "geodesic dome" are so firmly associated that they cannot imagine the one without the other.

Brian cherished the idea of building a dome right from the beginning, but he didn't argue much about it with Hal, who was supplying the money. Hal opted for a rectangular building.

Between buildings one and two, however, Brian became even more feverishly interested in domes. In the meantime, communes on the West Coast were putting them up and raving about them. Drop City had made them out of cartops. Brian checked on the availability and cost of cartops—the local junkyards wanted forty dollars each for them. Perhaps a dome could be made of polyethylene—two layers, insulated in between them? Or of plywood? The famous *Dome Book One* and *Dome Book Two* were not yet out, or at least we had not seen them, so Brian had a hard time convincing anyone that domes were a good idea. Dwight suspected that they might leak. Hal and Pete said simply that we didn't know how to put them up. Among those three people lay all the real construction skill that the Community had. Brian was not known for careful workmanship.

Brian was also not known for holding out against opposition, and the dome idea was set aside for the time being.

Brian contented himself with an overall plan that he and Dwight thought up, which featured twin domes as the eventual kitchen and dining room. Meanwhile, Oneida was rectangular.

But dome dreams crop up like mushrooms. Gideon conceived a passion for building one in 1971. The only problem was finding a good use for it. By this time we had *Dome Book One,* plus a whole file full of pictures of beautiful domes that had been constructed in various parts of the world for various purposes. It was no longer a question of their feasibility. This time the argument against them was that they weren't good for anything. Furniture, argued the opposition, is rectangular. How do you fit it into a pie-shaped room?

The pro-dome argument was partly philosophical. One adherent defended it simply because it was round (The universe is round. Why should man be imprisoned in cubes?). But it was not mysticism that moved Gideon. He simply longed to do something far-out and technologically advanced. He didn't want to be conventional.

Gideon finally got his way when we held a conference on our premises in the summer of 1971. For the conference we needed a large rain and sun shelter where the conferees could eat their meals. We had no building large enough. The conference participants themselves would be paying enough to cover the price of a simple shelter. A geodesic dome was the obvious answer.

We made it of two-by-fours and used slices of iron pipe for the hubs, connecting the two by means of steel strapping, according to instructions we found in *Dome Book One.* Unlike Brian's shaky edifice of tobacco sticks, Gideon's dome was sturdy and promised to be useful. After the basic structure came the problem of the skin. The only opaque plastic we could buy was black, so we stapled a black plastic skin to the giant triangles. Putting on the skin took more time and work than the structure itself and was less successful. In fact, it leaked. Fortunately, it didn't rain during our conference, and the dome served its purpose as a sunshade.

And then what? What do you do with a plastic-covered geodesic dome 42 feet across and 21 feet high? You can't live in it or work in it: it has no insulation, and besides, it leaks. We could leave it there for another conference, but it does take up a good portion of our hay field.

Of course we could finish it. But making a dome waterproof and properly insulated and at the same time goodlooking from the inside takes as much money as any other kind of building, and it is, indeed, difficult to justify the round shape when our next priority is additional dormitory space. Besides, we have members who complain that it looks silly alongside the other buildings we have already completed.

As I write this, the dome is still there, sitting unused and apparently unusable. Gideon says he will take it apart soon and use the two-by-fours for other purposes. His passion for domes died with the production of his firstborn. He is working on plans for building number three, which is more or less rectangular.

But even since that summer other people have taken up the interest in domes. One member was working on a dome greenhouse. Another considered a dome doghouse. Domes-in-the-woods have been suggested, for summer retreats (yoga and dance space).

That brings me to the question of overall plans. The hodgepodge appearance of domes and cubes next door to each other is only one of the basic architectural problems we have to solve before we go much further. It is fortunate that we are now attracting the attention of architects to help us out. Before we build more we have to determine what our probable ultimate size will be. Will we go to Skinner's projected 1000? Or will we find ourselves comfortable with the 200–300 of the average Israeli kibbutz? Several members are not pleased with dormitory living as a long-term plan and want to build smaller dwelling units to cut down on traffic noise. In order to stall for time, we are constructing building number three near our present buildings, so that the whole will become a circle of buildings around a central grassy courtyard. After that we can decide where the eventual dwelling units will go.

IX

They Come and They Go—
Selection and Turnover

You can always get a good conversation going at Twin Oaks by bringing up the subject of membership selection. It has been a controversial topic since before the Community began, and it still is.

There are two major points of view, with variations. One theory is that the Community ought not to select at all. There are some pretty good arguments on that side. The moral argument is the strongest. It says that we are here to provide the good life for as many as we can take, that we are supposed to be experimenting with social design that could work for human beings in general, not just a certain select kind of human being, and that if we select carefully, we will have ended up proving nothing except that it's nice to live with compatible people. Fraternities and sororities have paved the way before us!

The opposing side argues simply that we must select if we are to survive. There are a lot of times when we think that we ought to be even more careful than we are.

It is a luxury to be able to talk about selection at all. The first two years of Twin Oaks's shaky existence was a time when we were constantly afraid we would run out of people. Brian and Dwight and I would sit in planners' meetings and discuss how to increase the membership. "Somewhere,"

Dwight used to say, "there have to be more people like us." Dwight was uneasy at the slowness of membership growth. There were only five enthusiastic communitarians among the original eight members.

New members came and went during the first few months: Charlie, who didn't want to do any work; Marie, who did not not find a suitable mate after Charlie left; and Mary, whose juvenile selfishness was a drag on Community morale. None of them stayed long, nor did we really wish them to. Nevertheless, every time someone stayed a trial period and then left, we got the discouraged feeling of failure—failure to attract members with the kind of spirit we needed, failure to make profound changes in the mixed-up people who did come through. For the first few months it happened that new members came and went, and when they left, the same original eight remained. Then some of the original people began to leave. Quincy's rigidity and hostility became unbearable, and we asked him to leave. Sandy changed his mind about his personal goals and went to California to seek Expanded Consciousness. Jenny followed him a month later.

Jenny's leaving made me very unhappy. I was frightened both for her and for the Community. Though she was unusually self-reliant for her age, I had heard stories about teen-agers being picked up by the police and placed in detention homes. Would the law call me an unfit mother? Would she be locked up somewhere until she was eighteen? Hitch-hiking, too, I thought dangerous. And the Community sorely needed her energy and high spirits. But Jenny would not be deterred. She said she knew how to hitch-hike safely, that policemen were just men, and she could talk her way out of an arrest. She said my fears were far-fetched and the value I placed on her membership exaggerated. She said in any case she was going to California, and there was no way I could stop her. Brian, though he didn't want her to leave, backed up her argument. As usual he appealed to principle. By community tenet Jenny was a full member and entitled to make her own decisions. Had I not given up the concept of parental authority? If I hadn't, I did then. Jenny had her way, and I never again thought of myself as having any authority over her.

Hal, always a constant visitor, finally joined. For the entire first year we hovered around the dozen mark. I was constantly conscious of the problem of holding the group together, constantly afraid that too many people would leave at once and there might not be any community left. Carrie had black moods during which she put pressure on Brian to take her back to the middle-class world where she belonged. Would she be successful? Dwight was always pessimistic, always disgusted at the lack of progress we had made toward our goals. Would he give up? Jenny's defection destroyed my morale for a long time.

Looking back on this anxiety, I am amused. Finding members is the last thing that worries me now. We usually have eight to ten people on our waiting list, and we could triple if we made the slightest effort. But the worry was real enough in 1967. We took anybody who came through. Technically we had a rule that incoming members had to contribute two hundred dollars as an entrance fee. This was to discourage the use of Twin Oaks as a crash pad and to indicate a degree of commitment among people who joined. But in fact we waived this fee for the first four people who came along, because they didn't have any money.

There was talk of selection, even then. Both Hal and Fred were exasperated with Charlie, Marie, and Mary. Fred referred to them as belonging to a general class of drifters, spongers, and bums. He and Hal both saw that it was possible and even likely that our financial and emotional resources could be drained by noncontributors. Fred personally resented his labor going into food for people he did not respect. Hal talked of attracting a more competent type of member.

This general idea of competence has been the keynote for

much of the discussion of selection criteria throughout our history. It usually takes the form of frustration on the part of people who rightly consider themselves competent at various useful skills seeing their energy being wasted by people who do not contribute in those ways. Competent people can hammer a nail without bending it, tend to pick up after themselves, do not leave their tools out in the rain or try to saw through a rock with a chain saw. They change into rough clothes before climbing a tree. They clean off all the drainboards as an assumed part of the job of dishwashing. They can finish mopping the kitchen floor in fifteen minutes or less. They are familiar with the practical applications of arithmetic and geometry—or grammar and spelling. They prefer order to chaos, and they are willing to put out the effort to get it.

The opposite of "competent" is "irresponsible." This is the person who has to be awakened for morning milking, gets a substitute for a dishwashing shift because of a headache, takes fifty days to get through a forty-day outside work shift, rolls a cigarette and leaves tobacco on the table, opens a pound of margarine and leaves it out without removing the waxed paper. The irresponsible member makes work and manages to do less than his full share. The competent member often picks up after the irresponsible and usually does more than a normal share of the work in addition. He tends to accumulate labor credits.

Pete, an exemplary member of the competent class, once said to me, "People around here think that I work all the time because I like to work, because I couldn't think of anything to do with leisure time. Well, that's not true. I have a lot of things I would like do to, books I want to read but don't have time for. But we are trying to get this community off the ground, and there is a lot of work to be done. I figure that if I don't do it, I don't know who's going to. So I work extra, and I get a lot of vacation credits that I never get a chance to use up, because there is always more work that needs to be done. And what makes me mad is that while I'm doing extra work, the person who isn't working so hard is making more work for me to do."

It is easy to understand why the most competent members would like to have a selection policy to discriminate against the irresponsible. With a membership made up entirely of the competent, the Community would leap ahead physically and financially.

But there is another side to the argument. Historically, it has often been the case that competence has gone hand in hand with intolerance. It is true that, despite the labor credit system, the job of building the Community is often borne disproportionately by dedicated volunteers. It is natural that they should feel used, and they begin to resent it eventually. This resentment shows itself in angry accusations, or nagging, or general critical comments. Quite often they will begin to speak of the Community members as "they" and of Twin Oaks as "this place," divorcing themselves from any guilt for what they consider bad management and irresponsibility. What has often happened is that the nagging and criticism have got out of hand and the competent have earned the dislike, not only of those whom they criticize, but of every member who enjoys a peaceful and pleasant atmosphere. Most of us would like to see the buildings always clean, the tools always in their places, etc. But we would rather live in dirt and disorder than listen to the angry comments of people who cannot control their annoyance.

From time to time there has even been talk of selecting *against* those competent people who make life miserable for the careless. Some thoughtful people have suggested that we deliberately select members for their ability to tolerate standards different from their own, thus deliberately excluding people who want to raise the physical standards of the group and are willing to do some verbal pushing to do it.

Actually, we have done very little selection for either competence or tolerance. Now that we have a waiting list, what we actually do is vote applicants in, each member deciding for himself what the basis of his vote will be.

And of course there is self-selection. Our anti-drug rules select against people who are dependent on drugs, our scientific and pragmatic approach selects against mystics. By a similar process, a *de facto* selection works against the long-term membership of people who have difficulty getting along or who cannot attract a mate.

As time goes on it becomes apparent that competence and tolerance are not mutually exclusive traits. We have a growing core of members who can pick up after themselves and also after others, without feeling heavy emotions gnawing at them. Our standards are rising, albeit slowly, mostly because of people who know how to deplore a mess without condemning the messy. These people, considerate not only of other people's workload, but of their feelings as well, are the kind we are really selecting for.

The selection process itself has evolved gradually. At first, partly because of need and partly out of principle, we accepted anyone who wanted to join. By the summer of 1971 we had a waiting list. Most people didn't wait long, because turnover was still fairly constant. Sometimes several people left about the same time, and we could take in the whole waiting list at once. Eventually, though, turnover slowed down, and the waiting list got longer. It was then that we invented the entrance poll. There was strong sentiment among community members to choose the best applicants first, rather than taking people in the order in which they applied. They argued that a membership composed of strong, emotionally stable people would build the Community faster than a nonselected group, and in the long run enable us to support more people.

So we made up a questionnaire that the members fill out on each applicant for membership. It asks for comments on the applicant's ideas, work habits, and personality. Then there are two crucial questions:

From what I know so far, I predict that I will

_____ seek this person's company
_____ enjoy her/his company
_____ be indifferent to him/her
_____ avoid her/him.

Which of the following most closely represents your opinion on when we should accept this person as a provisional member?

_____ Immediately, even if it overcrowds us
_____ As soon as there is a regular space in our normal membership quota
_____ accept for available space unless someone special comes along
_____ only if our membership is getting dangerously low
_____ Never.

All applicants are required to visit for two weeks before the members fill out the poll questionnaire. The polls are turned in, and the Membership Manager derives a score from them. When openings occur in the membership, the applicant with the highest score is admitted first.

If the score is below a certain point, we don't accept the person at all. Over the past year I have had the unpleasant duty of telling five different people (one in every seven applicants) that they had been rejected.

We have used this method for more than a year now, and it has been criticized by members who feel that it is discriminatory. There are times when it is obvious that a high score means nothing more than a pleasing manner or even a pretty face. "What do we know about these people after a two-week visit?" asks Jenny, who opposes the method "All we have are some surface impressions. Really important things like commitment to community living aren't even visible for the first several months. Besides, the poll assumes that we have to *select* for good members, and I think we can *create* them." Over and over I have heard old members say, "I never could have got in if I had had to pass that poll."

On the other side of the question is the sheer fact of our pleasant social atmosphere during the year we have been using the poll. It almost seems that friction-causing people have been intuitively screened out. And so, with an uneasy group conscience, we continue to select from the top of the list.

The single biggest problem this Community had in trying to get on its feet was membership turnover. Turnover, more than poverty or youth or inexperience, has crippled us repeatedly and prevented us from going into skilled business. Until recently our statistics told us that we would lose 1.6 members each month. That is not entirely bad. Most of the members we lose are provisional members who have been here less than six months, who have been trying out the group to see if they fit in or not. Sometimes it is agreed all around that they do not, and their departure is not looked upon as a tragedy. Then, too, turnover used to be a lot worse than it is now, and we take pleasure in our gradually increasing stability. We have reached the point, at least, where our heaviest managerships are in the hands of people responsible enough to train a replacement if they should ever decide to leave. It was not always that way. A swift turnover in cattle managers in 1969 (there were four different managers within that year, most of whom left without warning and without leaving any written information for the next manager to follow) nearly caused starvation in the herd.

Why do people leave? This is the question thrown at us by lecture audiences, and by visitors, journalists, and new members. It is the obvious test question for any experimental community. For we are aimed at Utopia. We will admit that. We want an ideal life, and we think we have some good ideas for getting it. The test of a good idea about the good life is whether people indeed do find it good. Therefore if people come, test it out, and then leave, obviously we have failed to provide the good life. Logical? Perfectly logical.

We have one answer to that challenge, and we say it patiently over and over again as a basic answer to the question, "Why do people leave?" The answer is this: Because we aren't Utopia yet. We don't have a perfect life. There are things missing. There are problems we haven't solved. We have not achieved Walden Two. In short, we are not prepared to meet the test. We intend to meet it, but we aren't there yet.

But there are more specific answers. We once did a statistical breakdown on the reasons people leave. The heaviest percentage by a wide margin came in a category we called "Adventure."

Ralph left one spring because he had always wanted to travel across the country on his own, having no particular schedule, living off the land. We wished him well and urged him to come back to us if his adventure didn't work out. He was back within two weeks, reporting that it is impossible to find any land to live off of. Every time he tried to camp, somebody came and told him it was illegal to camp there. There just didn't seem to be any wilderness left for him. And he was hungry.

Maggie was another member who returned a sparse week after departing on an adventure trip to visit other communes. She had a similar problem with food. She says: "I was fed. People were nice to me and shared their meals with me. But all they had to eat was gray soup. I would look at the bowl of soup—barley and vegetables or rice and vegetables—and I would taste it, and it tasted all right. But then I would think, 'Is this supper?' I got so hungry."

Jenny and Leif also took off on an adventure trip but were back within a month. They had planned to go to Africa, Leif's birthplace. But they needed money, so they had to live and work in New York for enough time to save up the necessary cash for the trip. Says Jenny: "But I couldn't stand

New York. Everywhere I walked I saw the most incredible misery. People just standing there in the middle of the sidewalk throwing up, and other people walking by and not caring. I couldn't stand it. I kept saying, 'Something has got to be done about the system that produces these people,' and then I'd remind myself that I had just left the Community where we were making an honest effort to find an alternative. The African adventure seemed awfully far away, and I began to want to come home."

Ned's reasons for leaving were less definite. "I just don't see things the way the Community does," he said. "I don't think humanity's problems are economic or can be solved by changing the social system. The problem is within man himself. It's an internal thing. I have to go work out my internal problems. I just want to bum around for a while. I'll probably be back. . . ." He was gone for six months before he returned.

Not everyone comes back, but people who leave for adventure reasons tend to return, presumably because their adventures lack the luster in real life that they had in fantasy.

A large percentage of the people who leave the Community do so to escape loneliness. Many find love and happiness here, but some do not, and watching happy couples all around them only increases their desperate alienation.

Some people leave for solid ideological reasons. They simply do not like Walden Two ideas, or they used to like them but have changed their minds.

X

Some Big Ones That Got Away

The title of this section suggests that I am making a judgment about the value of the members of this Community. It says, in effect, that some members are bigger than others, and that some people's leaving was more significant than other people's leaving. This has a ring of contradiction to our basic equalitarian philosophy, but I don't think the contradiction is really there. It is true that all human beings are equally valuable—to themselves. It is also true that our Community recognizes that essential worth of every individual. Indeed, equalitarianism is based on it. But it is plainly not true that everyone is of equal value to the rest of mankind. For us, specifically, it is not true that everyone contributes equally to the building of the Community. Everyone makes a contribution, yes. Every time we wash a dish or play the guitar or smile and say hello we are making a contribution. But there are some kinds of contributions that seem to be necessary for the survival of the Community, assets and characteristics that are not common enough, not easy to find. I think I can be excused for the time and emotion I invested in trying to attract and hold members who in my opinion had a lot to contribute to the Community's overall goals.

Sometimes the asset is a highly developed work skill.

Both Hal and Fred had very useful knowledge and skills to offer to the Community. Sometimes, as in the case of Dwight and Pete, it is the quality of idealism that is of greatest value, their determination and dedication to our goals. In fact, all of the people I talk about in this chapter were both skilled and dedicated, in varying degrees and sometimes, unhappily, to different ends.

We lost them all, one by one, in 1968 and 1969.

Dwight

The summer of 1968 was the worst period in our history to date. We had had little turnover until that time—a few temporary people had come and gone, but most of the original people were still here. Dwight, Brian, and I served on the board of planners. Fred was still vacillating over whether to leave or stay. Pete and Rosa had arrived with their children and were trying to make a permanent home with us. Gwen, divorced with two children, had joined, and she and Hal found each other compatible companions. They later married.

It was a season of one bitter conflict after another. It started with Hal's desire to be on the board of planners. Hal had not been elected to the board at the beginning, for the simple reason that he had not been a member at the time. By the time he became a member, we knew him fairly well and were not sure we wanted to risk the Community's future to his ideas. For one thing we didn't think he was cautious enough with money. But apart from our fears of Hal's fiscal policies, there was another issue that made us wish not to have him on the board. There was something self-seeking about Hal's logic. When he took sides on an issue, it always developed that the side he took, if successful, was to his personal advantage. Thus, when he found that the logic of the labor credit system sometimes placed him at the sink washing dishes, he argued that the labor credit system was basically inefficient. And when Gwen's house trailer came under question as a special privilege, Hal argued in favor of private property. Granted that there is no such thing as true objectivity, still Hal seemed to have less of it than we did.

Gwen brought a three-bedroom house trailer with her when she joined. No one had ever told her that the trailer would become community-use property while it sat on community land, and she had taken it for granted that she and her children would occupy it as a family. Brian and I assumed the same—not because we approved of this entering wedge of private home and nuclear family, but because we were embarrassed to make a fuss over a matter about which we had neglected to give Gwen fair warning.

Dwight, however, was not embarrassed. He was still smoldering over Hal's attempted coup. In addition, he was not happy with the group of people who had joined the Community since its inception. Hal and Gwen, Pete and Rosa, four children, two teen-age girls, and a sprinkling of hippies worried him. What he had imagined before starting the Community was a devoted group of radicals, determined to change the face of the earth with a New Social Order and a New Man. What he found was a group that he could not help labeling The Bourgeoisie. Furthermore, this bourgeoisie was evidently determined to take control and make the Community into its own little comfortable world, with little thought for equality and justice for all. First Hal had attempted a power play. Next, Hal's overwhelmingly middle-class girlfriend brought with her a giant luxury house trailer and wanted to keep it to herself. It was time, said Dwight, to take a stand.

It was more than a stand against the bourgeoisie. It was a test for Brian and me. Dwight had seen us in the struggle over the plannership, and he was not satisfied with our ability to stand on principle. When Hal had laid down his ultimatum (either make me a planner or get off my land), Brian had considered giving him his way. I had avoided the head-on conflict by dissolving the board and calling for a new election. But Dwight had walked out of the meeting. We all felt moral indignation at Hal's power play, but only Dwight acted upon it. Now here we were at a new crisis. Would we allow that bourgeois woman to occupy that trailer all by herself on the dubious principle that she owned it? Or would we stand by our community principles—that it was a new Community house and as such should be divided into bedrooms and have each bedroom assigned to whatever member should win the toss of a coin?

There was the implicit threat that if we made Hal and Gwen too angry, they would leave the Community. But there was the more urgent threat that if Brian and I did not measure up to Dwight's idea of what a community government ought to be like, we would lose Dwight. We did not want to lose anybody, but if forced to choose, we would try hardest to keep Dwight. Therefore, Dwight did not have a great deal of difficulty persuading me and Brian to stick to a strict interpretation of Community rules. The trailer would go up for flips. For his part, Dwight consented to a phony, fixed coin toss for the master bedroom. We "tossed the coin" there in a closed planners' meeting, and it came up "Gwen," heads or tails.

Gwen and Hal accepted the decision with reasonable grace. Another couple moved into the back bedroom, and the Community used the living room as a schoolroom.

We had achieved a dubious peace on the trailer question (I was feeling rather awed at our ability to force through a no-compromise decision) when community emotions erupted over the outside-work question. This was the point when Hal was called upon to do an outside work shift, and he refused to go. Once again Dwight demanded that it be made a large public issue. Two open meetings were held. Terrible, hostile things were said in cold, rational language. The essence of it was that Hal did not think he should have to go on outside work and challenged the authority of the board of planners to make him do it. Dwight wanted to take up the challenge and actually expel him. I was trying to avoid having to make that clear choice. But Dwight would not allow any avoidance. He forced the board to a vote. He voted to expel Hal. I voted not to do so. Brian refused to vote at all. That broke up the meeting. Dwight and Brian spent the rest of the night discussing the issue by themselves. Hal placated the group by deciding to volunteer for a slight amount of outside work. The summer lurched sickeningly on.

Dwight never forgave me for my vote on the issue of Hal's expulsion. He considered me the Apostle of Expedience, said I had no principles at all except the principles of personal leadership. In a letter he wrote when he left he said, "To retain her position she will compromise any aspect of Walden Two. Any time the masses want something done, you will find her jumping in to lead them." What Dwight missed in his analysis was that I was trying to hold the Community together long enough to insure its survival.

The board of planners spent the next month arguing about proposed changes in our bylaws. The original bylaws were written largely by me and passed into law by a very lazy consensus that didn't even examine them closely. Dwight had never bothered with them, believing that written law has little to do with actual behavior. But in the issue of expelling Hal, I had based my vote on our expulsion regulations as laid down in the bylaws, where it specifically limits the reasons a full member can be expelled—and refusing to do outside work is not one of them. This caused Dwight to take a closer look at the bylaws, and he didn't like what he found.

Our bylaws are stated sufficiently loosely that even our form of government is not defined in them. They leave us free to experiment with government and to change it from time to time as we see fit, without revolution or constitutional revision. Furthermore, they are fundamentally democratic, in that they allow a two-thirds majority veto by the full members of any decision made by the governing body. Dwight had always been distrustful of democratic procedures. This ultimate appeal to democracy struck him as absurd and inconsistent. We argued about it a lot. I said that there had to be some protection against abuses by the board of planners, and he said that there had to be protection against the abuses of democracy. After a month of arguing, Dwight presented the board with three ultimata. He wanted the bylaws to specify the planner-manager government rather than leaving the government subject to change; he wanted a ten-year term for the planners; and he wanted the removal of two-thirds overrule. Though Brian and I thoroughly sympathized with Dwight's distrust of the irrationalities of democracy, neither of us would agree to those changes in the bylaws. Though we understood the nature of the ultimatum, and though we personally esteemed Dwight far above anyone else in the Community, we refused to change the bylaws. Why? I, because I really believe in the importance of good law; Brian, because he did not believe it was possible to keep Dwight any longer. Dwight had fought all summer against the bourgeoisie, and he was not satisfied with his victories. He was not satisfied with his companions in the battle. Brian and I had failed him.

Before he left, he wrote down his misgivings about the direction the Community was taking. I quote:

> I suppose Fred and Pete will be the next new planners. You might keep in mind that both of them favor the 75-hour week . . . I suspect that during the next few months or years there will be a strong pressure to keep out negroes, adolescents, intellectuals, psychologists, radicals, hippies, and college dropouts. This would be extremely unfortunate, I think. Even if you don't like the opinions and actions of these people, you had better keep them around to balance the right wing. I am afraid that within a couple years Fred and Pete are going to be the extreme left wing in this community, and not because they have changed any of *their* opinions. . . . As the Community grows

richer, the situation becomes worse, because more and more bourgeoisie decide to join. . . . What sort of utopian radicals are going to gather around Pete and Fred?

For all his virtues, Dwight was a poor prophet. Within six months Hal and Gwen, Pete and Rosa, and Fred had all given up and gone away.

Fred

What people don't understand when they hear the story of Fred and the Community is why a man like Fred would join a community in the first place. Hearing him speak with bitterness and sarcasm about Twin Oaks's institutions and prospects, one would think that he had always been a rugged individualist, selfish and opportunistic, always feathering his own nest and caring very little for anyone else. But this was not true. Fred became bitter through his community experience. He is one member who was a worse person for having lived here.

When Fred first read *Walden Two* he was getting his B.A. in psychology in Michigan. The communal structure depicted in the book appealed to him immensely. It made so much sense. Why have a stove in every house, when one stove would cook enough food for fifty people? Why a swimming pool in every suburban backyard? A big swimming pool would cost less and be better to swim in. Fred's interests roamed far. He delved into ham radio, photography, model building. All of these hobbies require expensive equipment. Sharing the gear with other hams and other photographers would make it possible for him to have excellent equipment available for much less money than owning it himself. The possibilities in joint ownership were exciting. Think of the library, the records, the electronic gear! As other men have dreamed of owning a lot of things, Fred dreamed of using a lot of things. They would be owned by the Community, and he would do his share for the Community. In exchange, all these things he wanted to work and play with would be his, in as real a sense as if he owned them.

There was nothing wrong with this dream except that Fred failed to see the intermediate steps that would have to be taken before we got there. He might have been happy in an affluent community or in one that eased into public ownership gradually, allowing each member to buy, own, and control a fair amount of personal property during the first years and only moving into group use when all the problems of organization and group care had been worked out. He was never happy at Twin Oaks.

Though one of the original eight, Fred was trapped in the city for the first five months of the Community's existence because of the payments on the city house. He kept his city job. What's more, he kept his income. That caused the first clash between Fred and the rest of us. Instead of sitting in general session (Sandy's consensus meetings) and arguing that he ought to be allowed to keep his income, or that he would postpone his technical entrance into membership until such time as he could quit his job and move onto the farm, he kept silent at meetings and let the total community-of-property decisions go through without dissent. He dissented simply by not turning over his paychecks. None of the rest of us had any idea what to do about it. We liked group harmony, and we certainly didn't want to alienate anybody. We couldn't afford to lose any members from that little group. I did point out to Fred that his income should go into the communal treasury, since he was a member. He just said that he was spending the money on the Community, and so it *was* going into the treasury, indirectly. It was true. Fred spent his money on baby ducklings, a brood sow, a water pump, and spray nozzles for a spray rig he was making. Whatever community project interested him, there he put his paycheck, thus deriving enjoyment from his weekends on the farm. He said that if he put his checks directly into the treasury, it would be diddled away, and he never would get the things he wanted. This was true enough, if by "diddled" he meant food purchases, light bills, etc. It was perfectly true that we would not, as a group, have given priority to a brood sow without figures to show that pig raising was profitable, nor to the spray rig unless it was agreed by the group as a whole that it was badly needed.

This beginning on a "watch out for myself" basis prevented Fred from being elected to the board of planners and deprived him of the respect of the group. For all the year and a half that he lived here, in all matters of spending money, distribution of property and the like, Fred worked against the rest of the Community, and the Community worked around and in spite of Fred.

Nevertheless he was a leader in important ways. No one could question his importance to us. He studied farming and poured his energies into the garden. He repaired our cars as they broke down. He did the electric wiring in the Harmony building. It is certainly true that the automobiles were worse off when Fred ceased to care for them, and that the farm went to pieces after his departure.

Our historical records are fortunate in Fred's case, for he left behind him a complete list of the reasons he decided to leave. I quote from the list:

> Too much frustration. It is like being the youngest child in a family. After I decide to do something I have to get approval of others and may be overruled. No autonomy of action.
>
> Hobbies very important to me. Not enough money. Not allowed to earn extra money.
>
> Feeling that everyone should take his turn on outside work. Do I spend summers accumulating extra credits on farm work and then do the same on a winter cash job?
>
> Community not likely to succeed. No one with business sense and urge. No agreement on business. No capital. No motivation to see a business to success.
>
> Too little privacy. Gossip. Bawling babies. Noisy people. No retreat in winter. I need a workshop that is secluded,

quiet, and where I can work on a project whenever I want to. Common use of tools, maybe, but a private work bench and a room to put it in.

Nothing given except if you holler for it. My pants for example. After griping for a month and making an official issue at a planners' meeting I am told to buy some pants. Am I supposed to make a special trip to Richmond to buy pants? Now two trips have been made to Richmond without a thought so far as I know about buying them. Same applies to car repairs—spend half of my time fixing cars, the other half lobbying for parts.

Need motivation. No enthusiasm in working for someone else. That is my personality. Saying you wish it weren't so and ignoring it serves no good purpose.

Party-type people who are attracted to our leisure time not the type who are productive. My brother wouldn't join.

Farming the only community activity that interests me, and that only if I am in charge. Sacrificing myself not satisfying to me. Making others happy no good unless I am happy too.

Things not being handled satisfactorily. Dental care, my clothes, farm equipment problems, tools.

Most of my labor here is going into kids. They all consume more than they produce. This week 120 credits plus cash money on them. At $1.00 a credit, that is $10 from each person. All I asked for was $5 a week allowance for my hobbies, and they wouldn't give me that.

There is no question but that we were glad to see Fred go. In spite of all his value as a worker, the difficulty trying to institute community norms of cooperation and sharing against the active opposition of a charter member were enormous. Twin Oaks was a peaceful and quiet place after he left.

Pete

Pete and Rosa visited us in the winter of 1967, bringing with them their twelve-year-old daughter, Arlene, and baby Maxine. They seemed the least likely people in the world to want to join. True, I had read Pete's letters and correctly comprehended their message of passionate interest in the communal ideal. I knew that there were years of thinking and longing behind this visit to Twin Oaks, that he had come with hopes of making this his communal home. Still, the circumstances were none too favorable.

For one thing it was clear from the beginning that Rosa was not ideologically committed to community. She was committed to her husband and family, and she meant to go as far as she could to help Pete make his dreams come true. They were not her dreams, maybe. When does a woman get her dreams, anyway? Rosa would try to be happy here for her husband's sake. Perhaps it wouldn't work out, and they could go away again. Pete would never be able to say that she had stood in his way. Or perhaps he was right, and the Community would become a prosperous and happy place where she would be glad to stay.

In addition to ideology problems, there was a glaring cultural gap to deal with. Talking with Pete was like talking to a foreigner. The simplest way to say this is that he was not hip. He was intelligent and had a Master's degree, but he lacked a certain kind of sophistication. He was unfamiliar with the youth subculture. Through all of his reading and thinking about community, he seemed not to have realized that people who joined a community in 1968 would use profane language or flaunt their sexual rebellion openly and insistently. His sense of humor seemed to operate on a different level from the rest of us. He would laugh uproariously about a mistake one of us made in farm nomenclature and never realize, when we joined in the laughter, that it was his mirth and not the original mistake that set us laughing.

The sheer physical difficulties in the way of Pete's joining the Community seemed the biggest problem of all. Where would we put them? They would need two rooms. We didn't have two empty rooms. We were still assuming that new people would live in barns. Would we ask Pete and Rosa and their children to live in a barn? Or in the attic? Somehow we couldn't. They were older and they were respectable, and the idea of their climbing up and down a ladder from their bedroom was more than we could imagine. The alternative was finding some excuse to put current members in those same barns or attic, thus giving obvious preference to the newcomers. In principle we were opposed to this. But no one said a word when we decided to do it. Everyone understood that it was not going to make anybody happy to ask the new family to accept this crude equality the first day they walked in the door.

Even with the room question solved, it was obvious that accepting a ready-made family was going to cost us money and effort that we might be putting elsewhere. First we put new tires on our old school bus and drove it to North Carolina and back twice to bring their belongings. Then there was the baby-care expense. Maxine's care absorbed the equivalent of two members' labor, and in addition she occupied the living space that might have gone to a productive worker. Ironically, it was also expensive for Pete and Rosa. They had to leave behind things they had accumulated and subject their furniture to heavy community use. Pete left a good job and took a risk with his future aligning himself with a peculiar organization. Would the government hire an agricultural agent who had been a member of a commune? Who knew?

Moving, too, is expensive when you have a lot of household goods. Pete and Rosa had not only household goods but three cows.

We sat down to talk about money problems, and things looked worse and worse. Pete had insurance policies he didn't want to give up. Were we going to pay insurance premiums for him? In Pete's mind, the ideal community did these things. In ours was the simple equality question. If we couldn't afford insurance for everybody, we couldn't afford it for anybody. We suggested that they pay the policy up for a year, so that if Twin Oaks didn't work out for them, they wouldn't have sacrificed their insurance. I believed they did this, but it must have been a hardship. There was no great bank account to take such money out of. They had always been fairly poor.

Also, they did not have cash enough to pay their entrance fee, and they asked us to accept goods instead of the $800 required ($200 per person). Unspoken in my mind and Brian's were irritation at Pete's conservatism and the thought that most of the other members had paid their entrance fees and donated their goods in addition, withholding nothing. Still, none of us had two children to pay entrance fees for, either. It wouldn't be easy for Pete's one income to pay for four people, even in goods. No matter how you looked at it, both the Community and Pete's family stood to lose financially by the merger. Both did lose, and heavily.

To me the expense was unimportant in relation to the step we were taking. I felt that getting Pete and Rosa and the children into the Community was a major step toward stability and taking ourselves seriously as a permanent establishment. Brian was less enthusiastic, sensing problems ahead. Fred was downright angry about it. He could not see why we should put labor into raising somebody else's children.

They moved down in June. We had emptied two adjoining rooms for them, and they crowded their belongings into them. Arlene shared a room with the baby. Their living room furniture was an asset to our public space. Our living room began to look more like a living room.

You might guess that our major problems with Pete and Rosa were centered on the theories of child care as applied to Maxine, but this was not true. There were some minor disagreements, which I will tell about in another chapter. But we had an unspoken agreement about Maxine's care, and it worked out fairly well. Everybody understood it, and everybody went by it. For their part, the parents agreed to go along with communal child care theory and split up all the labor of Maxine's care, even submitting to community authority on questions of policy. For our part we treated Maxine with kindness and love, watched over her constantly, and never did anything with her or to her behind the parents' back. If authority rested with us, responsibility was actually accepted by Pete. Rosa loved the baby dearly, but she was pleased to be free of constant child care. She saw that we became fond of Maxine and rarely expressed any criticism of anything we did. I think there was not much to criticize. We loved Maxine very much.

Nevertheless there was trouble. Two things about the Community Rosa could not accept. One was profanity. The other was dirt.

It was the year of the dirty word. Naomi had just come, sixteen years old and free at last from an environment where her language was disapproved. She was reveling in her new freedom. The fad caught on, and for a while it was a rare sentence uttered in a public room that did not contain at least one obscenity. Rosa's silent, tight-lipped presence did nothing to curb the exuberant profanity. Even Pete was heard to say "shit" occasionally, though he tried to stop himself, for Rosa's sake.

We probably kept a cleaner house when Rosa was with us than ever before or since. This was partly because Rosa herself put in extra time on the cleaning, and partly because, out of fear of her disapproval, the rest of us paid some attention to picking up after ourselves. Nevertheless, the difference between the standard we kept and the standard she could accept was enormous. Rosa wanted the house to look as clean as a normal, middle-class house looks—as clean as she herself would have kept it for her family. Twenty-two members and a dozen visitors inhabited the Community that summer, traipsing through the buildings with mud and manure on their boots, looking for a place to put away a bucket, or a sweater, or a cigarette butt, and putting them anywhere at all if they didn't see a good place. Rosa could not tolerate that level of disorder and carelessness. She complained to Pete, and Pete called the planners into session to discuss the problem. The planners listened dismally and tried to propose solutions. We would have cleanup campaigns, or education programs. We would try harder. Pete tried to be satisfied with that, but he never noticed the improvements that we tried to make in our behavior. The gap was too big, and the improvements too small.

In return, Brian pointed out to Pete that the nagging, resentful, critical behavior he and Rosa exhibited was a drag on Community morale and was not particularly helping the cleanliness problem. He suggested that Pete try different techniques of social control. Brian pointed out carefully (trying to relay the urgent message of the Community as a whole) that caustic criticism and nagging, while temporarily effective in getting a mess cleaned up, have long-range side effects that do more harm than good. Pete thought this over, but he didn't agree. He said that his criticisms were always honest, and furthermore, they were generally right. Now if any one of us believed that he was wrong, and could support that belief, he, Pete, would retract the criticism and apologize. But as long as the fault existed, Pete reserved the right to criticize it. The Community's anti-gossip restrictions he found annoying. He said they interfered with communication.

Pete's style of attack was indignant, schoolteacherly sarcasm. "Did you want those beans to burn?" he asked Naomi, when she had left the burner on too high under a pot. "Well, did you? Did you?" Pete never stopped demanding "Did you?" until Naomi said tiredly that No, Pete, she had not intended to burn the beans. "Well, that's what it looks like," said Pete.

Or, "Who left that bushel of apples out for the ducks to eat?" he asked once. No one, of course, had intended to feed the ducks at all. Someone had simply forgotten about ducks and probably about the apples as well. Pete never understood why we should object so strenuously to the way he said things. "It doesn't matter how a person says it," he would say. "It means all the same. Doesn't it? Well, doesn't it?" Yes, Pete, maybe it does.

But then again, maybe it doesn't. We could disagree with Pete, but if we did, we were in for hours of discussion, for Pete did not give in easily (in fact, I never knew him to admit he was wrong unless about some trivial matter of fact), and he wanted the argument pursued until it was settled. He believed that people could argue until they agreed. Neither Brian nor I expected people to work that way. We knew all too well that most people simply give up arguing when the going gets tough, either logically or emotionally, and perhaps pretend to agree, but keep their same stubborn opinions. It is a rare person who can change his mind in the middle of an argument. So we wouldn't argue beyond presenting our points and having them rejected. We avoided discussions because of our dislike of being bullied with Pete's "Well, isn't it?" and Pete was disappointed. He loved to engage in discussions.

For all his foibles, Pete was much respected. He was a thoroughly honest person, and by his lights self-disciplined and considerate. He thought slowly, but he thought well, and once he committed himself to a person or an idea, he was a long time giving it up. We lost no time appointing him to the board of planners.

Pete on the board (he took my expired term) made a difficult situation for Brian to adjust to. Our first board had worked together easily, understood each other with few words. Pete did not start with the same understandings at all, and his manner intimidated Brian. The board was not effective. The decisions they made as a group they had to vote on, rather than reaching easy consensus, as the previous board had done. This was because Pete did have rather different opinions on some issues, and Brian lacked the verbal courage to fight with him. They disagreed on the manner of

handling community clothing purchases, Pete wanting each
member to have a cash clothing allowance and Brian (and
most of the rest of us) preferring to keep our clothes purchases communal and only buy what we had to buy as the
needs came up. Then there were various issues involving
eventual property arrangements with members, Brian wanting us to move faster toward the totally communal and Pete
wanting the Community to let property holders keep their
property. He didn't want us to seem grabby, and he thought
we ought to succeed financially on our own. Pete won temporary victories on the questions of property, but they were
all reversed as soon as he left.

It was dirt and "irresponsibility" that did us in. We could
have lived with Pete's mannerisms forever and loved him in
spite of them, and he could have happily hammered away at
the wall of our silent refusal to argue. But he could not face
Rosa's unhappiness about dirt, and he began to believe that
as a group we were too irresponsible ever to make a successful community.

Pete could (and did) point to dozens of examples of what
he meant by irresponsibility. The problem was real enough.
It still is. He meant starting a job and not finishing it properly. Like canning the tomatoes and then leaving them in
the kitchen for a week before remembering to take them to
the basement or even wiping them off. Or rendering the lard
and not cleaning up the grease that spilled on the stove. I
remember those two because they were things that I was
guilty of. But I was not, unfortunately, the worst culprit.
Naomi and Jenny at sixteen were not models of responsibility. If they felt like taking off for a drive with an exciting
visitor, they took off, dumping their work on whoever would
agree to get stuck with it, whether or not that person was
capable of doing it. Pete's tirades about this behavior were
made worse because we shared his indignation. On the other
hand, our indignation was muffled by our annoyance with the
tirades.

Compared with Pete and Rosa, the whole lot of us were irresponsible. They really were careful with tools. They really did put things away when they were through with them. They always cleaned up after themselves. They had done so since childhood, probably. Their twelve-year-old daughter Arlene did the same. Their training technique worked well on Arlene. It was a simple case of avoidance behavior. At that early age it really is easier to do one's work properly than it is to take nagging, sarcastic criticism. The same techniques didn't work on us adults, though. We had more choice. We could just avoid Pete.

For ten months Pete struggled to reduce Rosa's demands to a place where the Community could meet them and to raise the Community's standards to a point where he and Rosa could believe in our potential. But he had taken on more than he could do. He had overestimated his own stamina. Between Rosa's tears (behind the thin walls I could hear her crying and saying, "Oh, how I hate those people") and the Community's careless habits, his resolve to stick it out finally crumbled, and he decided to leave.

Rosa was not the only one to cry. For me, losing the battle to hold Pete and Rosa in the Community was a major, bitter defeat, sinking me into a depression that took months to recover from. Pete's losing his faith badly affected mine. We had already lost Dwight and Fred. Were Brian and I to be left to build the Community alone with a handful of kids? Was it to be a pattern that the Community would attract high-schoolers with their heads full of rock and roll, while the adults who might help would just stand by and judge us for our weakness? If we couldn't hold Pete, whom could we hold? I left the Community on a business trip and spent some time alone in the city, trying to put my faith back together. Brian, in the meantime, was doing outside work, and the Community's day-to-day affairs went along leaderless on their own momentum.

I still think of Pete's defection as a tragedy—more now for

him than for us. We have found other leaders, other people of strong purpose and integrity, and we will be all right. But where are Pete's dreams now? He can never again risk the financial blow of trying out another group. Nor can he make himself give up his belief that he belongs in community. We spoke to him not long ago, and he told us that he hopes some day to build a community of some sort on his own land. We wish him well.

Oh, Pete, if you had only timed it a little differently! Suppose you had joined in 1971 instead of 1968. Could you dig that workshop, with its neat rows of labeled boxes, color coded and kept in order? What would you say to Naomi and Jenny now, grown up and pulling their full share of the responsibility load? Wouldn't you like to come to one of our Feedback sessions, where we let down the no-gossip barriers and speak our minds about what is bothering us? But it's no use. One of the reasons we are on our feet in 1971 is that we have closed our doors temporarily to families with children.

XI

Children in Community

For over three years now there have been no children at Twin Oaks. All of our experience with children dates between the winter of 1967–68 and the summer of 1969. During that period there were nine children of different ages and at different times. Four of them were Simon's family. There is little to tell about them, so I am leaving them out of the narrative. They were happy children, played together, and got along all right both with Simon and the Community. They made a lot of noise, and we were grateful for the silence after their departure, but we never had a crisis over them. All of the others made waves in the Community, mostly over the issue of where the authority lay for decisions regarding their education and training, occasionally over real questions of child-raising policy itself.

Timothy was the charming four-year-old son of Marie, a short-term member early in our history. Marie was divorced and had turned to clerical work in order to support Timothy and herself. Holding a full-time job and leaving the baby to sitters was far from an ideal life, and Marie was naturally attracted to the Community when she heard about it. Here she could support Timothy and be with him at the same time. She could stop worrying about the bad influence of the baby-sitters, the television, and the neighborhood children.

Little Timothy would be brought up with pleasant adults, animals, and her own gentle care. Perhaps Marie would find a good man in the Community, too, and both their problems would be solved at once.

Marie visited the Community first and obtained our permission to bring the child. She had settled on a place in one of the barn lofts for their bedroom. At this period we were very short of living space. Both barn lofts had been made into bedrooms by dividing them down the middle with a wall of hay bales. Brian and Carrie lived in the same loft as Marie. Carrie's side of the loft was nicely decorated, made to look as much as possible like a real bedroom in a middle-class home. Carrie's king-size bed and the matching pieces of her bedroom suite were there. Drapes lined the walls, and there were lamps and pictures. Marie had not yet had time to do much with her side. She just had a mattress on a stack of hay bales.

The night she brought Timothy to the Community and tried to take him to their bed, Timothy objected. "I don't want to sleep in a barn," he told her. "I want to sleep in the house."

"Well, you can't sleep in the house," she answered. "Come on. It's a perfectly good bed. I'll sleep with you." Timothy got into bed with his mother, but he was not happy and did not fall asleep. Just as Marie was drifting off to sleep she heard Timothy say, "I'm not going to sleep in a barn. I'm going to sleep in the house," and get up and start across the room.

Carrie, who could hear from the other side of the wall of hay, felt some sympathy with little Timothy's objections. But she had made the adjustment, and she helped Timothy to make it. She called to him. "Timothy," she said, "why don't you come over here? It's nice over here, not like a barn. See the big bed? See the dresser and the curtains? It's just like a real bedroom. Why don't you come and get in bed with us?" Timothy was persuaded. He had met Carrie only that evening, but she spoke a language he understood. He crawled into the big king-sized bed with Carrie and Brian, put his head on the Dacron polyester pillow, and slept soundly until morning.

If Marie felt a twinge of jealousy, she never showed it. She was proud of Timothy's poise and verbal ability and pleased that he so easily made the transition to group parenthood. Timothy had some minor behavior problems. We appointed Brian as Child Manager, so that we would have some structure for dealing with them. Brian's experience with children was zero, but he had a gentle manner, and we trusted him. Timothy threw tantrums. They were the classic throw-yourself-on-the-floor type of tantrum that were very easy to cure. Brian easily persuaded Marie to ignore them, assuring her that she was not being a cruel, unloving parent, and that Timothy would not hurt himself by holding his breath. Marie was frankly relieved to share the burden of Timothy's behavior training. She went along willingly with any suggestion Brian made. Timothy, a very intelligent child and not severely disturbed, got over his tantrum behavior in a few days. Brian timed the tantrums. Fifteen minutes for the first one. Five minutes the second one. Two minutes the third. There never was a fourth. We were delighted with Brian and with ourselves.

It was harder to get Timothy to leave Marie any peace for her private life. She had fallen in love with Charlie, and they often wanted to be alone in the late evening when Timothy might have been in bed. But Brian did not want Timothy to be forced to any particular bedtime, so Timothy was naturally aware of his mother's whereabouts and wanted to be with her. We talked a lot about this problem. Brian defended the child's right to determine how much sleep he needed; we all defended Marie's right to spend time alone with Charlie. The obvious solution was that Timothy should stay up if he liked, but leave Marie alone. But Timothy did not see it that way. When Marie went into Charlie's room and closed the door, Timothy started to cry. Marie held out against tantrums, but she could not help responding to his new techniques as he invented them. His favorite was calling softly at the door, "Mommy, Mommy. [No answer] Mommy. Marie! Marie! Please let me in. I want to talk to you." The combination of his reasonable tone and his conforming to the Community Code by addressing his mother by her first name never failed to win Marie's heart. She always opened the door.

We never solved this problem, because Marie left the Community after only a few weeks. When she left, she placed Timothy in our care. This was our idea. We were interested in Timothy and felt that he would be much better off being raised by us than by relatives and baby-sitters. Marie was lonely (Charlie had left) and needed to go back to the city to look for a husband. But what did Timothy stand to gain from that world? As far as we could see, he belonged with us on the farm.

We were not bad parents. We were courteous with Timothy, gave him respect and liberty, tucked him into bed and told him stories. But in offering to care for Timothy we had underestimated his need for companionship. Because he needed someone to play with, he naturally sought to be with all of us, or any of us who would tolerate him. And the fact was that none of us was so interested in child raising that we wanted to spend time with him for our own pleasure and benefit.

He wanted to work with us. We gave him a limited freedom of the shop. He used hammers and nails, the saw, plane, chisel, and hand drill. (If he had stayed with us, he probably would have been a decent carpenter by the age of six.) This contented him for a while, but he wanted more than anything to work *with us* at the same tasks we were doing. His skills were not sufficient, and we could not let him. It was an adult's world, and Timothy encountered "no" oftener than we would have liked. "No," he couldn't eat more than his fair share of the oranges; "No," he couldn't use the power machinery, the electric typewriter, or the automobiles; and oftenest, "No," we didn't want to play with him right then. It was then that we understood fully why Skinner had suggested separate children's quarters. The idea is not to get children out of the way of the adults, but to put them in a place where they are not frustrated by things they can't have.

We put "playing with Timothy" on the labor credit system. Carrie did a lot of it. She took him sledding and played ball with him. Some of us went for walks with him, or played puzzles and games. But it was full-time companionship that he wanted, and we did not have time or desire to give it to him.

He quickly found which ones of us could be teased into giving him attention. Hal was particularly vulnerable. Hal had no theories about behavioral engineering. He didn't follow the arguments about reinforcement and extinction. When Timothy said, "Tell me a story," Hal would say, "Not right now," or, "I'm busy. Maybe later." But Timothy soon discovered that he didn't really mean it. If begged long enough, Hal would take Timothy on his knee in the traditional fashion and tell him stories.

Hal complained to Brian that Timothy was a nuisance and ought to be put to bed so as to be out of the way when adults wanted to spend time in the company of other adults. Brian eventually gave in on this argument, but he was frustrated at having to resort to regulation when it could have been avoided. He said that Hal could quickly extinguish Timothy's unwanted pestering if he would just use simple extinction techniques, and that Timothy, being bored, would go to bed by himself. But Hal could not stand to see the child standing lonely and disappointed, wanting someone to play with. So he "reinforced" the pestering and continued to complain about it. This situation, to one degree or another, was multipled by the number of members. Few of us really believed hard enough in the principle of extinction to apply the technique in the face of Timothy's bright, pleading eyes. So, with no regulation and no behavioral engineering, he became a little spoiled, and a lot of the adults ceased to enjoy him. When his mother came and took him away to his grandparents for a Christmas vacation (from which he never returned to us), we were relieved to be temporarily free of the problem.

Our next child was baby Maxine, the one-and-a-half-year-old daughter of Pete and Rosa. Her joining was a big event. For Pete was very serious about living in community, and we felt we had a good chance of raising Maxine all the way to adulthood. Maxine was probably the world's happiest and most placid child. She was large-boned and plump, almost twice the size of the usual baby her age. On her wide pumpkin face she wore a perpetual smile that won the hearts of everyone who took care of her. Maxine was prepared to approve of everything and everybody. She had never learned fear. She had known nothing but love from her adoring family. She came to us whole, undamaged. I am glad to say that she left in the same sound condition.

Pete had read *Walden Two* and understood that we did not want a nuclear family arrangement on Community grounds. He persuaded Rosa. In fact, Rosa was glad to share the baby care responsibilities with the rest of us. The only person who objected to the arrangement was Maxine herself, who wanted her mother to be on call at all times. But it was not a serious problem. Maxine was always happy with her substitute mothers. She just wanted Rosa to be part of the party, too, and Rosa, who had other things to do, sometimes had to sneak around to avoid being noticed by the baby.

We divided Maxine's day into seven two-hour shifts. Rosa always took the early, wake-up shift, and Pete generally signed up for a shift during the day. There were eight other people who took part in child care. Maxine seemed to love us all. She beamed happily at us when she woke up from her nap, was pleased to get lunch from our hands, and delighted in playing with us or taking us for walks.

She was particularly fond of Jenny and Naomi. These two girls tried to carry on their own lives with Maxine as a party to their activities, rather than setting aside a clear babysitting time. They would take her to their room while they were trying to read or talk or work, and Maxine would busy herself with whatever toys were available, mostly full ashtrays and half-emptied Kool-Aid glasses. One of the devices she discovered for amusement was taking off her shoes and socks. She loved to be barefoot, and she liked the activity of removing her clothes. Naomi and Jenny could not bring themselves to get excited about it. True, it was winter, but the house was heated, and it seemed to them that it would do Maxine no harm to run barefoot for a while. Pete and Rosa disagreed. They reminded Naomi and Jenny that the floor was not carpeted. They pointed to the numerous colds that Maxine had caught and insisted that she be kept warmly dressed. The girls responded sullenly but patiently by holding the squirming baby down and putting the shoes and socks back on. Maxine, of course, just took them off again. The trick was to get them on her often enough so that her parents did not see her barefoot. Pete went into tirades on the subject.

Where was the Child Manager then? Why did he not interfere and tell Pete that the Community's children would be allowed to go barefoot inside the house? Brian, like the rest of us, was cowed by Pete. Pete never actually said, "This is my child, and I will determine how she is raised," but he might as well have. As long as Maxine was with us, no matter what title we had conferred on Brian, it was Pete who was *de facto* child manager.

On two occasions members challenged Pete's right to make decisions about Maxine. Both times Pete worked honorably through channels, never allowing himself to pull legal rank as the child's parent or threatening to leave if he didn't get his way. Nevertheless, the pressure was there. None of us could stand up against it, and he always got his way. The fortunate thing was that we agreed on most things, and issues didn't come up very often.

The first challenge to Pete's authority was brought up by Jenny, who wanted to take Maxine to nearby Louisa with her in the car. Jenny had a driver's license and was a careful driver. What she was trying to do was enliven her baby care shifts by doing something interesting in them. She wanted to put Maxine in the car, take Naomi along for company and to keep Maxine under control, and go into Louisa on community errands. Thus the child care shift would pass swiftly, and Jenny could get the shopping done at the same time. Pete objected. He didn't just object—he said Absolutely Not. Jenny went to Brian, and Brian, unwilling to deal with the question by himself, called in the board of planners. We argued for an hour. Pete said he did not trust the young girls with the baby in the car. They might get to talking, he said, and forget what they were doing. He felt that the addition of the baby made an accident more likely. Jenny argued bitterly that Pete's objections were not out in the open— that he was really punishing her for having been "irresponsible" in some unrelated area, like not washing a drainboard or not getting up on time for milking. She said that she had as good a driving record as anyone in the Community and objected to being the victim of a prejudice against youth. She felt quite confident that she and Naomi would look after the baby as well as anyone else, and she challenged Pete to show any evidence that she was careless with human life. Pete stuck to his opinions (or emotions) and charged general irresponsibility of character. The planners secretly agreed with both of them. We privately thought that the girls were probably less responsible than older people might be; we also thought that the chances of an accident were extremely small and not worth making a fuss about. Any of us would have risked our own children, if we had had them, to the same two girls without worrying. After long debate, in which Brian argued that we could not use vague, prejudiced intuitions as a basis for legislation, and I argued that Pete's emotions were strong and needed to be considered, rational or not, we finally decided to prohibit Maxine's being taken to town in the car. The girls could not take her. But neither could anybody else, including Pete and Rosa.

An almost identical issue involved whether Naomi should be allowed to bathe with Maxine. Again, Naomi was trying to fill the child care hours with activity. Also, she realized that the baby rarely saw a naked human, and didn't want her to grow up believing that only the clothed body is suitable to be viewed. So it was not just a bath that she had in mind, but a cultural lesson as well. When Rosa objected, most of us thought that it was precisely this cultural lesson that she objected to, though Pete adamantly denied it. Her ostensible objection was that Naomi might let the slippery baby fall and hurt herself in the bathtub. In addition (Pete confided to me privately), they feared that Naomi might have some venereal disease and pass it to the baby in the bathwater. This was so absurd that it was difficult not to laugh. I assured Pete that Naomi did not have any venereal disease (Naomi, despite behavior that made her appear promiscuous, was still a virgin at the time), but Pete reserved his own' opinions. It just wasn't worth taking a chance, he said.

Once again the planners were called into session. Once again the decision went against the bath, on the grounds that Pete's anxiety, however irrational, had to be considered, and that Maxine didn't care one way or the other.

But that was not the real reason for the decision. The real reason was that none of us could stand up to Pete. He shouted, and he waxed indignant, and he never stopped arguing until he got his way. Considering that Maxine didn't really give two hoots whether she took a bath with Naomi or not, we asked Naomi to swallow her pride and forego the

communal splash. Naomi was angry, felt she had been betrayed, that the whole Community had been betrayed by
the board's fear of Pete's temper. And perhaps it was.

Rosa's worries about communal child care did not always
come to planners' meetings. Quite often Pete took care of
them privately. One occasion had to do with a member
named Toby, who signed up for child care and then spent
the time reading. He was reading the Tolkien trilogy at the
time and decided to read it aloud to Maxine. He had read
somewhere about an experiment that had been done with
preverbal children, reading to them aloud for an hour every
day when they were only a year old. According to the report,
those children later developed excellent vocabulary and
language skills. Maxine was just the right age for the application of this experiment, and Toby was enthusiastic about
science. So he put Maxine into a hammock and read to her
by the hour. Rosa did not like this. "Maxine doesn't understand anything that book says," she complained to Pete.
"She would rather get up and run around and play. It seems
to me he's the one that wants to read that book." But Pete
observed Toby and Maxine and decided that no damage was
being done. "It won't hurt her any," he said. "If she didn't
like it, she wouldn't sit there and listen." So the readings
went on, and Rosa learned to look on with tolerance. Sometimes Maxine would drift off pleasantly into her nap in the
middle of the story.

By spring 1969 we realized that Pete and his family were
going to leave the Community. They had wavered for a long
time and finally made up their minds. But they stayed for
several months after the decision had been made, so the
Community lived for those months with the knowledge that
all the child care we were doing was irrelevant to our goals
and wasteful of our energies. Pete and Rosa, meanwhile, had
earned a great many vacation credits, and took their earned
vacation in half-quota, week after week. We were low on
members, high on work. The work quota was steadily in the

fifties (over fifty hours of work per member per week). Maxine's care became aversive as it became pointless. We still loved the baby, it is true, but we no longer had any hope of raising her. "What difference does it make now?" said Naomi bitterly. "In a few years she'll be just another little Rosa." The labor situation was so pressing that we considered combining child care with other tasks, like laundry or housekeeping. But Pete would not allow it. One of us might get involved in the housekeeping and forget all about her, and she might wander off and get into something. In exasperation I said that millions of children all over the world are cared for by housekeepers. Pete said that in those cases there were mothers who cared for the children, but he didn't have any confidence that the Community members could do as well. He meant, of course, Jenny and Naomi. By now he knew that we would not discriminate against the young without solid evidence. So we continued to throw away fourteen hours a day on caring for a child who didn't belong to us, and we resented every hour of it. It was then that I made up my mind to recommend that Twin Oaks not accept outsiders' children any more until we had our own permanent children's facility away from the biological parents' interference. In fact, Twin Oaks needed some time to get on its economic feet without the drain of nonproducers. But we couldn't make a decision against children right then, because Carrie was pregnant.

Carrie conceived Bonnie with the full approval of the board of planners. She called a meeting about it, and shyly asked whether we felt we could afford to have a child. We gave our delighted consent. Actually, the consent of the board of planners was less difficult to obtain than the consent of her husband. Brian had been reluctant to bring a child into their family, because Carrie's attitudes about the Community were less than enthusiastic. He did not want to raise a child in the outside world. He told Carrie that he would be willing for her to bear a child, provided they stayed in the Community.

Carrie's desire for a baby was very strong. She had lived in the Community for eight months and had many times wished to leave, but had never been able to persuade Brian. Brian's attitude toward childbearing put a new light on Community living. Here she could have a child—right away. Carrie put away her doubts about the Community and determined to be happy here. The change in her was remarkable. She became a stalwart member, tried to believe in our institutions, and succeeded fairly well. For a while, she even served on the board of planners. Part of her happiness was her pregnancy.

Carrie always had the emotions that a character in a *True Romance* magazine would have. She sighed over her wedding pictures, treasured her matching bedroom suite, and felt tenderness for the developing fetus in her womb. She might have developed fondness for outlandish foods, but she knew we would make fun of her, so if she desired pickles and ice cream in the middle of the night, she never said so.

It was a *True Romance* tragedy that destroyed Carrie's happiness in the fifth month of her pregnancy. Brian, who had never been interested in the possessive aspects of traditional marriage, began to act on his radical theories and pay attention to another girl. The girl he chose was a teen-ager named Marjorie who resembled Carrie in many ways. Like Carrie, she was very pretty and not very smart. She looked up at Brian with adoring eyes, just as Carrie must have when she had first met him. Carrie watched them exchanging the glances and signals that she recognized, and she became miserably unhappy.

Everyone in the Community was indignant at Brian's behavior and said so. He endured criticism not only from Hal and Gwen and Pete and Rosa, but also from his close friends. Even visitors got into the circle of outrage. We were having

encounter-group sessions at the time, and Brian had to listen
to people tell him how badly he had timed his affair, how
he was basically just rebelling against his parents by his unacceptable behavior, and so forth. Brian listened in silence
and remained unmoved. He offered Carrie an every-other-
day arrangement, whereby he would give his attention ex-
clusively to her one day and to Marjorie the next, in exchange
for freedom from recriminations and guilt. Carrie tried to
accept this for a short time, but her pride rebelled. She
would have a whole husband or none. So she got none. Brian
devoted all of his free time to his new affair, and Carrie spent
her days sitting quietly staring out over the fields and thinking. Meanwhile, little Bonnie was rapidly developing toward
her entry into the world.

The baby arrived at the local Louisa Hospital with all the
accouterments a magazine heroine is supposed to have. Relatives had sent her baby clothes and blankets and rattles and
stuffed animals. Carrie had the usual record book to record
Bonnie's first smile, first tooth, etc. We fixed up one of the
rooms into a nursery and put Bonnie into our newly completed
air crib.

By the time the baby was born, Brian and Carrie had put
their marriage back together to a limited extent. Marjorie
had left, under some pressure from the Community. (In fact,
she had been denied membership by a vote of the board of
planners, Carrie and I voting 2 to 1 against Brian. This em-
barrasses me as I look back on it, but at the time I sincerely
thought that Brian's affair had been a silly mistake, that he
recognized it as such, and that it would not happen again if
only we could get rid of that particular girl. It was only later
that I realized that the breach in the marriage was permanent
and that neither legislation nor guilt would put it back together.) Carrie's life was still not happy, but she made the
best she could of it and devoted herself to the child.

Bonnie, of course, was a Community child. Here, if anywhere, we had to assert the Community's right to make de-

cisions about her upbringing and education. Brian was still Child Manager, however, and his relation to Carrie made it difficult for him to cross her. For three months Carrie had the exclusive care of Bonnie. Breast feeding made this arrangement practical to some extent. But mostly we were just diffident about insisting on group care when we all knew that the baby was all that remained to Carrie of her dreams.

Eventually, though, the issue had to come up. When were we going to put Bonnie's care on the labor credit system? The pressure came once again from the young girls, Naomi and Jenny. The resistance this time came from a strange quarter—from our hardest radical, Dwight.

Dwight's defense of Carrie's possessiveness arose out of a contradiction in Dwight's own philosophy. For all his belief in personal liberty, for all his insistence upon the basic Walden Two ideas, he was himself strictly monogamous and ardently wished everyone else to be so. He was deeply upset by Brian's infidelity and identified strongly with Carrie in her loss. He recognized the necessity of a shift to communal care for the baby, but his sympathy with Carrie made him for once a conservative force.

Carrie didn't mind if someone held the baby for a while when she was busy doing something else. Like Mrs. True Romance everywhere, she gladly accepted a baby-sitter for an occasional afternoon off. But to accept the role of concerned adult among other concerned adults and give up the proprietorship involved in the role of "mother" she was not prepared to do. She attended a planners' meeting and explained her feelings to us. "I know the rules," she told us, "and I don't want to be kicked out of the Community. I like it here and I want to stay. I think I can adjust to Community child care after a little while, but I'm just not ready yet." We asked her when she expected to be ready. Bonnie was already four months old. "I don't know," she answered. "I'll let you know as we go along. I can accept certain people caring for Bonnie on certain days, I don't mind Jenny or

Rosa or Arlene or Dwight or Brian . . ." Her unfinished sentence said that she definitely did object to Naomi and to me.

I personally never made an issue of Carrie's objections. But Naomi was tired of being called "irresponsible." She demanded good reasons for being disqualified. Dwight backed up Carrie in the objection, saying that it was obvious on the surface that Naomi was irresponsible—that she might leave the baby on the edge of a table and forget about her, and so forth. Brian was contemptuous of the argument. "Yes, she might," he admitted, "and so might Carrie, for that matter." Once again the reason given was not the real reason. The real reason was that Carrie suspected Naomi of being Brian's new lover. In *True Romance* fashion she had once confronted Naomi and begged her with tears in her eyes, "Please leave my husband alone."

Brian's new love was not Naomi, but he did indeed have one. This time Brian did not act in the open but carried on the affair clandestinely, a course of action he disliked intensely. It didn't work, anyway. Carrie found out, and when she found out, she left the Community. Bonnie, of course, went with her.

There were a few other children. Their stories illustrate the same general conflicts and problems we met with Timothy, Maxine and Bonnie. Parental worries, parental jealousy, Community theory, Community inexperience. Gerald, Gwen's seven-year-old son, used his mother and the Community against each other just as any clever child uses his parents when he knows they don't agree. "I am a member of the Community, just like you, and I don't have to do what you say," he once told Gwen. It was theoretically true. The only authority he had to accept was from the Child Manager, who didn't exercise any. Gwen said to us, "I don't mind that the Community is supposed to be the authority over the children, rather than the parents. I would be glad to pass over the responsibility. But I just wish the Community would *exercise* its authority." The Community did not do so, however, so Gwen felt she had to remind Gerald to wash his face, brush his teeth, get to bed on time, go to school, tuck in his shirt, put vegetables on his plate. . . . The sound of her whining, nagging voice was part of the background music for the awful scenes of the summer of 1968.

In 1969 we definitely clamped the restriction down. No More Children. Not until we have a children's house and a children's staff and can take care of them properly, not until we have our own children who aren't going to get up and leave, wasting all our time and energy and emotion.

Recently a visitor with small children told me that he had visited Twin Oaks during the weeks immediately following this decision against the children of outsiders. "I had come to see about joining the Community, and I found out you had just made this new rule. I was pretty angry. I still am a little angry. What happened to you was that you got a bunch of bad people, and you generalized. If you had accepted me and my wife and our kids, you wouldn't have gone through those hassles. We would have accepted Community child care. We would have agreed with you about letting babies go barefoot and bathing with adults. *And we wouldn't have left!*" (He went and found other people and formed another community, so maybe that proves it.)

Perhaps he is right. Perhaps Twin Oaks was just the victim of the wrong bunch of people. Perhaps if we had been very careful and accepted only families whose child-rearing theories were very similar to our own, and who, in addition, were very much impressed by *Walden Two*, it might have worked out better. I don't know. But I doubt it. I don't think it was the selection of people. I think that the problem of supporting little children in a fledgling organization that can barely support itself is enough to explain what happened, without blaming anybody. Trying to force communal child care onto parents who had no faith in it was an effort doomed to failure. Pioneers in community child care must, I think, be people who have a heavy investment in the theory.

Our early experience with children simply showed us that Skinner was right, and that a controlled environment is absolutely necessary in order to demonstrate better child raising than liberal America elsewhere is doing with laissez faire. We could be parents now and let children grow up in a communal environment as best they can. They would be better kids than most, probably. Timothy and Maxine were children nobody would have been ashamed of. But better than most is not what we are aiming at. We aim to produce a whole generation of kids free of hangups and neuroses, able to enjoy both work and play, to be rational and (in the best sense) religious, to preserve themselves and still watch out for the rest of mankind. When we have done this we will write another book.

Our plans call for beginning to raise children (our own or adopted) just as soon as we have built a proper building to house them. We hope that will be within a year. We may take outsiders' children again after we have demonstrated with our own that we know what we are doing and that we don't intend to engage in any arguments about where the ultimate authority lies.

After all, the core of our success as a community will lie in the kind of people we produce. We are changing ourselves as best we can, but making a fresh start with newborns is a very appealing prospect. Our next set of parents have to be people who are committed communitarians *first*. The way things look now, that shouldn't be too hard to arrange.

XII

A Sense of Community—Interpersonal Relations

The social planning of the founders of Twin Oaks was largely limited to considerations of equality, and especially economic equality. I am not ashamed of that. Achieving a cultural norm that assumes real economic equality is no simple task, as the stories in this book show. The effort we put into this task, which we considered basic and indispensable to our aims, has been repaid, I think, by the smoothness and pleasantness of our daily lives now that the struggle has been won. Our labor and property systems really are fair. We really do all get a fair share of the Community's wealth, such as it is, and the managers and planners really do make the best decisions they can for the benefit of the whole group—they have no reason to do anything else. We have been called "dogmatic" and "doctrinaire" and "rigid" and "nitpicking," but our net result is a peaceful and pleasant life style.

At first I thought that this thorough and determined economic equality, plus a little common sense, would be all that was necessary to insure good human relations. What are most quarrels about, anyway? Do they not arise out of envy? And if we removed the causes of envy, would we not be removing the causes of the quarrels?

I now think that this idea was naïve. It is true that we removed a lot of the causes for discord, and it is true also that we have reaped the rewards of that planning. But there is more to human antagonism than envy, and we do not have the capability of even doing away with all causes for envy. Our systems did not touch the problems of loneliness, rejection, and unrequited love. We had no way of dealing with envy caused by superior social talents or disgruntlements over appointments to public office. We were continually plagued by dissatisfactions over the failure of members to agree on standards of workmanship, cleanliness, or courtesy. In short, there were problems in human behavior that our institutions just didn't reach. They were problems, we would say to each other with wry humor, for "behavioral engineering."

Well, what does that mean? In theory, we were for it, but what is it?

We have never been hindered by the usual conception of behavioral engineering as the manipulation of people's desires and preferences by a group of scientists in white coats, while the poor dupes under their control find themselves helplessly doing things that they really do not want to do, just because they "want to." We had read *Brave New World* and *1984* and were not impressed. The writing is great, the logic downright silly. If there were to be manipulators, we were it. But we would also be the manipulated. We would have to be both puppet and puppet-master. The logic of equalitarianism is inescapable on this point. The board of planners might think of a program for changing behavior, but they would themselves be subject to that program.

We were not hindered, as I said, by silly prejudices, from using behavioral engineering. But we were hindered, nevertheless. It is precisely the equality ethic that makes the problem complicated.

Great strides have been made by the behaviorists in mental hospitals and schools by the use of token economies. The staff are given tokens of some kind. The students or patients are told how they can earn these tokens by certain desirable behavior—doing homework, taking a bath, cleaning up a room, or what have you. The tokens can be traded for sweets or privileges. Behavior quickly conforms to the desired norms without the use of punishment. Fine. But Twin Oaks is different from these institutions in a fundamental way. There is no staff. There are no students. We divide the labor—some people have the labor of making governmental decisions—but we do not seriously have hierarchies. We are all on the same level. Token economies necessitate someone handing out the tokens. Who would do it here? The planners? Resentment over such blatant presumption and authority would topple the government. We would refuse to earn the tokens. We would tear them up and demand our rights to those sweets or privileges as citizens of a people's state. No, token economies operating from a premise of controller-controllee will not do.

Or perhaps manipulation could be more subtle. The planners could reward desirable behavior without the members knowing what was happening. But how? With what? Do we not distribute equally every reinforcer we can get our hands on? What is there left to manipulate with?

In short, the only way we can apply behavioral engineering to adults is with the cooperation of the whole group. Given that, we could use token systems if we chose. We could just draw lots to see who hands out the tokens. Group cooperation in behavioral engineering means that we as a group want to change our behavior to meet certain standards, but we have trouble doing it. We ask for the help of the rest of the group. We can then inventory our available reinforcers, decide which ones are appropriate, and start the program. The reinforcers might be labor credits, cash, or approval. We could waive our absolute equality norms for a time for the sake of the mutually agreed upon program.

So far Twin Oaks has rejected token economies altogether.

They have been suggested numerous times without success. It is not certain that we will never use them. But we haven't done so yet.

Discarding the simplistic token idea, there are still areas of techniques of behavioral engineering available to us. We know that the approval of our peers is a powerful reinforcer. Also, peaceful and pleasant human relations are reinforcing, as is the solution of sticky problems. That throws the area of behavioral engineering open to the consideration of all techniques that have ever been used for social control: law, admonition, persuasion, criticism, encounter groups. Under the general heading, "It is reinforcing to get along together," we can try anything that looks as if it might help and legitimately call it behavioral engineering. Thus if we try some encounter techniques invented by Skinner's theoretical opponents, we are not thereby placing ourselves in some philosophical camp that is inconsistent with our admiration for behaviorism. We are, like *Walden Two*'s Frazier, combing the literature for suggestions of technique.

The simplest and maybe oldest of all deliberate techniques of social control is the making of rules. Walden Two had them. We have them. They are not backed up by force, but they are there as a kind of guideline and goal. Item Four of Twin Oaks's Behavioral Code says that we will not speak negatively about other members behind their backs. This was our interpretation of the hint in *Walden Two* that "gossip" was prohibited by the Walden Code. Actually, we interpreted "gossip" to mean something quite different from its ordinary connotations. Commenting on someone's love affairs is not considered gossip at Twin Oaks. To call it so is to imply that there is something somehow wrong or shameful about sexual relations, an implication we did not want to make, even indirectly. "Gossip" in our definition is talk that does damage. Exasperated comments on the quality of someone's work is gossip, as are disparaging remarks about personal characteristics. If you have something negative to say, says our rule, say it to the person's face—and when there is nobody else listening. (For this reason the words, "May I speak to you alone?" have an ominous sound.)

Can we do away with negative speech just by writing a rule against it? Experimental evidence backs up common-sense assumptions on this point: No, we cannot. But the rule, viewed as a desirable norm, does have the effect of curbing negative talk—we don't do as much of it as we might. After all, we wrote the rule; we signed a contract saying we would try to go by it; we generally approve of it. So we sometimes lose control and violate our agreement? So what? Tomorrow we can try again.

The anti-gossip rule has been under attack on various occasions. Pete disliked it, saying that honesty was desirable, even if negative. Several members throughout our history have shared his feeling. They were frustrated that work was not done as well as they wanted, or that somebody left the gate open and the cows got out, and they wanted to complain about it loudly and publicly. Rule Four says they shouldn't. People will even get up and leave the room if they do it. The rule can be changed, of course, any time we find, as a group, that it does not have desirable consequences. But out of the three meetings I can recall on the subject, the conclusion has always been that as a group we really do not want to listen to public statements about other people's sins (or our own). The rule stands.

That leaves us with the question: What *can* one do about frustration with other people's unacceptable behavior? What are we supposed to do when we are just sick and tired of having the cows get out, or seeing the kitchen improperly cleaned—or for that matter, of hearing other people violate the gossip rule? We have tried several structures, all with some success, to handle legitimate criticism.

The first was the appointment of a "Generalized Bastard." Brian thought of the idea, and we unanimously appointed him to the task. It was his job to relay unpleasant information. If I wanted to tell Quincy that he wasn't doing his share of the work, I was supposed to tell Brian, and he would tell Quincy without mentioning my name. Brian quickly found that he lacked the stomach for face-to-face encounters and reduced the system to note-writing. We lived with variations on this system for over three years. Now we have a box with a slot in the top called the "Bitch Box," where we can air our grievances if we lack the courage to go directly to the offender.

It works like this: Suppose I am unhappy about the waste of money involved in making too many automobile trips to Richmond. I notice that one person in particular seems to make extra trips. I write a note for the Bitch Box and can sign it or not. There is no need for me to restrain my temper for the Bitch Box, and my note might go something like this: "I am goddamned sick and tired of seeing Community cars being run back and forth to Richmond for nothing. Three trips have been made this week, in addition to the regularly scheduled one, two of them by John. John doesn't seem to care whether he wastes Community money, Community time, and Community automobiles. He just likes to go for rides. His excuses for this week's trips are pretty weak ones, considering that it costs us $10 a trip in wear and tear and gasoline. I tried to talk to him about it, and he just said he needed to get some things. I say he doesn't need to get those things. He could wait for a regular Richmond trip."

The Bitch Manager would get my note, but he would not deliver it directly to John. He would probably speak to John about automobile trips in general and say something like this: "Some people have been noticing that we have been putting a lot of automobile mileage into trips to Richmond, and someone particularly mentioned your name in this connection, questioning whether the value of the trips was really worth the ten dollars per trip it costs us." John will probably explain why he thought the trips necessary, and the Bitch Manager will probably respond sympathetically.

He may or may not relay this information back to me, depending on whether it will be likely to mollify me or just make me madder. In any case several things have been accomplished: I have expressed myself vehemently to someone who cares, without having gossiped in public and made other people uncomfortable; John now knows that trips to Richmond really cost ten dollars each, something he may not have thought of; and John now realizes that his driving does not go unnoticed, a form of gentle pressure that probably helps the situation if he is indeed driving more than he ought.

The Bitch Box helps a little. But it isn't enough. Some interpersonal friction is caused not by illegal or inconsiderate behavior that one can reasonably bitch about, but by overriding personality traits that need to be discussed. It was to this problem that we addressed ourselves when we started the Group Criticism sessions.

In 1969 we had an educational project called Utopia Class. It amounted to a weekly group meeting to read about communities of the past and to discuss the possible applications of their systems, ideas, successes, and failures to Twin Oaks situations. A great many ideas came out of these sessions. One of them was Group Criticism, which we borrowed from Oneida Community. Like the Oneidans, we found each other's behavior less than perfect, and we wondered if smooth group functioning might be helped by more direct information—that is, some regular and accepted means of getting across negative feedback to members. A lot of us professed ourselves willing and interested in hearing what the rest of the group would say about us. It amounted to an invitation to criticize. One of us at a time would volunteer, and the group would gather to talk about the volunteer.

I was writing a journal during this period. I quote from my notes:

> *Penn.* Criticism of Penn tonight. Jenny, Penn and I had all volunteered to be the first subject for Group Criticism,

so we tossed a coin, and Penn "won." There was some feeling that this was a bad place to begin, because it was obvious to practically everybody that there wasn't much to criticize in Penn's behavior. He is good, kind, considerate, and fun to be with. What can you say about somebody like that?

Everybody in the Community attended, including the little kids. We read the ground rules aloud. Then we started around the group clockwise. Everybody said something to the effect that they couldn't think of anything to say. Brian's criticism was that Penn sometimes left him and Jenny alone together when his (Penn's) company would have been perfectly welcome. Also that his thinking is irrational, that he believes things that don't have any evidence for them. Dwight criticized Penn's fuzzy thinking ("Maybe you don't think the moon is made of green cheese, but it isn't at all clear why you wouldn't. There's as much evidence for that as for some other things you do believe.") and for his lack of political commitment ("Why don't you join the Community?"). Jenny just said "The same as Brian," and Simon and the children all said Penn let himself be taken advantage of too easily, and that other people had no way of knowing when they were exploiting him, because he accepted exploitation so cheerfully. I said that he had leadership qualities (people tend to do what he does) and that he ought to pay more attention to where he was leading people. My example was the apple diet he and some others have been on. Apple diets don't do much harm, probably, but there must be better things to do.

Penn was pleased and embarrassed by so much oblique praise, and he said he had learned that he hid his faults well. Dwight commented that nobody else would get by so easily. The meeting had the effect of making other people want to be "it," and of setting a tone of helpfulness and courtesy for the meetings that followed. But no meeting since has been so well attended.

Me. About ten people present. Brian said I ought to get the newsletter out oftener than I do. Also that I am too easily bored, which I interpret to mean that I show my boredom too openly. Simon said that I ought to drink a little beer and hang around and party a little—loosen up and be part of the social life instead of worrying about the Community all the time. I understand what he is trying to say, but it amounted to telling me to be somebody else instead of me.

Dwight, from whom I feared the sharpest criticism, confessed to coming unprepared to the session. He said, "I feel that I should have a great deal to say, but I haven't thought it out." I was disappointed. But later he did some thinking and wrote me a criticism in a letter. It was devastating, and I only wish it could have been said in public, where I could hear other people's comments on it. The core of it is what he called "imperial attitudes." He says I exhibit a "condescension toward the group—a certain regal airiness," that I sometimes act "as if Twin Oaks were my duchy." I sense that Dwight is saying (at last) something a lot of people have felt but won't say, and I feel a mixture of defensiveness and gratitude. He cited incidents and quoted comments of mine which I recall with embarrassment. He completely misinterpreted the things I said. But then, probably everybody else misinterpreted them, too. That's the point. I have got to change my verbal behavior!

Jenny. We met in Brian's room, and there were only six or seven people there. Practically everybody said the same thing—that her work was sloppy, and she is careless and inconsiderate about leaving things for other people to do. Also some people said she made sharp comments to people without meaning to hurt as much as she does. Simon said she talks as if she is Miss Twin Oaks and knows all the answers.

Kurt. A lot like Penn's session, except only five people were present. Hardly anybody could think of any valid criticisms. Brian said Kurt talks too loud, especially after quiet hours. But Dwight set the tone. He said that Kurt should damned well join the Community, and the rest of the time after that we spent talking about why Kurt should

join or not join. A couple of days later he decided to join,
but then later he changed his mind again, unable to face
not having a college education to fall back on in case the
Community doesn't make it.

Simon. Very few people attended. Sheila told me
privately that she disliked him too much to attend the criticism, that she didn't feel helpful and couldn't express herself reasonably. She just wants him to go away. I don't
know if other people felt the same. Dwight, Brian, Kurt,
Naomi, and Penn were there. Most of the talking was done
by Dwight and me. Dwight expressed his dislike of
Simon's fundamental ideology, his me-firstism and lack
of commitment to anything important beyond himself. I
forget what else he said. He talked for a considerable
length of time. So did I. I talked about public bitching,
boasting, how I detested his going around saying the
Community owed him a better sex life, and his heavy-
handed criticisms of Dwight and Brian in front of me,
continually hurting my feelings and making me mad. I
also gave him a couple of unexpected compliments. I told
him he would be the first person I would go to if I were
in personal trouble and needed help, and that I liked him
as a man, underneath all the crap. Simon commented afterward that he wasn't much impressed with Dwight's criticisms and mine. He already knew that we didn't approve
of him, and he didn't much care. What surprised him was
that the other, less articulate members also mentioned
his public bitching. He said, "I knew that the planners
didn't like it, but that doesn't matter a whole lot. I didn't
realize that the rest of the Community objected to it. In
fact, I had the general impression that they agreed with
me."

Sheila. There was a large group tonight. The biggest
things said were mostly about her getting too excited
about stuff that doesn't make any difference. "Overreact"
was Brian's word. Kurt said he couldn't stand her wearing
T-shirts. Simon said he loved T-shirts. Also, people talked
about her obvious black moods. Simon said he would like
her to wear a sign or something, saying she was in a

black mood, so he wouldn't have to feel guilty and wonder if she was mad at him in particular. Her angry face makes everyone uptight. My criticisms were specific. I told her I couldn't stand the way she comes up to me and folds her hands in front of her like a little girl and says, "May I ask you a question?" Why doesn't she just go ahead and ask the question? (She stopped this behavior instantly.) I also said I was made uncomfortable by her aggressive driving. She said, "Why didn't you say so before? We've been driving together for months." And she is quite right. I should have. She has stopped that, too.

Criticism sessions went on for a year and a half and have fallen into disuse only in the last few months. I never missed a session, and I feel that I ought to have a better idea than I do of whether or not they have been effective, whether they did more good or more harm. The truth is that I still feel ambivalent about them. They seemed to serve very well the function of reassuring timid and modest people that they are appreciated and liked by the group. They also allowed some of us to let off steam about behavior that particularly annoyed us. Occasionally we could even notice changes after a Criticism.

But the major benefit of the method in my opinion was simply the attitude it induced in us of being admittedly imperfect and willing to listen to the opinions of our peers about our conduct. We said, in effect, "I am not defending my bad behavior; I want to know how I come across; I care what you all think about me." I found myself more tolerant of somebody's foibles if I had already told that person about them.

Also, I am personally glad to have gone through the experience. I certainly know more about my social self than I did before I came here, and I am much more sensitive to group opinion.

Nevertheless I am not unreservedly enthusiastic about Criticism. It did not succeed in its major aim—which was to

impart to every member of the group the consciousness of
being responsible to the rest. It worked only for volunteers.
Dissenters to the system simply did not attend the sessions
and did not volunteer to be the subject. They claimed that
public criticism was nothing more than authorized gossip,
and that it had the same bad effects as the unauthorized kind.

The right not to attend is fundamental to Twin Oaks's
sense of liberty. As the number of nonparticipants grew
larger in 1971, the subjection of the individual's ego to the
criticism process ceased to be the norm. For a long time, too,
the people who would volunteer for criticism just weren't the
people we were mad at. There wasn't much to say. Interest
flagged.

Or maybe there was another reason. There was one thing
about Criticism that I always objected to and never could do
anything about—and that was a sense of hypocrisy that prevailed in spite of ourselves. We resolved to be courteous,
and we were. We would take the most damning statements
and phrase them in such a way as to take the sting out of
them. Thus, instead of saying, "You drive me crazy with your
bitching all the time," a member would say, "Well, I have
sometimes noticed that you do public bitching." The person
being criticized could hear the content of the criticism, but
he missed entirely the emotion behind it and thus never
really got the message. A common phenomenon was the subjects' taking the criticisms back to their rooms and carefully
rationalizing them so as not to have to take any serious action on them. "I've decided," a member told me once, "that
what people mean by telling me that I am bossy is just that
they don't want to be reminded when they're not doing what
they're supposed to be doing." This might well have been
true, but she missed the point of the criticism.

One other personal problem-solving technique has been
tried at Twin Oaks with some success. When two people
cannot get along with each other at all but are nevertheless
forced by circumstances to be in each other's company, we

sometimes get them together with a moderator and ask them to talk the problem out.

The first time we did this was a problem between Hal and Charlie, back in October of 1967.

You will remember that Hal was our oldest member, then about forty-two. He had been our benefactor in the land purchase and had made personal sacrifices to get the money to build our first building. He was our Construction Manager and our most skilled, most knowledgeable resident in practical and technical matters. Furthermore, he was a cheerful, amiable person, and at that time most of us liked him.

Charlie was a newcomer. He was our first new member since the formation of the Community. He was without assets of any kind except intelligence and good looks. He was not at all fond of working. And, far from being amiable, he spent his days making sarcastic comments about the Community's structure, comparing it unfavorably with his own philosophy. It was Charlie who made the complaint against Hal. He said that Hal treated him in an authoritarian and disrespectful way on the construction site. The situation was not promising for profitable encounter, for I felt that the two men were just not peers, and that we would be heavily prejudiced on Hal's side. But we tried the technique anyway, and it turned out that I was wrong.

What I didn't know was that Charlie was not the only person to resent authoritarianism on the construction job. Sandy and Brian smarted under it also. As the session went on, and Sandy seconded Charlie's accusations in a quiet way, Hal lost his arrogance and began to listen. "It's the way you phrase things, partly," they told him. "The other day you said, 'Hey, bring that hammer over here,' as if I were a servant or something. I wouldn't have minded if you had said, 'How about handing me that hammer.'" "It goes further than that," said Charlie. "You probably could have got your own damned hammer."

And thus they hit on the behavior problem that was to

plague Hal as long as he lived with us. After this session, he made a genuine effort to curb his dictatorial speech and phrase things more pleasantly. Charlie, of course, didn't stay in the Community long, and the rest of us valued Hal enough to be tolerant of his slips into bossiness. But the fundamental problem was that he felt himself our superior, and we, like Charlie, would admit to it only in limited ways. Though we worked together for some time successfully, our relationship was always marred by Hal's inability to deal with us as peers.

Another of these head-to-head encounter sessions—again with the rest of the Community moderating—involved Hal again, this time with Marie, our first Negro member. Marie felt that Hal regarded her as a nigger, and Hal felt that he was innocent. His problem was a combination of the high-handed way he talked to everyone, which Marie interpreted racially, and his heavy Southern accent. I don't remember that much came out of this meeting, except that Hal was castigated for saying "nigra." "But," he protested, "that's just the way I pronounce things." And it was true. I listened to his speech after that, and noticed that he consistently made final *o*'s into *a*'s—tobacca, potata, winda, etc. But Marie wasn't satisfied. "Any educated man can learn to say 'Negro,'" she said. So Hal learned it. It sounded odd with the rest of his speech, a Yankee word thrown into the middle of his drawl, but he made the effort, anyway.

In the last year or so we have been getting members at Twin Oaks who have not been content with our social aims. It is not enough, they say, just to reduce interpersonal friction. The Bitch Box, gossip rule, and Group Criticism could all be dispensed with, they claim, if we all just loved and trusted one another. When I first heard this kind of talk I responded with exasperation and contempt. Sure it would be lovely if we all loved one another, but we don't all love one another, so let's use what techniques we can find to minimize the friction. But the young people joining the Community these last two years have not been willing to settle for that. They do not believe that mutual love and trust are out of our reach. They think that hatred and suspicion and jealousy are just results of misunderstanding, and that increased understanding would bring increased affection. I find this difficult to swallow. I can see a great many antagonisms born of perfectly good understandings, clear perceptions of conflict of interest. My skepticism notwithstanding, I have had a keen interest in every trial we have given to Group Encounter techniques. After all, at least *some* bad feeling is traceable to mistaken perception. What do we have to lose by trying?

Brian thought we had quite a bit to lose when encounter groups were first suggested in the summer of 1968. He was the only one among us who had any experience with them, and he said they were dangerous. When people get under pressure, he predicted, they will probably leave the Community. We are no casual group meeting for a weekend retreat. We have to live with each other. The proponents of encounter group were Pete, who had been reading about Esalen Institute, and certain of the new people who had just joined the Community. Brian resisted. I, being ignorant, followed his lead. "If they want encounter group, why don't they just call it?" he complained. "Why does it have to be done by the board of planners?" But the summer wore on and got worse and worse. Eventually it was Brian who called the encounter group, figuring we had nothing to lose any more. "Who's afraid of an hour of silence?" read the notice on the bulletin board. "Group tonight at 8:00."

Contrary to prediction, we did not sit in silence. Naomi got us off to a running start with a direct question to a new member—"Why do you dislike me, Harry?" she asked. We spent the rest of the session finding out why Harry disliked Naomi, and in the process uncovered passions that most of us hadn't known existed, including the love of one of our male members for the adolescent son of Gwen, who was sitting right there in the group listening.

It must be said to Gwen's credit that she took this information in her stride, never interfering in the friendship between her son and his admirer. The younger people didn't do as well. The principals of the first meeting did not attend the second. As the weeks went by and more and more difficult problems were aired, more and more members dropped out of the encounter group. In the end, only Pete and Rosa, Brian, Naomi and I remained, and we dropped it out of boredom. What was there to talk about that we hadn't already discussed *ad nauseam?*

As a matter of fact, there was plenty to talk about, but we were afraid to go beneath the surface. The major problem of the summer was the tension between Rosa and the rest of the Community. But nobody ever talked about it at encounter group. Pete we could talk to. He might not agree with us, but he didn't crumple under attack. But if we let Rosa know how we felt about her nagging, critical public unhappiness, she would, we were sure, insist on leaving the Community. She didn't want to be here in the first place. We were desperately holding on to Pete, hoping against increasing unlikelihood that we could get them to settle down and decide to live out their lives here. So naturally we didn't level with Rosa, and encounter group got boring.

The second attempt was in 1970. It was lower-keyed this time, aimed simply at gathering in little groups and talking about things—just a getting-more-deeply-acquainted device. We called it Grouprap. It, too, died quickly of the same disease as encounter group. The combination of lack of leadership and lack of interest did it in.

But we don't give up easily. This year we got a lot of help from a pair of professional Group Encounter leaders, who donated their time and talents to us out of interest in the Community. They lived with us for several days, asked us in depth about our internal conflicts, and used their skills deftly and effectively in the lively group sessions that gathered during their stay. A lot was accomplished, a lot of useless old hostility was exposed and discarded. It was like a religious revival, and the effects still linger at the date of this writing.

XIII

Which Way to the Orgies?—
Sex, Love, Marriage,
and Women's Liberation

"Sex is an interesting question," said B. F. Skinner in an interview for *Mademoiselle*, "because nobody can say anything against it." This is pretty close to the stand Twin Oaks took on sexual morality from the beginning, but we didn't derive it from *Walden Two*. Written in 1947, *Walden Two* portrays a society in which couples marry at an early age in order to get around the problem of adolescent sexual frustration. The fictional community put a high value on abiding affection—loosely equivalent to monogamy, and presumably backed up its value system with behavioral engineering. Not so Twin Oaks. Though most of *Walden Two* was nearly sacred to us, we ignored this solution to the sex problem. We figured Skinner would have written it differently if he had been writing in the sixties instead of the forties. In any case, our standard was freedom, and it continues to be.

It was a freedom that was largely academic in our first year. Monogamy was so common among us in the beginning that single people found life with us intolerable and were immediately forced into more or less monogamous relationships. This pattern broke down in the summer of 1968 when a large number of young people joined the Community at about the same time. From then until now sexual freedom has been the Community's norm, both in theory and in practice.

This, of course, includes monogamy. We don't have anything against monogamy, as long as it is desired by both parties. What we object to is one of a pair's being happily monogamous while the other is not. In such a case, the weight of Twin Oaks's social pressure is against the jealous, possessive person and in favor of the one who wants to get free.

Under these circumstances it is reasonable to wonder how marriages fare at Twin Oaks. There are institutional reasons why marriage should naturally be weaker in community—any community—than on the Outside. No economic bonds link pairs here. Everybody supports himself with his own work. Likewise, children need not provide a vital connection, for the Community will certainly care for its children, regardless of whether their parents like each other or not. In short, the only reason for a married couple to stay married in community is that they like each other.

Out of the nine married couples who have at one time or another been members of Twin Oaks, six stayed married and three broke up. Occasionally a couple will leave the Community because they fear the influence of other available partners on their unstable relationships. Toby was one of these. "I agree with the idea of dissolving the nuclear family," he told us when he left, "but I always thought of it in terms of parent-child, not husband-wife." Toby's wife had begun to prefer other company to his. Their marriage didn't last more than six months after they left the Community, so it is doubtful that, even had they stayed, the Community could have been called responsible for the break.

It isn't always another partner that splits up a marriage. At least once the break came because one partner wanted to leave the Community, and the other refused to go.

Twin Oaks has made marriages as well as broken them. Hal and Gwen met here, Leif and Jenny, Dwight and Sally.

We have also provided the courtship scene for visitors who are now married or engaged, including the reporter from *Time* who fell in love with a reporter from *National Geographic*.

Even the pristine arrangements of *Walden Two* left room for nonsexual friendship between men and women, but we had one member who defended his married virtue to precisely the same degree that he would on the Outside—avoiding even the appearance of a compromising situation. This was Pete. Though a sexual liberal—he believed in freedom for others—Pete was very circumspect in his own behavior. Once when he was giving flirtatious Jenny a class in chemistry, she reached out to him to straighten his shirt, which he had buttoned improperly. Pete jerked away from her gesture, saying, "I can button my own shirt." On another occasion, I asked him if he would show me the new calf in the lower pasture, and with some embarrassment he said that I should have Fred show it to me, since viewing new calves was something that he and Rosa had always done together.

Nevertheless, nonsexual friendship across sex lines is commonplace at Twin Oaks. It is particularly common where there is some strong reason to leave sex out of the relationship. If a pair is monogamous, for instance, and everybody in the Community knows it, neither of the pair is thereby cut off from friendship. Partly because of a fairly large age difference, I have not participated much in the mating games here, but I have always had good male friends, people I sit and talk with for hours, take walks with, go for drives with, even travel to other cities with.

Sometimes friendship with the opposite sex is easier than friendship with a person of the same sex. We went through some soul-searching on this subject in 1971. The women discovered that they were competing with each other and saw each other as rivals rather than as potential friends. Just getting together and talking about this helped a lot. Several of the women deliberately sought the company of other women, just to force themselves out of old habits. Men began to do the same. New friendships came about that have been continuously rewarding, lacking the terrible ups and downs of love affairs, making up in stability for what they lack in excitement.

There isn't much I can say about the love affairs themselves. For one thing, I don't know much. Lovemaking continues to be a private thing at Twin Oaks. Even though demonstrative public affection is common, you can't tell just from looking at two Twin Oakers holding hands that they are lovers. They may be and they may not be. Nobody asks, and nobody much cares.

Jealousy, of course, is a problem. Jealousy caused us to lose Carrie and Bonnie in 1969, and it will probably account for some turnover this year and next. We have not solved this problem. We have, however, taken steps to ease it. Sometimes we succeed and sometimes we don't, but for what it's worth, here is what Twin Oaks couples have come up with to help the tensions caused by either multiple relations or changing ones.

One technique is simple scheduling. If a woman cares a lot about two different men, and the men don't like each other, it may be possible for her to agree to spend one day with one, the next with the other. This has been tried various times at Twin Oaks, and it always breaks down after a short time, but it helps to ease the interim. The reason it breaks down is usually that the person in the middle really does prefer one partner to the other and shows it. This leads to withdrawal by the less-preferred partner out of hurt pride.

What has been more successful is for the three to spend a lot of time together as a trio. Thus the people who would otherwise be rivals are able to learn to appreciate each other and to gauge the depth of the affair all around. Even if one of them discovers that things aren't ideal for him or her, at least he or she isn't sitting around alone being tortured by imaginary scenes. It is easier to be right there dealing with a real situation than to be imagining one that may or may not exist.

Multiple relations have succeeded best when both ends of the triangle like each other. Otherwise they are practically impossible in community. In any case, they have not lasted very long. I have sometimes thought that triangles are really just a process of getting gently from one pairing to a different one.

The biggest bulwark against jealousy is our heavy communal disapproval of it. This is why sexual freedom is easier in community than it is on the Outside. Here we stand behind it as a group. Nobody gets group reinforcement for feeling or expressing jealousy. A surprising amount of it is wiped out by that fact alone.

What can't be accounted for by public pressure can be attributed to personal idealism. Strange as it seems to our parents and the rest of the straight world, the stand against personal possessiveness is a moral stand, and most of us here do not approve of our bad feelings when we have them. Just as a person with a puritan conscience can often control his erotic impulses by reference to what he believes, so a person with a communitarian conscience can control his possessive impulses by reminding himself of what his principles are.

Twin Oaks has taken a firm stand in favor of sexual freedom and nonpossessiveness, and that brings its problems with it. But problems notwithstanding, we did not have any real choice about taking this stand. Any group that settles on monogamy as a norm has to figure out how to defend it. Without a heavy puritan religious bias this is very difficult. Philosophy isn't the only problem with monogamy, either. Sexual rules are hard to enforce in any society, and more so among free-thinking communitarians. The closer people live together, the higher will be the incidence of opportunity for attraction. A commune has to take the choice between dealing with jealousy in an open way or dealing with complicated questions of sin, dalliance, adultery. I conjecture that a group norm of free choice in sexual matters is not only philosophically consistent but literally easier to manage than any compromises would be.

In any case, we are rather pleased with our progress in this area. We are managing fairly well to live what we believe. Members do whatever seems right for them, and wrong choices do not shake the Community itself at all. A good many unconventional sexual arrangements have worked out perfectly smoothly and successfully here, probably because the individuals involved were prepared for them.

There have been three stages in Twin Oaks's sexual revolution. The first was just the step away from the standards that we learned from Mom and Dad, away from a sense of sex being connected with sin. That was the easiest. A lot of our members came here with that battle years behind them. The next was the fight against personal possessiveness and jealousy. That one is harder, but we are winning.

The third step, one that has become necessary partly because of the liberation achieved through the first two, is the ongoing struggle against sexism.

Sexism is the assumption that one's overall worth is measured in terms of one's desirability to the opposite sex. Outside society is heavily sexist, and women, in particular, suffer from it. We weren't conscious of this problem when we started the Community, but when Women's Liberation consciousness hit the rest of the nation, Twin Oaks naturally started thinking about it too. We examined our attitudes, and they were not entirely free of sexism. We still thought of each other in terms of physical attractiveness, and "cute" men and women were rated above plain ones, just as they would be on the Outside. Well, what could we do about it? We have all been raised to respond to certain types of beauty, as well as to status-linked styles of dress, certain hair styles, and so forth. Being products of the youth culture did not change this. True, our women liked only long-haired men and spurned the advances of anyone with a crewcut, but the

reasons for this were just the same as the ones that make a
sorority girl choose a date on the basis of his acceptable appearance. For a woman the criteria were even more stringent. Twin Oaks men, like men elsewhere, found that they
preferred women who didn't chase them but just smiled and
waited to be approached, that they were turned on by girls
who let them do most of the talking, and most of all that it
mattered a great deal to them that women have long hair
and bodies that somewhat resembled that of a *Playboy* fold-
out. Here, as elsewhere, the closer a girl came to the standard
stereotypes of beauty, the more she received the attentions
of men.

On a sexual level this is very hard to eradicate. Adult
sexual responses have already been conditioned to certain
kinds of partners. We mean for our children to grow up without these kinds of prejudices, but for ourselves, we are stuck
with our conditioning. The only thing that helps this situation is the fact that the longer a member is here, the less
physical appearance matters. All of us are beautiful, and
the status-giving power of certain kinds of beauty fades after
a few months of living together.

On other than strictly sexual levels, there is a great deal
we can do about the roles men and women are expected to
play. We had meetings on the subject and discussed the
problem. Was it true that men did most of the talking at
meetings? It was. Was this because the group did not respect
women? We thought not. The dismal fact was that many of
the women did not know as much as the men, had not
thought as much, and therefore did not have as much to say.
The remedy, then, was with the women themselves. They
began to read more, talk more about Community policy, and
then speak up at meetings. In a matter of a few months we
had a heavy liberation norm going that drew newcomers
into it as soon as they got here. For a while the women
tended to discriminate against new male applicants for membership if the applicants were caught making male chauvinist

remarks, or even if they openly preferred pretty girls to plain ones. But after a few weeks the women began to relax as they realized their own power as a group. "All males are chauvinists when they first come here," one woman member commented to me, "but in a week or two they learn better."

We are all learning better, but not all at once. So much of our thinking is colored by assumptions about masculinity and femininity that it is hard to get free of them. What we are aiming for is to relate to each other simply as people, appreciating each other as human beings without regard to gender. Even now we are closer to this ideal than most places. We have no sex roles in our work. Both men and women cook and clean and wash dishes; both women and men drive trucks and tractors, repair fences, load hay, slaughter cattle. Managerial responsibility is divided almost exactly equally—this in spite of the fact that our women are on the average two or three years younger than our men.

Sensation seekers looking for communal orgies would be surprised to hear that one of the acceptable behavior patterns at Twin Oaks is celibacy. Once free of the necessity of proving oneself worthy by finding a mate, a person can really decide whether or not he or she is interested in sex. Every once in a while, somebody isn't. And that's all right. Your love life is your own business here, and if you don't want any love life, that's your business, too.

As for orgies, I don't think there are any. I have no way of being sure, of course. We don't have any anti-orgy rules or anything. For all I know there may be one every night, and I just haven't been invited. But I doubt it. Sex is very important to us, but at the same time we don't make a big deal of it. It is part of our daily lives, but we rarely discuss it. Like eating and working and going for a walk and playing the guitar, it is a part of the good life.

XIV

Health and Sickness

Sickness has never been a major problem at Twin Oaks, but a group living as close together as we do and eating in a common dining room naturally has to watch out for disease, and we have had a brush or two with illness.

Among the original eight we had Carrie, a registered nurse. Carrie had just graduated and had done her practice nursing in a psychiatric ward, so her experience was not extensive, but her degree gave her an aura of authority that gave us confidence. When someone came down with a fever or an earache, Carrie would say decisively, "I'm no doctor; go to Louisa and see a doctor." The Community of course paid the bills, which were few in those early days. Carrie never had to do much beyond bandaging a cut or a burn and giving permission to visit an M.D. We had very little money the first year, and the microbes considerately stayed away.

After Carrie left in early 1969 there were no professionals to take the Health Managership. Just the same, somebody had to make decisions about whether to go to a doctor or whether someone with a sore throat should be fixing meals, and so forth. I volunteered for the job. My main interest in the Health Managership was trying to put a stop to the spread of the common cold. My idea was that anyone who came down with the slightest sniffle should go into isolation. Better, said I, to sacrifice the temporary happiness of one member than to spread the cold throughout the Community, where it dragged a little bit on everyone's happiness. It was one of those decisions that are easy to make and impossible to implement. The first two people to come down with colds were Brian and Dwight, both of whom refused to be separated from their mates, regardless of the spread of germs. Rather than sleep alone, they both ceased to believe in the germ theory. If Dwight and Brian, stalwart Centralists both, would not obey a managerial mandate, what point was there in even trying to enforce it on other people, who had less theoretical backbone than they? I gave up the isolation idea and concentrated on the use of face masks. In this I was inspired by pictures I had seen of the cities of China and Japan, where these masks are a commonplace sight. People over there evidently don't feel they have a God-given right to spread disease and are doing what they can to prevent it. I purchased a box of face masks, and I believe I persuaded at least two people during the following year to wear them. Then I read somewhere that the spread of colds takes place mostly during the days that precede the symptoms. If this is true, the Japanese and Chinese are wasting their time, and so was I. I gave up on the common cold.

Anyway, by then I had more serious things to worry about. Two members came down with identical high fevers. I sent them to the doctor immediately. The doctor gave them penicillin and instructed them on the technique of taking stool tests, which were to be sent to Richmond for analysis. One of the sick men sent the stool test off immediately, and one of them delayed over the weekend. The results of the tests were sent back, not to us, but to the doctor, who immediately relayed the information from the first test to the County Health Department—Diagnosis: typhoid.

If Kurt had typhoid, then how many of us might have it soon? Did typhoid not come from bad water, or from contamination from feces—possibly carried by flies from our outhouse? (We had a flush toilet but used an outhouse in addition.)

The Health Department was professionally concerned and unprofessionally moralistic. They came out to the Community in force with inoculations, three weeks in a row. The head of the Health Department came with them, just to look things over. They sent out a man to test our well. They looked over our sewage system. We stopped swimming in the river for a while, fearing it might be the source of contamination. One of the nurses said to Simon's oldest child as he lined up for his shot, "You ought not to be in a place like this; why don't you go home?"

The well got a clean bill of health. The sewage system didn't prove to have typhoid either, but our drain field was leaking, so they ordered us to put in a large septic tank and drain field within thirty days.

But odd things were happening. The second sick man had sent in his stool sample and the results came back negative. No typhoid there. Furthermore, even Kurt, whose analysis had been the one to start the scare in the first place, was showing consistently negative on subsequent tests. Also, both men were back on their feet and feeling fine within four days after the fever hit. Was this typhoid?

Nobody knows for sure, but we think it was not. Kurt had been inoculated for typhoid just a week before coming to the Community, and it might be possible that this influenced the first laboratory test.

So we all took painful typhoid shots for three weeks, and we were forced to divert money from our new building fund into expensive septic and drain-field systems, all for a disease that we probably didn't have. But we would in any case have needed the drain field within a few months, so we didn't lose anything in the long run.

Medical expenses have not been a big problem so far. In the first year we didn't go to the dentist unless we had a tooth that actually ached. We began having regular dental check-ups in 1970 when the income started coming in more regularly, and we spend about sixty dollars a month for this purpose now. Most of us go to the same dentist in Richmond, who just bills the Community. We wouldn't go all the way to Richmond for dentistry if there were a dentist in nearby Louisa, but Louisa is hard up for medical people generally. It is a small town serving a large rural area, and doctors have a lot demanded of them for small pay. City hospitals draw them away. We daydream about the day that Twin Oaks might attract an M.D. of its own, who would work part time in Louisa and provide a service to the entire surrounding community as well as to ourselves. People ask us whether, if we had a doctor among us, he would be required to wash dishes and weave hammocks like the rest of us. In theory he would, of course, if there wasn't enough medical work to be done. But while the entire county is short of medical personnel, it seems likely he would spend most of his time at his profession, working Outside and earning labor credits.

In the meantime free and nearly free clinics in Richmond keep us from having serious trouble. Any suspicious symptom is checked out in those laboratories. Twin Oaks members are about as healthy as most farm people—better than some. Even our incidence of colds seems lower than on the Outside, probably because we spend so much of our time out-of-doors. Of course we take ordinary precautions, using a three-well sink and disinfectant in the rinse water for our dishes, having an isolation room available for any serious disease that might come along.

From time to time we think about getting hospitalization insurance, but all research to date has shown it to be far too expensive for us. We have so far had to pay one hospital bill. That was for Doreen in 1971.

What Doreen thought (and hoped) she had was a pregnancy. In spite of her IUD it looked as if she might have conceived. Though Twin Oaks was not really quite ready for children, still one little baby could be managed somehow. She went to the clinic to get the IUD removed so that she could go through her pregnancy without worrying about possible damage to the baby from the device. But it wasn't a pregnancy. It was an advanced ovarian infection, and the ovary had to come out right away. Doreen's husband had her admitted to the hospital to be prepared for surgery, then called the Community. She would be in the hospital for seven days at least. The doctor would not charge for his services, but the hospital bill was likely to come to nearly $100 a day.

It was good that this happened in 1971 and not earlier. We had a building fund to fall back on, and cattle in our pastures to sell, if it came to that. We could have managed it somehow at any stage in our history, but in 1971 we did it without sacrifice, simply borrowing from the building fund, to be paid back in small pieces over the following months. The bill came to over $900. Doreen's in-laws sent a love-present of $100, over the insistence of her husband that we did not need it. ("Oh, we have plenty of money," he told his parents. Communitarians have their pride.) Most of it we paid in cash, but we got a break by being allowed to make up as much as we chose of the bill in donations of blood. The hospital, suspecting perhaps that we might find the bill difficult to pay, offered us $15 off the bill for every pint of blood we donated to the blood bank. We swiftly accepted the offer. We were the talk of the blood bank for several days, as one after another we went in to sell blood for the sake of our bank account. I think it looked nobler than it was. They must have thought that we were all volunteering blood out of friendship for Doreen (did she have an accident? they asked us), not realizing that it was our own common benefit that we were serving and that group underwriting of medical expenses is a basic assumption of communal theory.

Communes don't have to be unhealthy places. I have read

a lot about sickness in communes, but it doesn't have to be a result of living in groups. I suspect that when a whole commune comes down with a disease and spreads it far and wide through visitors and transient members, it is because of extreme youth, ignorance, and fear of authorities more than because of communal living arrangements. It is true that enteric diseases have a better chance wherever there is a common kitchen, particularly if the kitchen is not kept clean or if the cooks don't wash their hands. But consider that every restaurant, hamburger joint, and ice-cream parlor in every city is institutionally the same kind of risk. What keeps most such places relatively harmless is the attention that their managers give to cleanliness. Exactly the same thing can be true of communal kitchens. Twin Oaks has never had much money, and we are always struggling against dirt, but we have managed with a minimum of effort to prevent the spread of enteric disease. The two occasions when a member has had symptoms of infectious hepatitis, we have been able to isolate the disease immediately, and no one else caught it either time. We didn't have any special hospital facilities or sterilization equipment. We had very little made out of stainless steel. We did have medical advice and common sense, and that's all we needed. The same has been true of the occasional epidemic of intestinal trouble. Occasionally something—perhaps salmonella?—sweeps through half the Community. The other half copes. We get the best medical advice available and take it.

Airborne diseases are less prevalent here than in the cities. The very fact that we are not mixed with hundreds of people every day in schoolrooms and factories undoubtedly accounts for this. Communal living, from this point of view, is healthier than suburbia.

The problem we watch out for, of course, is venereal disease. Venereal disease is on the rise nationwide, especially among youth, and it would be over-sanguine of us to assume that we will never be hit. Our greatest defense is education.

Some time ago the Health Manager called the group together to listen to a visiting doctor, who told us precisely what the symptoms of venereal disease are. We discussed frankly the fact that statistically there is no way we can escape ever being touched by it, and that what we have to do is to think of it simply as a disease to be cured, not as a divine visitation for sin. Once we free our minds from the association of VD with shame, we can be assured of getting rapidly cured and not spreading it. So far, however, we have been lucky and have not had a case.

Mental health is a different problem. Twin Oaks is pretty confident that we will not as a culture actually cause or allow the development of mental illness in the people we raise here. This hope is not farfetched. It is supported by reports that mental illness is virtually unknown among the children of the Israeli kibbutzim, who are raised by a system and in a community somewhat similar to ours.

The first generation, nevertheless, has to face the problem of extreme emotional disturbances. These days we try to screen out the emotionally ill, since our success as a therapeutic community has been very slight. But before we started screening we had quite a lot of experience with people who either had already been in mental hospitals or were to go to them after leaving here. The memories are unpleasant, and I feel no desire to tell these stories in detail. There have been several incidents, and the pattern in all cases is similar. I will just generalize briefly.

The person comes and stays for a little while, then asks for admission as a member. We are short of members and accept him. Usually he is very quiet and unaggressive, though occasionally the opposite will be true. The person's behavior at first is not classified as abnormal. He is just a little odd, perhaps, a little self-centered, lacking in social skills. What is certain is that he does not make friends. He is alone. In a community where almost everyone is happily involved socially, the newcomer's isolation is very acute. Sometimes a member will feel sorry for him and go out of his way to be friendly. But the friendship is unrewarding for the giver, and the lonely person tends to demand more and more attention, usually forcing the idealistic member to withdraw his offer of friendship, which was only based on pity in the first place.

The exact line between "well" and "sick" is unclear. But the members I am referring to at one point cross it, and everyone realizes that their behavior is too strange to be tolerated. In our most extreme case to date, the person stood at the sink for hours, running hot water over his hands, also tore paper napkins into shreds and piled them by his plate at every meal, poked through his food painstakingly "looking for soap," and entirely lost his ability to control an automobile and to type a coherent sentence. In less extreme cases the behavior has consisted of staring into space for days at a time and not responding to anybody or anything. There have been a couple of attempted suicides.

These incidents tear the Community's morale to shreds. We are behaviorists, after all, and we know very well that we don't rid ourselves of responsibility just by labeling somebody "crazy." Mental health is a continuum, and we continually hope that we can bring the sick person's behavior enough into line so that the person and the Community can be mutually beneficial. We can sense that in almost all cases the source of the problem is lack of love, and many of us believe that if we could give the love, even at this late date, we could cure the problem and redeem the human.

When I say that the problem is lack of love, I am not speaking behaviorist language. We are aware that it is precisely in mental hospitals that reinforcement techniques have been most successful. We once discussed the possibility of using a token system for rewarding normal behavior, but we ran into extreme resistance. Many members were squeamish about placing the sick person on a different level from the other members of the Community. All felt that if they

were to be asked to participate in any deprivation (like
telling the sick member that he couldn't play the record
player until he had done such and such), they would refuse to do it. Our situation—living and eating as a group—
required that all should cooperate if any such program were
to be tried. In fact, none were willing to take on the authoritarian role.

But beyond that, we recognized that just getting the member's behavior within acceptable boundaries with respect to
the record player, food, and hot water tap was not going to
make that person a happy and functioning member. The
problem still boiled down to whether anyone would extend friendship. Since the sick person had little to bring to
a friendship, no one would spend much time with him.

I am not certain that Twin Oaks will never undertake this
task successfully in the future. I know only that our sporadic
attempts in the past have all failed. We may have a secret
meeting and decide to be loving and treat the person like a
normal person, and so forth. But it always comes out that we
have other things to do and other candidates for membership
to consider, and we need every member to be functioning
most of the time. We did not set out to be a therapeutic
community, at least not for psychotics. We see perfectly well
that the task of treating the mentally ill is a great one and
worthwhile, and that few institutions are doing it very well.
We see also that we might extend ourselves to be such an institution, perhaps with some success. But that is not what we
are interested in doing.

So what happens is that these people eventually go away.
Usually we do not force them out, but just try to hold them
to basic Community norms (you must do your share of the
work; you may not play the same record over and over a
dozen times; you must take your turn at an outside job), and
they go away voluntarily when they find themselves unable
or unwilling to comply.

And then everybody feels terrible for a while. We judge

ourselves harshly. At least one good member left the Community because of the hardness of heart he thought he discerned in Twin Oaks's leadership when we failed to provide for our worst psychotic. We have never discovered any way to rid ourselves of the mentally ill and still have a clear conscience. These days, as I said before, we try to avoid taking them in the first place.

A member of Camphill Community, a group that successfully offers communal life to the mentally retarded, once told me that Twin Oaks would not have any social significance unless we undertook some worthwhile social work, presumably like curing the mentally disturbed. Our answer, then as now, is that we are too busy doing socially significant work to get ourselves bogged down in patching up the messes that society makes of its outcasts. We have no quarrel with Camphill. Caring for the retarded is necessary work. Any society, however utopian, may produce retardates, and must deal with the problem of sharing the good life with them. Our work, however, is to experiment in ways of making a sane society. Floundering in guilty half attempts to cure the mentally ill only slows us down.

XV

Getting Along with the Neighbors

We were afraid to let our neighbors know what we were up to when we first moved to the farm. That was because we had heard stories about other communes being shot at or railroaded out of town or closed down by the health department. So we were cautious.

Even when we were looking for land we were careful. Fred and I did the scouting, and we never said a word about community to the real estate men who took us around. We just said we wanted to farm and that we had a big family. And so we did. Sometimes real estate men didn't want to bother much with us. I think we didn't look very prosperous. In order to explain that we really did want to buy a farm and that we really did have money behind our purpose, we told them about Hal but made him part of our family. Sometimes I said he was my brother. Other times he was a cousin.

Then when Hal actually bought the land, he explained the whole plan to the former owner, real estate agent, and lawyer who handled the sale. By then perhaps it was too late for them to consider whether they wanted a commune in their midst. At any rate, Hal was paying cash, and everyone was very friendly.

We resolved to be pleasant, pay our bills on time, not argue with the neighbors about politics or religion, and gen-

erally mind our own business. It was hard to explain ourselves, because the word "commune" was not yet in common
use in the press—we did not use the word ourselves until
1969. When questioned we explained, "We are a group of
people that came from the city, but we don't like city life.
In the city you have to work for a boss, and we want to run
our own lives and not be told what time to come to work
and what time to take off for lunch. None of us had enough
money to buy a farm by ourselves, so we pooled our resources. That's the only way we can afford to live in the
country." Then we told them that our system was share-and-
share-alike, that we ate together and shared expenses.

Since we all came from city backgrounds, we at first expected to be left alone by our neighbors, just as we had been
in the city. But people in the country have different cus-
toms. On our very first day people dropped in to see us.
They always brought something for us when they came, a
dozen eggs or a sack of apples or some tomato plants. We
didn't know for sure what was expected of us in return, but
Carrie generally gave them some of our blackberry jam, to
be on the safe side. To this day we are not quite certain how
to act when neighbors visit us. We show them around if they
haven't seen the place before. But it isn't always a showplace
that we are proud of. More often than not it is untidy or even
dirty, and we sense that they would certainly not receive
company in their homes unless they had cleaned up first.

In this rural area, you have to have lived here for at least
two generations before you aren't considered newcomers,
so we didn't really expect to be accepted as active participants in local affairs. All we really wanted was a general
feeling of friendliness and cooperation with the people who
live near us. In this we have been fairly successful. We hear
from time to time that some people talk about us—do not approve of our moral or religious views, but after all, people
talk about each other everywhere, and there is no reason we
should be an exception. We don't worry about the talk. At

least in face to face contacts, the people have been consistently courteous, friendly, and helpful.

The local businessmen and the people in the bank, for instance, smile and make small talk while we do business. We have opened up a number of charge accounts locally and have good credit. We make it a point to spend our money in Louisa unless a really great price discount draws us elsewhere. Some of our members have from time to time attended the local branches of their denominational churches. For a while, Carrie, Jenny, Hal, and I sang in the Methodist choir. Hal, in particular, was valued for his fine tenor voice.

A few Twin Oakers are registered voters, but most of us forget to vote when the time comes. We have not yet got around to studying the local political situation, and the national problems seem rather beyond our control. It is not very usual for candidates to seek our votes, either, though occasionally an enterprising vote seeker will visit us. The last one to do so got a tour of the commune, like other visitors, while we questioned him about his views on issues about to come before the Legislature. He was amazed to see a young woman working the drill press and ventured to ask her if she was sure she knew what she was doing. She glowered at him. "Of course I know what I'm doing!" she told him.

There is something nice about small towns. Once I was in Richmond and found myself unable to cash a check because I had forgotten my wallet and had no identification. The Richmond bank called the Louisa office and talked to the manager. The manager of the Louisa branch was able to identify me over the telephone by describing me to the cautious downtown manager, and I got my check cashed.

Another thing about small towns is that news gets around fairly fast. We once got a phone call from a woman who knew me from the church choir. She said, "I understand you people keep bees. Well, there's a swarm buzzing on my rosebush, and I sure would like to get rid of it. Would you come and get it?" We did, indeed, want the bees, but we were curious how she knew that we kept them, since we had only had bees for about a week before she called. The answer turned out to be simple. She was related to someone in the Post Office, who remembered the buzzing package that had been sent to us from Sears, Roebuck.

And everywhere we get Southern courtesy. The man who baled our hay for us cut his price because we had the bad luck to suffer rain loss before the hay was dry. The same man gave us a whole barnful of straw that was buried under a rickety structure that had been knocked over during a windstorm.

Closer to home we know local people we call our friends. Our closest neighbors are Mr. and Mrs. Jonas. They have put themselves out to lend us a hand almost since we first arrived. They gave us plants and seeds, and lent us big pots to render lard and a grinder for the sausage. (We broke the grinder and hunted all over Richmond before we got an identical replacement.) More important, the first time we slaughtered hogs, they came over as a family and spent the day with us, teaching us to cut up the meat and helping us to cut the lard and render it. During the winter days of 1967, Mr. Jonas came over almost every day to help us strip, sort, and tie the tobacco, preparing it for market. We tried to reciprocate by going over to his farm as a crew in haying season and helping him put up hay. Eventually this mutual exchange of favors got to be burdensome to both parties, because nobody was sure who was in whose debt, and we were both more comfortable when we put our crew labor on a simple cash basis. But our friendship continues just the same. As we get more competent and affluent, there are more things we can do for them. We keep their car repaired, for instance, charging only a minimum wage for the labor. We can weld tractor parts and do other simple maintenance jobs. Mr. Jonas's advice is very helpful, especially if we have a sick

cow. It was he in 1969 who let us know that we had a nutrition problem with our cattle, and advised us how to fatten
our cattle before trying to sell them.

In general we like to listen to the good farming advice of
our neighbors, and to hear them tell stories of the Depression
years. We do not do exactly the same kind of farming as most
of them, so some of our knowledge we must get from other
sources, but their experience is quite often applicable just
the same.

We have one neighbor, however, who does not approve
of us, and says so. This is Mrs. Gardiner, widow of Daniel
Gardiner, who used to have the peach orchard. I say "used
to have." When Mr. Gardiner died in 1966, his widow discovered that she could not keep up the fruit business. She
couldn't get the labor at the right price, and she was getting
too old for heavy work. She noticed that people were beginning to steal some of the peaches from the trees that kept
right on bearing. That made her mad. Not that she was un-
generous. Lots of times Mrs. Gardiner herself had been
known to pick peaches and pack them nicely in bushel
baskets and take them to her friends. But when people not
her friends didn't wait for the bushel baskets but just came
onto her property without her permission and picked the
fruit and carried it away, Mrs. Gardiner did not like it. So
she hired a bulldozer to come in and remove the trees. There
was no more theft at Mrs. Gardiner's place.

With a sense of private property like that, you can imagine
how Mrs. Gardiner felt about having a communal experiment
going on practically right next door. Our relationship with
her began one night when we saw smoke rising above the
trees about a mile from our farm and rushed down there to
help put the fire out. We didn't have much fire-fighting
equipment but took along some burlap sacks drenched in
water to beat out the flames with. When we got to the scene
of the fire, we were chagrined to find that it was a regular
yearly grass-removal that was being done by Mrs. Gardiner's

brother, that everything was under control and no help was needed.

Word got around, and Mrs. Gardiner felt moved to send us a note of thanks. Silly as our rescue mission looked to us, it struck our neighbors as being well-intentioned. Mrs. Gardiner invited some of the ladies of the Community to visit her. We chose a delegation of three—Rosa, Carrie, and I, the most respectable-looking of the group. We visited her one afternoon. She told us about her childhood and girlhood in this same area, told us herself the story we had already heard about the peach trees, and explained that she just didn't like to have people stealing. Then she asked us about ourselves, and when we had explained the Community a little bit, she said, "Oh girls, girls, I feel I must warn you you won't be happy in a place like that. You are throwing away good years of your lives. Wouldn't you rather have a nice little home of your own?" When we left we carried with us a lovely basket of Early Golden Delicious from one of her apple trees, chosen and packed by Mrs. Gardiner's own hands.

Other than that, most of our relationship with Mrs. Gardiner has not been face to face. We think that it was she who called the County Sheriff and urged him to come down and investigate us because she was sure there must be something illegal going on. But mostly we hear about her from visitors who innocently knock on her door and ask if they are on the right road to Twin Oaks. "Oh young man," she told one of them, "don't go there!" She explained to him that we were good people ourselves (hadn't we once offered to help her brother fight a fire?) but that we were the dupes of a Communist conspiracy that had its roots in a sinister organization from California.

To us, when we meet on the street, she is still courteous. We discuss the weather, or the dogs, bid each other good afternoon, and continue on our way.

The first few visits we had from the Sheriff were either about traffic citations we had forgotten or questions about runaways. Had we seen such and such a girl or boy who had left New York or Philadelphia with a copy of our newsletter in his pocket? He or she was wanted by parents or other wardens. With the exception of Felix, whose story I have already mentioned, we never did have any contact with runaways and we could always answer the Sheriff's questions with complete candor and a clear conscience.

But one day the Sheriff invited me to get into his car, because he wanted to talk to me. (Although we have several times invited the Sheriff to come into our buildings to talk, he always prefers his own territory.) He had heard, he said, that we had a peculiar way of life here, and he wanted to know what our philosophy was. What kind of a commune were we? People called him up, he said, and complained of goings-on. How much truth was there in these suspicions? We talked for perhaps half an hour. I assured him that we had no runaways, no drugs, and no illegal businesses. The Sheriff was more concerned about what we believed. Were we part of the New Left? Did we sympathize with the Black Panthers? What did we think of demonstrations? I explained to him that we were opposed to violence. I said we had no connection with any of the New Left groups that advocate violence. I said that our political persuasions were somewhat varied, and I couldn't really speak for the members as a whole.

The Sheriff seemed satisfied and went away. A month later he was back, this time with an FBI agent in the seat beside him. The FBI man had been told to look in on all the communes in the neighborhood and check them out for fugitives. Had we seen any of these people? He showed us glossies of Rap Brown, Bernardine Dohrn, and Cathy Wilkerson. No, we hadn't seen them. I tried to explain to them that the more violent sectors of the New Left held communes in contempt, and that even if we did not abjure them, they would in any case have nothing to do with us, but the FBI man said he just had to check. So he checked. He comes back from time to time, whenever a bomb goes off in a public building somewhere, to ask us to look at his latest collection of glossies. By now we both know that it's just a form, something that he has to do as part of his job. He told us once that he had considered bringing his Sunday School class down to visit us as a field trip, but he never did.

The last time we had a visit from the Sheriff was when we were planning our summer conference. "I hear rumors," he told me after I had obliged him by getting once more into the back seat of his patrol car, "that you people are holding some sort of a love-in rock festival, and that over a thousand people are expected." That was news to us, and we set the Sheriff straight. We were holding a conference for families with children, families who were interested in perhaps starting communities something like ours—but in other states— and we were expecting perhaps a hundred people. He wanted to know if these would be mostly married people who would be attending, and I said I didn't expect to ask to see their marriage licenses, but most people with children are married. He said that the conference sounded all right with him, as long as there wasn't going to be a large crowd, but that we should let him know if a lot of unexpected people showed up, especially undesirable types. We were glad to be assured of his help in case anything got out of hand, though his idea of undesirables might have been somewhat different from ours. He probably had in mind something like Hell's Angels. What we were worried about was drunken local youths, making themselves unpleasant with the women of the Community.

If we can be said to have any problem with the people in our area, that would be it. We are always made uneasy by the carloads of young men who drive up looking for excitement. Sometimes they are white men and sometimes black. Whatever their color, their purpose is always the same. They want to have a party. They will supply the beer, if we will supply the girls. We always demur. We show them around the farm, sometimes explain the labor credit system to them as we would to any other visitor. But everybody knows that they don't care about labor credits and the only sight they are interested in seeing is a pretty girl. The women, meanwhile, keep to their rooms.

Occasionally a man will drive up under the mistaken impression that we have love for sale. We just send our visitor-greeter out to tell him gently that we are not in that kind of business.

Some of the blacks have challenged our philosophy. They heard we weren't prejudiced against blacks. Is that right? Yes, that's right. Well, then, if a girl liked a black man, would it be all right if they went out together? Yes, it would be all right with us. Well then, couldn't they come over and talk to our girls some time? Yes, they could if they were invited by one of the girls and if she wanted to talk to him.

On a few occasions I have tried to explain the real situation to some of these male visitors of both races. I have vaguely hinted that there are educational and cultural differences that prevent the women from being interested in them. In spite of that, they sometimes say they want to join. They have heard somewhere that Twin Oaks girls will have nothing to do with any man who isn't a member of the Community, so they are prepared to become members. The best way we have found to deal with that is to tell them the simple truth: Twin Oaks members are not allowed to have their own cars; they get only seventy-five cents a week, and that has to buy all their cigarettes, Cokes, and beer. Occasionally one of them will say that the gains would be worth the price, in which case we will explain about the required two-week visit at $1.50 a day, sober, all by themselves, and without their carful of buddies. So far none of them has taken us up on it. If they ever did, we would treat them like anybody else.

XVI

Wheels

It ought to be obvious to anyone who thinks about starting a community that the maintenance of vehicles is going to be a major concern. When every car has a dozen different drivers, and the Maintenance Manager is also in charge of six or eight other areas, one must expect breakdowns. But for some reason, when we were calculating the cost of living in the Community, we overlooked transportation costs entirely. We thought about the price of food, spent a lot of time figuring the cost of housing construction. But we had cars, and we must have just thought they would keep on running.

It may be just as well that we were unrealistic about the cost of living. If we had been able to forecast the figures accurately, we might have been too timid to undertake the project. We went into it ignorantly, and we have survived various financial storms without heavy debt. We know a lot more these days. We know, for instance, that we have to budget three hundred dollars a month for automobile maintenance expenses, provided that we do all our own mechanical labor. That money is just for parts.

The first summer we used to get in the VW to drive across our own property to the river to go swimming. Some of us would walk (as we all do these days), but others, accustomed to driving everywhere, would pile into the VW with their towels and inner tubes and drive down the bumpy path through the woods, over big rocks and tree roots that eventually tore the shock absorbers to pieces. Some members even used the car to get the mail from the mailbox at the end of the driveway.

And trips to Louisa! The first day of community life we drove to Louisa three times just to get the right kind of tomato sauce for Sandy's spaghetti recipe. We were making three or four trips a day until we organized our errands into the single daily trip system we use now.

Brian and Carrie had brought the VW sedan. I contributed a little old Saab. Fred had a 1957 Pontiac, but he would not let the Community use it. He set it up on blocks and stored it. Technically we had a rule against private cars being stored on the premises, but it is hard to make rules like that stick when you are dependent upon every member for the survival of the group. We shrugged our shoulders and pretended that the Pontiac was not there. We also had the use of Hal's Dodge.

At first it seemed that whenever we got a member who was skilled in anything useful, like auto mechanics, he was always somebody with a very marginal understanding of community principles or *Walden Two*. Fred maintained the cars the first few months. When he needed money for parts, he would snarl at the board of planners that we could either release seventy-five dollars for fixing up the VW or he would let it run aground. We couldn't get him to explain what parts of the car he was going to fix, or to consider priorities with us. We wanted to have information about how important it really was to the car to get its shock absorbers fixed—whether we might choose to let them rattle and put the money elsewhere. Operating on that level of poverty so annoyed Fred that he would refuse to discuss the matter. We had no choice but to write the checks and get our cars back on the road, but it didn't make for close community feeling.

After a while Fred simply resigned as Automobile Manager

and told us we could pay a garage to do the work. He refused to do it any more on the kind of budget we were
forcing him to and the kind of information we kept asking
from him. He felt unappreciated. We tried to reason with
him, saying that there was just so much money to go around,
and that we had to consider where it ought best to go. To
that he would only reply that we ought not to be so poor—
and that if we didn't keep taking in stray hippies and useless
bums (we had just been through Charlie and Mary), we
wouldn't be so poor.

With Fred's resignation the maintenance of vehicles
passed to Chuck, a new member whose self-confidence
greatly exceeded his abilities. Before he left he wrecked two
engines, not while fixing them but while driving them.

Simon was not only a competent mechanic but a cheerful
one, accustomed to low-budget repair work and willing to
work within our narrow financial limits. It was a relief to
turn our cars over to him when he joined the Community in
1969, for we had been without a mechanic of any kind for
over four months. Simon brought with him a panel truck, a
former bread delivery truck which he had painted bright
orange. We were pretty glad to see that truck. We had been
without a heavy vehicle since Chuck had wrecked the school
bus eight months before, and we sorely needed one for haul-
ing grain and lumber.

We talked to Simon very carefully about the arrangements
with his truck. Did he understand that we could not guar-
antee the condition of the truck, that in bringing it into the
Community he was risking it? He laughingly said that he
was accustomed to risks, and he figured that he could always
fix it up, no matter what happened to it. Simon told us from
the beginning that his stay would be of only one year's dura-
tion. He wanted to live with us a while, then go to Canada
and homestead. We were willing to accept this arrangement,
but we knew that the chances were pretty good that some
time during the year the truck would need a major repair

and that the Community would not be willing to pay for a major overhaul of a vehicle that would soon be leaving.

What we should have done, it seems clear now, was to make a simple rental agreement with Simon about the truck, guaranteeing a certain degree of upkeep but limiting our liability. Instead, we simply told Simon that we would assume no liability whatever for the truck, and that if he brought it with him, it would be at his own risk. Simon professed ideological reasons for bringing in the truck—"The Community needs a truck; I have a truck." From each according to his abilities, etc. Our informal agreements, therefore, were entirely to the Community's benefit. What we didn't know at the time was that Simon was not in the habit of contributing to anybody's benefit but his own, and that he could see ways of making sure that at the end of the year he would come out ahead. What he intended, it developed, was to limp along on marginal repairs until he was about ready to leave, and then, with the authority of the Auto Maintenance Managership, give the truck a major overhaul.

It was, from Simon's point of view, a good plan. But Community carelessness intervened, bringing matters to a head several months before Simon was ready to leave, and forcing his departure.

I think it was Brian who ruined the engine—driving it without oil or something similar. Anyway, Brian accepted the blame, and the Community officially admitted at a planners' meeting that it was our communal carelessness that had done in the engine of the orange truck. We pondered what to do about it. As always, we were short of money. Our contract with Simon was a temptation to us. After all, we didn't *have* to do anything about the truck. We could just let it sit there with a ruined engine. Our contract protected us from liability. But we felt uncomfortable about taking that line. It might be reasonable to treat a full member's vehicle that way, but here was a man who was leaving, had always intended to leave, who had lent his truck to us as a goodwill gesture, and we had wrecked it by carelessness. Could we say to him, "Too bad about your truck, but that's what you get for associating with a community"? We chose not to say that. We tentatively suggested that we pay Simon part of the repair expenses—that part which presumably reasonably corresponded to the damage we had done, enough so that he would not have lost greatly by his association with us but would not have made a profit off us either. The amount we offered was $250.

The offer didn't satisfy Simon. It spoiled his plan to get a new engine out of the Community. He wanted $450. What he did about the difference was to steal it directly from the checkbook.

It was a pretty dramatic happening. I remember when our bookkeeper first reported that a signed check was missing from the checkbook, and we called the bank in order to stop payment on it. I put in the morning calling other major places in Louisa where such a check might be cashed, stopping payment at the Safeway and the local feed store. But Simon cashed it right at our bank, the clerk of course recognizing him and not having been informed by the bookkeeping department of the probability of the stolen check being passed. So he came home with the money in his pocket and a smug expression on his face. We called a general meeting that night, and I told the story of the truck from start to finish for the benefit of those members who did not know what was happening.

The end of the meeting was confusing. Simon kept saying that he was willing to stay around for a few more months, provided we fixed up his truck, and we kept saying that we would like him to leave the premises, please, within seventy-two hours, and give the bank its money back on his way through Louisa.

The theft relieved us of our feeling of moral obligation to

Simon, but he got his money. He had withheld outside work paychecks and finagled other monies that more than covered any loss he sustained through his association with us.

As for Twin Oaks, we got the use of the truck and the services of a good mechanic for the six months of his membership. When he left, we were back where we started—lots of idealists and philosophy majors, nobody who understood the insides of an automobile.

It was in 1970 that our automotive maintenance problems began to be solved in what looks like a permanent way. This time it was not a mechanic who joined the Community, but a Community member who became a mechanic.

Gideon dropped out of Antioch College in his junior year. He was bored. He wrote to Twin Oaks asking permission to stay for the summer, then quickly changed his mind and decided to become a permanent member. Like many college dropouts Gideon suspected that he was capable of learning a great variety of skills, but in fact his education had not prepared him to do anything very useful. It occurred to him to develop a skill in auto mechanics. He chose that field because Twin Oaks had an acute need for this skill at the time he joined. This was the period when our cars were all grounded, and we did not even have any vehicle to tow them to a repair shop with. We didn't have a great deal to lose by letting a beginner experiment with our old cars, the newest of which was over ten years old. Gideon learned what he could from repair manuals and from casual visitors who had some automotive experience. Most of what he now knows, however, he learned directly from the vehicles themselves. It took him about eight months to get to the point where he could handle all of the common automobile maintenance problems. By this time, another mechanic had joined the Community, and one of the Community women had begun to train as an apprentice. We now have mechanics who are not likely to leave, and who are not at odds with the central thrust of the Community's priorities. Fred would be bitter if he could see how easily these mechanics get money for the maintenance budget. They get anything they ask for, because we have confidence that they have the Community's priorities well in mind when they ask. These days we have an indoor garage and are gradually building up a Community-owned automotive tool set. We rebuilt three engines last month.

Some of the Community's transportation problems are not essentially community problems but the problems of poor people everywhere. When we were very short of money, we used to drive members' cars with their out-of-state license plates for months, sometimes even after the plates had expired in their state of origin. We learned not to do this after it cost us $105 in fines and court costs in a single, hard-pressed month. Driving without a proper driver's license, having a taillight go out, or a brake light, or a turn signal—all these little things have cost us a terrible amount of money. We have learned at last to do everything strictly legally—it's cheaper.

No Twins Oaks member has ever been ticketed for speeding, drunk driving, or recklessness. Felix got a ticket once for what the officer deemed reckless driving. But we reviewed the case at a planners' meeting and judged Felix innocent. He had caused an accident, but it was a matter of misjudgment based on inexperience. The judge at the juvenile court where the case was heard was annoyed that the Community was going to pay Felix's fine. He figured that Felix would learn something through earning the money to pay his own fine. We understand that theory. The difference was that *our* court found Felix not guilty.

Maybe the juvenile court would have agreed with our findings if we had been able to appear in court at the prescribed time. But it happened that the court date in January found us without a vehicle of any kind that could make the trip to Richmond. Every car was either stuck fast in frozen mud or dead for some mechanical reason. So we didn't get to court until a month later, and the judge found Felix guilty in his absence.

One of the heaviest hassles the Community board of planners has ever had to deal with has been the question of individual liability for fines. At one time Dwight and I forced through (over Brian's resistance) a resolution to make individual members responsible for fines and court costs if they were involved in illegal, avoidable activity. Dwight thought this legislation would act as a deterrent; Brian thought it would not. For my part, I didn't care if it did or didn't. I just wanted to get some money someplace to pay the fines with. It seemed to me reasonable for the person who caused the expense to go out and work to pay it off. That regulation is still on the books, but it has rarely had a peaceful application. Every time an instance comes up, the basic theory comes up for question again. We have debated the punishment question and the deterrent question and the money question perhaps four times. Sometimes the decision goes one way, sometimes the other, depending mostly on who happen to be planners at the time.

What makes the whole personal responsibility theory a problem is that we have never even tried to apply it in any area except fines. We do not, for example, ever consider whether a member who leans too far back in a chair and breaks it is responsible to pay for it, or whether we ought to charge individual members for carelessly wrecking a perfectly good pair of jeans, or breaking a drill bit. We have always assumed that the solution to better care of group property lies in education and training. The exterior imposition of traffic fines made them seem somehow different. But the difference is hard to defend, and the personal liability rules for traffic fines seem likely to fall into disuse.

Some of the problems I used to think about with regard to vehicles, back when I was dreaming about community, have never come up. That is, they never come up with members. Like the sports car problem. I used to theorize a lot about the use of sports cars and pleasure vehicles. Is it reasonable to ask the owner of a sports car who joins the Community to give up his personal use of it and let any Community member drive it any time? What about the feeling he has for his car? A sports car is not a vehicle—it is an extension of the owner's personality, etc., etc. I will admit that we have had lively discussions on this topic in Community—but always with visitors. By the time a person has joined Twin Oaks, he has long ago dispensed with such trivia as sports cars. The problem is still real. Perhaps ten years from now we will be attracting members who will not be ashamed to argue its pros and cons. At present, however, the inequality that would result from one person's having a private car is so gross that it would not even be considered by any serious member.

XVII

The Pets

Anybody who lives on a farm will be familiar with the pet problem. City people buy a puppy, or accept a kitten, and as long as it's a puppy or a kitten, they manage to hide it from the landlord. Then it grows up. The children have long since lost interest in feeding or cleaning up after it. It bothers the neighbors, or chews the furniture, or comes in heat. It is obvious that the animal needs a better place than a city apartment. It needs a farm.

Twin Oaks is, among other things, a farm. It is perfectly true that all of our animals are ecstatically happy here. All eleven cats. All nine dogs.

The first pet to arrive, along with a visiting family, was a chicken of undetermined sex. Chickychick, as we called it, had been hatched in a second-grade science classroom, its hatching behavior having been duly observed by thirty fledgling scientists, and had then been awarded to little Stephanie for good behavior. Stephanie took Chickychick home, where it lived in the dining room for several weeks. When it got old enough to fly onto the table and the mantel-piece, Stephanie's family started looking for a better place for it. That's when they heard about Twin Oaks.

We printed the adventures of Chickychick in our news-letter for several issues. She was an unusual chicken, having had an unusual background, and besides, there wasn't, in those early days, much else to write about. I never thought of Chickychick or those articles as having any particular symbolic or ideological significance. But after a couple of issues we began to get letters about her. There were pro-Chickychick letters and anti-Chickychick letters. The "pro" people told us that it was nice that we were such warm, human people and not at all like the white-coated specialists they imagined when they read *Walden Two,* and the "anti" people told us that nobody would ever take us seriously as a community unless we wrote about something more significant than a damned chicken. I continued to write about Chickychick, just to keep on encouraging the timid sentimentalists who are afraid of behaviorism, and we started writing more serious articles, too, in the hope that somebody would take us seriously. My theory was always that nobody would take us seriously, anyway, until we had been around for a few years to prove ourselves, and that it didn't matter what we wrote about, as long as people heard that we were still here.

Our first dog was given to us by visitors who thought we ought to have one. Our second was a purebred collie that we hoped to breed and sell her puppies for profit. After that the dog population just grew as the human population did. For every four members who join the Community, one will have a dog—a dog that cannot be left behind because of the affection its owner has for it. We tried once to make a rule against admitting more dogs. But it was useless. We made exceptions every time a new member came along. "I just cannot face a pet owner and say no," complains the Pet Manager, who himself joined the Community with a big Airedale. "The new member doesn't have any experience with our dog problems. He just feels that any place that doesn't have room for one more dog doesn't have room for him. What possible difference can one more dog make?"

For a while we told ourselves that we could make money selling the puppies of purebred dogs, so we accepted a purebred St. Bernard in addition to our collie. Neither of them has made any money yet, but we are very fond of them. For one thing, our dog pack protects us. Whenever official-looking strangers drive up in big, black cars and want to know what our philosophy is or whether we have any runaways, they are greeted by six or seven barking dogs, several of which are big enough to knock them down if they felt like it. They don't feel like it, but the officials don't know that.

Cats haven't been as much of a problem as dogs. They find food for themselves if they must. They're quieter and cleaner and just plain *smaller*. Kittens are very sweet while they last. They don't last long. If the dogs don't kill them, the foxes do. Perhaps the main problem the cats have caused was the controversy over whether or not they should be fed.

We appointed a Pet Manager some time ago, and one day the Pet Manager decided that it was unnecessary to feed cats. He argued that while dogs are pets and need pet food, cats are farm animals, useful for catching mice, and that they won't bother hunting mice if they are full of cat food. The decision did not meet with universal approval. To put it more accurately, the decision was vociferously resented, argued, and finally retracted. An entire planners' meeting was given over to it, mostly arguing the pure matter of fact of whether or not a cat would indeed continue to hunt if it is fed, or whether it has to be motivated by hunger. That question was finally settled by an appeal to an authority—a statement in a book about cats, though just what data the author had to support his statement is still in doubt. At any rate, both cats and dogs are now fed.

Another running controversy on the animals has been the question of whether they should be allowed in the house. Several times we have had meetings and decided to keep them out-of-doors. If members want to bring them indoors, we generally say, let them take them into their private rooms. Public rooms should be reserved for the exclusive use of the human members of our Community. The difficulty with this decision is that it is always defeated by the animals themselves. Once a dog or a cat gets in, it is more work than it is worth to put it out again. So decisions go for nothing. If you want to sit on the living room couch, you have to evict a dog first.

A visitor once told me that he "could tell what kind of people we were by the way we treated our animals." By that I think he meant that we are gentle and humane. But one might as easily deduce that we are suckers for soft fur and big brown eyes and just never did learn how to say no.

XVIII

Everybody Wants to Visit a Commune

We had visitors the first day we started the Community. I don't recall who they were now. We were much too busy getting acquainted with each other and unpacking our things to bother too much with them. In one way or another that has been true of our entire history with visitors. They come here to talk to us, and we're usually too busy. Certainly we must have been a disappointment and a puzzle to the people who visited us our first year. We paid them no attention at all unless by some accident we were working with them or discovered a topic of mutual interest, or unless the visitor went out of his way to make friends. The shy ones got very little from their visits, I'm afraid. They slept on the floor in their sleeping bags in whatever spaces we could find for them. And for this they paid $1.50 a day. Nevertheless, they kept coming. We kept saying in our newsletter that we really welcomed them (in theory we did), and they kept taking us at our word and discovering when they arrived that we were too busy to make them comfortable.

It took us a while even to realize that visitors were always going to be a part of our lives. The first few weeks Carrie would go into a mood whenever a car drove up with strangers in it. She had difficulty enough adjusting to the enlarged family of Community members (what she really wanted

was a normal family life), and each group of visitors seemed
to her like unexpected company, something a housewife
justifiably gets upset about in the outside world. I remember
four college students showed up in the middle of the night
once, and Carrie found them in the kitchen the next morning,
eating pancakes and smoking cigarettes. She stood still and
glared at them as if they were beings from outer space, then
turned to me and asked, "What are those?"

"Those" were visitors, a prelude of many hundreds yet to
come. Carrie adjusted to them eventually, as the rest of us
did, primarily by ignoring them. She would just ask, "How
many of them are staying for supper?" and multiply the
chickens accordingly.

We had been on the farm less than a week when the
Rutledges arrived. They had vacation time from their jobs
and decided to spend it with us. There were six of them—the
two adult Rutledges, two small children, a teen-age son, and
a cousin the same age as the son. Carrie and I were in the
kitchen making blackberry jam when they arrived. Jenny
breezed through the kitchen and said, "There's a family of
six just come, and they've got a tent, and they're intending
to stay a couple of weeks." And there they were.

The Rutledges brought with them a problem that we have
been fighting ever since. The teen-age cousin was obviously
high on one drug or another, and we had formed no policy
about drugs, nor did we yet have any government structure
that could make policy in a hurry. Most of us felt that we did
not want dope on the property. What complicated the issue,
however, was that the young man had long, wild, curly hair.
Remember, this was 1967 when the hippie movement was
just getting started. Somehow our reaction to dope and our
reaction to long hair got all mixed up. All of our own men
wore their hair short, feeling that they owed something to
our local reputation. We didn't want to be known as a hippie
farm. After a great deal of worried talk about the entire
question of drugs and hair, we called a meeting of the whole

group to make a decision on it. It wasn't a very good meeting. People voiced a lot of opinions, but there wasn't any mechanism to get a decision made. We talked for two hours and then went away from the meeting not knowing whether we had decided anything or not. The two opposing points brought up at the meeting were these: (1) long hair will make people think we are kooky, and we want to make a good impression; if we accept visitors who look like hippies, other hippies will start visiting, and we will become a place for hippies to visit, and we don't really want that kind of people around; and (2) the length of one's hair is so obviously one's own business that it would be a moral defeat if we made any policy about it.

It was the latter point of view that we eventually opted for. Dope, no; hair, yes. Within a year, almost all of our men had grown long hair or beards or both. We are indeed known as the hippie farm, and it is indeed difficult to persuade our neighbors that we really do not have drugs on the property. But we are pretty sure we made the right decision.

Most visitors come because they want to take part in community life, to try out the life style, either to write a paper about it or perhaps to test whether they might want to join. But some people visit just because they have no place else to go. One pair that I remember particularly well we called the Apple Tree Couple.

They arrived hitchhiking, with packs on their backs. He was bearded and dreamy-eyed. She was vague-looking and about six months pregnant. They asked for a place to pitch their tent. I explained our visitor policy to them—that they work while visiting, pay $1.50 a day, and eat with us. The man (he always spoke for both of them) accepted all of our terms, or seemed to, but called me aside later and asked if they could build a campfire and eat their own meals, because they couldn't really afford the $1.50 a day.

Decisions like that always bother me. On the one hand, we are trying to build a community here, and a policy of letting drifters camp on our land would be disastrous if carried very far. There are people who have a philosophy of providing free land for whoever wants to stay on it, but that is not what Twin Oaks is about. On the other hand, here are these very poor people, one of them a pregnant girl, asking for a small privilege that costs us nothing. I felt the usual conflict between a long-range "no" and a short-range "yes." I said yes.

So they camped under the apple trees and fixed their own meals. He cooked for her and cared for her tenderly. "She was pregnant once before," he confided to me, "but we were on a strictly macrobiotic diet, and she lost the baby because of malnutrition. Now we're being very careful this time." I told him to feel free to pick and eat our spinach, which was all we had in the garden at the time.

When they had been under the apple tree three days, we began to be annoyed that they had not volunteered to do any work. (We were still trying to take the position that they were visiting our community, not just camping on our land.) Carrie took the initiative. She walked up to them and said, "After visitors have been here twenty-four hours, they generally help out with the work. I can use some help in the kitchen, and Fred would be glad to use you in the garden." They listened in silence but did not volunteer. Later that afternoon, though, Fred spotted the man in the potato patch, apparently planting something. Fred went over to investigate, and found that Mr. Apple Tree was carefully planting summer squash seeds between the rows of potato plants. "Look," said Fred carefully, as he might have to a child or mental patient, "if you want to plant those squashes, I can show you a row where we didn't finish out the beans, and they might do all right there." The man kept on planting. "Because," Fred went on, "this is a potato patch, and we bring a cultivator through here, and the cultivator teeth will tear the squash plants to pieces."

"I like to do things on impulse," the man said. He waited

until Fred shrugged his shoulders and went away, and then kept on planting.

"Did you get him to do any work?" Carrie asked Fred at supper time. "No, and I'm not going to," Fred told her. "I've got too much to do to be bothered with crazy people. Let him work when he feels the damned impulse."

After five days the annoyance had reached a peak, and the question remained simply one of who would ask them to leave. By this time their campfire had become an institution. Other guests who would ordinarily have spent their time with us, investigating our methods and ideas, were gathering with the Apple Tree Couple and digging their free philosophy. "They're very interesting people," our guests told us. "Well, they're being interesting at our expense," we replied, and it was thus that the Apple Tree Couple heard that they were not welcome. One of our other visitors let them know. They left, and so did our other visitors, none of them liking us very well. It was one of our more miserable failures in human relations.

More difficult still was Ivan, the Magician, who visited in the early part of 1970. By this time we were a well-established community. Our planner-manager system was working, and we had clear ideas about the role a visitor should play. We were long past allowing anyone to camp under our trees. Anyway, Ivan and his girlfriend didn't come to visit. They came, they announced, to stay. He introduced himself to me. "I am a builder," he said, and paused to see what effect that would have. "A builder and a magician."

Arnie was in the room at the time. "What kind of a magician?" Arnie asked. "Do you pull rabbits out of hats or what?"

"Prestidigitators are a dime a dozen," said Ivan loftily. "I do real magic. But don't be afraid. All my magic is white magic." I wasn't afraid of anything at the moment except having to spend time talking with this absurd man, so I escaped as quickly as I could and left Arnie to handle him. Arnie would talk to anybody about any theoretical matter, no matter how ridiculous the subject or how insane the conversationalist. It is one of Arnie's golden virtues. As I walked out I heard Arnie begin, "Well, now, how do you define magic?"

As it turned out, Ivan was indeed a builder. Or at any rate he was a worker. He could and did work three times as hard as any member of our community, and he quickly grew contemptuous of our haphazard, lazy ways. Our grounds were on the unkempt side, and one day he got tired of the mess and decided to clean it up. Within an hour or two he had gathered a huge pile of combustibles and was preparing to set fire to them when a member stopped him and asked him what he was doing.

"This trash has evil spirits in it," Ivan explained. "Evil spirits cannot live in a clean, neat place. If we burn this pile, the spirits will go and seek some other abode."

"But that's our scrap lumber," objected the member. "We make things out of it. And besides, you don't just do things like that without even asking the manager."

Ivan desisted from his fire-making. Perhaps garnering all the evil spirits into one pile satisfied him temporarily.

Evidently the objects that harbored the worst spirits of all were the two defunct automobiles that were sitting in our parking lot with their engines exposed. Ivan decided to put them in a less offensive spot. He hooked the tractor to them and dragged them off to the storage barn, where they still remain. He had hooked the tractor to the crippled school bus and was trying to drag it away, too, when Arnie came out to see what was going on. Ivan explained once more about the spirits. "Look," said Arnie, "you are a visitor. You are supposed to be doing work on the labor credit system. But even if you were a member, you don't just up and decide to move these cars. If you want them moved, you ask the Automobile Manager, who happens to be me."

"You," said Ivan, "are not fit to be a manager. God is my manager, and he tells me to move these cars." Evidently God intended the school bus to stay where it was, because Ivan couldn't budge it with the tractor.

By this time Ivan had moved into the empty furnace room in the new building we were completing. He had decorated it nicely, and had candles and incense burning. We believe he did incantations. He also did beautiful artwork. When he left (we threatened him, finally, with civil authorities if he continued to trespass), he did so with a turn-the-other-cheek gesture of giving us the things he had made. To me personally (I was the villain of the piece, who actually delivered the message) he presented a lovely amethyst set in silver, evidently his own work. To other members he gave his paintings and wood carvings, all exquisite. We joke, sometimes, about the objects being cursed, but I think the gifts were meant purely to heap coals of fire upon our heads—a fairly successful device, by the way. We all felt guilt mixed in with our relief.

Most of our visitors aren't crazy, but they often get confused. Take the man who mistook the word "Dishes" printed on his labor credit sheet for "Ditches." The kitchen was shorthanded for two days before the mistake was discovered, but in the meantime, yards of beautifully dug drainage ditches appeared in the cow yard. How did such a mixup go two days without discovery? "Well," says the Cow Manager, "I didn't remember asking for so many hours of ditch digging, but here was this visitor saying he was supposed to dig ditches, and I'd been wanting them dug for a long time, so I didn't argue with him. I just showed him where to plant his shovel." And the Kitchen Manager said, "I saw that he hadn't done his dishwashing shift, but I saw him working out-of-doors and thought perhaps someone had drafted him for emergency work, and being a visitor, he didn't realize that kitchen work takes priority. The second day I finally got up nerve enough to ask."

Richard had come just out of curiosity, because he didn't have anything much to do on his week's leave from his Navy

base. While he was here he read *Walden Two* and all of our
material and talked to members. We talk to a lot of people,
but I don't recall ever having converted anyone quite the
way we did Richard. It was rather like a religious conversion.
He saw the communal light, at it were, saw it as the answer
to all of society's problems, and began to spread the word
zealously. The first thing he did was call his mother on the
telephone. "Hey, Mom," he told her, "I'm a Communist!"

"Yes, dear," said his mother, "we'll talk about it when you
get home."

Richard did talk to his mother when he went home, according to a letter he later sent us. He says he has her almost
convinced. We half expect to see the two of them sign up for
provisional membership when Richard's tour in the Navy is
finished.

My favorite visitor memory is of Wolfgang, a prospective
member who flunked the entrance poll. I liked him, and if it
had been up to me, he would probably be a member now,
busily trying to overthrow Twin Oaks's government and
monopolizing all of our meetings with his excited Teutonic
speech. But the membership voted in favor of peace and
quiet, and Wolfgang didn't get in.

He came to spend two weeks and to apply for membership
if he liked what he saw. His bright blue eyes took in everything, and he commented on everything. He told us with
great frankness about the failure of his last communal attempt, in which struggles for leadership, dependence upon
a single income, and disagreements about dope led to dissolution in a matter of months. Then he unhesitatingly gave
us advice about our community, forgetting entirely that the
principles he was touting had just failed to work in his recent
experience. He asked questions, and we answered him, but
he listened only to disagree. Debate was meat and drink to
him. He never considered actually changing his mind in an
argument. He spoke, not as a participant in a discussion, but
as a persuader. He was always fully convinced, never ques-

tioned whether there might be a valid point of view different
from his own.

Though Twin Oaks members usually do not argue heatedly
(we have learned that nobody is ever persuaded in a heated
argument), Wolfgang brought out the old fighting spirit in
me and in some other members, and he never failed to find
adversaries for his debates. All during his visit, the kitchen
and dining room echoed with theoretical discussion, Wolfgang against Rod, Wolfgang against Naomi, Wolfgang
against me, and sometimes Wolfgang against a whole group
of annoyed communitarians, defending their way of life
against calumny.

This was all old-culture fun (competitive conversation),
but it *was* fun, and most of his most adamant opponents in
argument thoroughly enjoyed him as an antagonist.

Where Wolfgang made his mistake was in trying to start
a revolution.

From time to time Twin Oaks has been plagued by mis-
understandings and group friction that has polarized the
Community into mutually hostile groups. This polarization
never lasts long, and with each issue that divides us, the
division takes place along different lines. Such divisions as
planners versus ambitious nonplanners, competent people
versus tolerant people, agriculture lovers versus agriculture
critics, new culture versus youth culture, and so forth, will
find any given member first lined up with certain others,
then with a different group on a different issue. At the time
Wolfgang was here, he sensed that there was a division, and
he hastened to define it as he understood it. According to
him, Twin Oaks was divided into two basic groups of people:
the Economics group and the Personal Relations group. The
Economics people, as he saw it, were those who worked
hard, who saw the Community as having a future worth
working for, and who were committed to its physical goals
of growth and development. We (I was part of this group)
took pleasure in putting up new buildings, getting industries

started, and making a success of the farm. Our interest in the labor credit system and the governmental system was based on their power to get work out of the lazier members and get on with our basically physical goals. The Personal Relations people, on the other hand, were interested not in the future but in the Community here and now. They wanted, not growth, but love and trust among the members who live here. They preferred a smaller group, because only a small group could become truly intimate with one another. They were people of sensitivity, quiet people, and they tended to be run over by the leadership group, which consisted of the Economics-type people. Wolfgang explained this classification to several representatives of the Economics group one evening, and we listened in astonishment. I began to sort out the members in my mind as he talked, figuring out whom he had put in which group. It was pretty simple. The highly articulate people whom he spent time debating with were all Economics people. The planners were all in that group, *a priori*, and all the hard-working managers. The other group would then be those whom Wolfgang had probably talked to late at night while listening to records—the people who were less involved in the inner workings of the Community, the ones who talked less, didn't go to meetings, spent more time at their private recreational pursuits. Among them were two or three people who really did have grievances against the Community, who really did feel left out and unrepresented by the leadership. But the biggest part of the group that Wolfgang had in mind were people who had just got here and had not yet found a niche in the Community, or people who were entirely out of range of our philosophy and were on their way out, or people who just don't care about leadership and are perfectly happy doing their quota and being left in peace to pursue their own interests.

Wolfgang conceived it as his mission to straighten the Community out. He wanted to see a reversal of power. It was no trouble to him to figure out that personal relations were far more important than economics and that people who valued them should by right direct the Community's paths. Their problem, as he saw it, was that they had no articulate spokesman. And that was where Wolfgang came in.

Wolfgang's class analysis of Twin Oaks was badly mistaken. We have no members who would place economics and personal relations in opposition to each other and consider that we had to sacrifice either for the sake of the other. Even if it was true that some people emphasized one thing and some another, Wolfgang had not correctly named the parties. Some of the people he grouped together as partisans were actually serious antagonists on important issues. Some of the planners were the most personal-relations-conscious people we have ever had. We tried to tell him all that, but listening wasn't Wolfgang's strong point. Toward the end we didn't try to tell him things any more.

Wolfgang didn't pass the entrance poll. But what is interesting is the lineup of the votes. There were only four people who favored his admission. All four of them were articulate, strong-minded people whom he would have placed in the Economics party. Without exception the quiet, the disenfranchised, the lovers of peace voted to exclude him. They said he talked too much, he talked too loud, he was always trying to stir up trouble, and he might try to overthrow the government.

This threat never worried me, because it was obvious that Wolfgang didn't know how to go about overthrowing a government, but it worried the people whom Wolfgang thought he represented.

There is a moral in that story for would-be revolutionaries. It is very, very difficult to be a spokesman for a class you do not belong to. Wolfgang, for all his attraction to the softer philosophies, was raised an intellectual, a hard worker, and an articulate debater. Even if Twin Oaks had really been divided along the lines that he imagined, he would still not have been successful in representing the quiet ones. He acted too much like the other side.

Sometimes visitors come in groups. We went through a period when we wouldn't take groups, because we couldn't integrate them into our lives, and they always ended up being a subculture and learning nothing. Then we went through another stage where we preferred groups, because they could work together as a team, entertain each other, and leave us to carry on our private lives in peace.

There is a particular kind of visitor that makes the whole Community uncomfortable, but we continue to invite them, because they bring in much-needed cash. I refer to the psychology or sociology classes from nearby colleges. They come as a group, along with their professor, are shown around the buildings and farm, then get a two-hour lecture and question period, after which they get back into their cars or chartered bus and go back home. We charge them two dollars a person for this dubious privilege, and we haven't run out of customers. We even get the same professors back the following term with a new group of students.

The trouble with these people is that their interest in community is minimal. They are just taking a course. Twin Oaks is a field trip, and they have to write a paper on their impressions. They generally come to us immediately after reading *Walden Two*.

On two occasions the professors have been kind enough to Xerox the papers written by the students and send them back to us. We sit around the dining room tables reading them aloud to each other. Some of us laugh. Others just swear. "I suppose," one student wrote, "that I ought not have expected the Community to be like Walden Two when they have been going such a short time, but nevertheless that is what I did expect, and I certainly was disappointed. I don't understand how any Americans can take pride in such a gruesome-looking establishment."

There have been times when we just had too many visitors

at a time, when we felt surrounded by strangers, aliens in our own world. Sometimes they literally outnumber the members, especially at semester breaks, Easter vacation, and Labor Day weekend. I am very glad never to have been a visitor to Twin Oaks during those crowded times. I can imagine how I would feel if I were greeted by someone whose first remarks were "Oh, God, another visitor."

Crowded seasons of visitors invariably lead to group meetings during which we decide to "do something about the visitor problem." One such time, we called a meeting for members only, to discuss visitors, and the visitors, in retaliation, called a meeting of their own to discuss us. Afterwards the two groups met and exchanged information. It turned out that the visitors sympathized with our problem more than we had thought they would. Only one of them resented being ignored and made to feel unwelcome. The others appreciated the chance to look the place over and didn't expect us to knock ourselves out being hospitable. Visitors mostly profit by their Twin Oaks experience in relation to what they expect to get out of it—the higher their expectation, the more likely they are to be disappointed and even bitter. The most casual drop-ins have sometimes turned into converts. The best attitude is a neutral one, expecting nothing.

There is another side of the visitor question. Our visitor policy is not all altruism, movement orientation, or even simple need for money. Visitors have a definite role to play in our labor pool.

At least half the dishwashing is done by visitors, more than half of the gardening, quite a bit of the haying, digging trenches, and other manual labor. Members do these tasks, too, of course, and it is not a deliberate plot of the Community's to dump its most tedious tasks onto defenseless guests. It happens because, in an effort to divide the work equally, the Labor Manager necessarily gives the visitors that part of the work that is not specialized, for which no training is required. It is a rare visitor who can be of help with our idiosyncratic printing press, or who is prepared to take full charge of getting out a meal for forty people, or who happens to be a skilled mechanic, or who even knows how to milk a cow by hand. The longer a member is here, the more he tends to find work to his liking, work which no visitor can help him with. Little by little our long-term members become free of jobs they don't like. So who does those? The members who haven't specialized, the new members, and the visitors.

Few visitors complain. I remember one girl who did bring the matter up, though. She came to a meeting and told us, "I have washed dishes and cleaned house all my life. So I come to a community, because I want to have a chance to do something different for one week out of the summer, and what happens? I end up washing dishes and cleaning house."

Sometimes members feel uncomfortable about this accidental exploitation. But there is very little we can do about it. We have given the visitors a lighter work load to compensate, and we try to divide their work in such a way that they don't get *all* dishwashing or *all* gardening. Fortunately, we can teach them to weave a hammock if they are staying as long as a week, and that helps.

We have had a lot of meetings about visitors. Members sometimes complain of feeling that this is no longer their home, that they are living in some transient hotel, or perhaps in a zoo, where they are the exhibits. At such times pressure is usually put on the Visitor Manager to cut back on the number of people. The manager complies, and there is a lull for a while, with only a few visitors. But the work quota goes up.

The truth is that having visitors is part of Twin Oaks life. Our membership turnover would long ago have killed the Community if we had not been able to fill the empty spaces with people who originally came here as visitors. Three quarters of our current members were visitors at one time.

Our dilemma has become simply a matter of deciding how

long a visitor should be allowed to stay. The longer they stay, the more useful and specialized work they can do. Besides, they become our friends, and we sometimes even forget they are not members. But if we fill our spaces up with long-term visitors (and we easily could), it would cut down seriously the total number of people who could come and see the Community. Half the time it isn't the long-term people who are really interested in joining, either, and while they are here, they are keeping away someone who might really be a good member, or who might be inspired to start his own community. So we vacillate and do a little of everything.

Nearly every day we get a letter from someone who is very excited about visiting us in order to gather material for a paper he or she is doing for some class. We talk about discouraging the paper-writers in favor of those who actually are investigating communes as a possible alternative for themselves. The trouble with that policy is that you can't always tell which is which. Anybody can *say* he's serious about communal living, and half the time the college students who admit they're writing papers are wavering on the borderline of dropping out of school and joining a commune. We have had three members who originally came here to do research on us.

Perhaps we need a large barracks building for transients. But if we put out the money to build any kind of structure, we would naturally choose to build it for more members. It isn't just visitors who want to get in. The waiting list for membership is always pressing on us.

XIX

What Do Your Parents Think of All This?

One question we never think to ask a prospective member unless he's under eighteen is, "How do your parents feel about your joining the Community?" Most people who are ready to join a commune are ready to do so whether or not their parents approve of it.

"People keep asking me, what did your parents think?" commented Emily after her mother and father paid her a weekend visit. "Who cares what they think? I left home *years* ago."

Some members care. Howard cares a lot. He teetered between joining and not joining for several months, mostly because he could not bear to break the news to his mother. "She reads about communes in the newspaper," says Howard, "and she imagines drugs. Then her political opinions tend to be conservative. She's worried about my being a victim of a Communist conspiracy." Howard travels to visit his mother as often as he can, shaving off his beard each time he goes. "You see, most people here have years of history of teaching their parents that they are independent people. But I have never done that, and I have it all ahead of me," he explains. "She wants to visit me here at the Community, but I don't think it is a good idea. If she saw two people sharing the bathroom, it would upset her. And she would just take one look around at the people and say 'Hippies.' "

Many parents visit. These visits are often a little bit of a strain. The whole Community is conscious that there are people present who are: (1) older, (2) straight, (3) probably disapproving; and that one of our members is likely to be embarrassed by almost anything that happens. So we tend to watch our language, refrain from any public display of affection, and almost not talk with the member whose parents are visiting. Emily's mother commented on this as she saw it. "I don't see that anyone here is making any effort to show that they care about each other," she said. "Isn't that what's wrong with the outside world?"

Most parents manage to take a "Well, you're happy here, and I guess that's what counts" stand, but Brian's mother and father abandoned it when they visited him once and found him ill. Brian had come down with something that had symptoms similar to infectious hepatitis. The treatment for that disease is simply to rest, and the problem for the Community was just to keep other people from getting it—simple enough with our flexible labor supply. But Brian's mother was visiting just as the disease was tentatively diagnosed, and she found him lying in another member's room, feeling ill. The room he had chosen to borrow (I forget why he wasn't in his own) was not a model of cleanliness. In fact it was a filthy pigsty and not the sort of place to which one invites one's mother. (Brian had been raised in a home so clean and nice that there were objects in his own bedroom that he was never allowed to touch.) Though Brian was twenty-five and married, and had been away from home for several years, his mother took one look at her helpless son lying in filth among hippies and Communists and decided to rescue him. She wanted to take him home and nurse him back to health in more antiseptic surroundings. Her only problem was persuading him. She brought pressure to bear by getting the doctor to advise Brian to go home with her.

Brian was moved by this. He did not want to endanger the Community. But the argument did not make much sense, for the entire Community had already been exposed and already been inoculated, and isolation procedures are very little trouble to a community. Brian talked to me, and I told him I saw no reason for him to leave. He was one of the central people in the group, both administratively and socially, and his loss would have been a severe blow to morale. He was not very ill at all, and spending weeks recuperating at his parents' home would have been terribly boring to him. Brian agreed and told his mother no. Then she came to me. "You are an intelligent woman," she began, and then followed probably the most unpleasant quarter hour of conversation that I have ever engaged in. I was put in the difficult position of defending dirt. Since I don't much like dirt myself, I couldn't argue without embarrassment. I insisted on being rational about hepatitis:

(1) Brian's already got it; (2) it isn't caused by sleeping on a mattress without a sheet, or by being surrounded with dirty clothes and cigarette butts and coffee cups; (3) being cared for in a nice clean house would not make him get better any faster.

In my frustration and embarrassment I am afraid I stooped to attack where I suspected she was vulnerable. "Brian is a grown man now," I said. "He left home years ago." And she glared at me with pure hatred. If Brian wouldn't go home with her, she decided, she would stay here and take care of him. She arranged with her husband to leave her to spend some weeks at Twin Oaks and began thinking in terms of cleaning up that room. I don't think she ever did know it wasn't his room. But she had to tell Brian her intentions, and that's where she met her match. "You can stay," Brian told her, "but if you stay, I'm leaving." She was gone within the hour.

So we rearranged some rooms and gave Brian private quarters for his illness (I made sure it was nice and clean).

We put isolation signs on the doors and processed his dishes
and laundry separately from the rest of ours. We talked to
him through the window, and he read a lot of books. Nobody
else got the disease, and subsequent lack of symptoms and
negative tests cast doubt on whether Brian had ever had it,
either. The breach between Brian and his family was healed
in time, too. His mother called him later that same week to
say that it was just as well he hadn't accompanied her home.
She had caught the Asian flu and her husband was having
to take time off work to take care of her. Did anybody at
Twin Oaks have it? No, the Asian flu passed us by.

Rosemary's father became violently angry when Rosemary
first joined the Community. "My father," says Rosemary,
"thinks the John Birch Society is a liberal organization. He
doesn't like Blacks and he doesn't like Jews, and he doesn't
like commies or pinkos or hippies or liberals. When you
come down to it, there aren't too many people left for him
to like." Rosemary remained determined to join the commune, and her father tried bribes. He promised her an air-
plane if she would come back home. When both anger and
bribes had no effect, he got adjusted to the idea. "When I
went home for Christmas, he was very nice to me," she said.
"He said the Community must be good for me, because I am
quieter and more self-possessed now. He told my grand-
mother (who was disapproving) that it wasn't a bad place
after all; it was a very good place."

For some parents it is not the commune itself that upsets
them. As communes go, Twin Oaks is pretty acceptable. It is
the fact that their son or daughter is not going to school.
Maggie's story illustrates the point.

> "When I graduated from high school I talked to my folks
> about what to do next. They knew I was interested in
> Community, and we read the Twin Oaks material together.
> I was wavering between coming here and going out to
> San Francisco to college. My mom suggested I come here,
> so I did. Then when I had been here a couple of weeks

and decided to join, I called her and told her. She was pretty surprised and not too pleased. It was like her plan had been upset: I was supposed to have visited Twin Oaks and been disillusioned. But I wasn't. My mother is a liberal. She got adjusted and figured it would be a good thing to do for the summer. But as September came around, she kept writing 'What am I supposed to do about your registration? The school keeps sending registration materials here.' I wrote back and told her to throw them out—that I wasn't going to go to school. On the last possible day of registration she came out here to visit me. I kept telling her I had no interest in college. I told her how I was into a study program on my own, reading in psychology and various other subjects, and she said 'Well, if you're going to study, why don't you go to school and get *credit* for it.' She urged me to take even correspondence courses, in order to get the credit. It took me some pains to explain to her that I didn't care about the credit— it was the education I was interested in. Finally she stopped trying to persuade me of anything. She can see my point about wanting to live in a commune. She has imagination enough to be excited by the idea. But she is really concerned about my future. She says 'You can't live there all your life.' But I'm very young, so she isn't too worried. She finally decided to set aside $100 a month for my education, and so then when and if I do want to go to college, it won't be difficult for me."

An occasional parent manages to fit in comfortably with the group. Usually it is a single parent who can do this, someone who will stay for several days and get acquainted. Jere's father is a favorite. He is a Baptist minister who shocks his congregations with radical sermons. I recall he brought a case of beer with him on one of his visits and was quite surprised to find how slowly it was consumed by the members. His son Jere suggested he also bring soft drinks. "The Cokes went as fast as the beer did," said the surprised donor. Hilda's father stayed for nine days and wrote a big article about us after he left, which was printed in his home town paper. He is a lawyer, and we typed a brief for him while he was here. He was pretty surprised to find secretarial skill at a commune. He sat in a hammock in shorts and a T-shirt and did some high-priced work for his firm in Michigan.

Some parents could easily fit in as members. Naomi's mother is one of these. She has the kind of vitality and flexibility that would laugh at the generation gap. But we haven't been able to persuade her yet.

My own mother lives too far away to visit and doesn't have the money to travel. I have been away from her for many years, but I remember her as a tolerant and adaptable person, and for a while I wrote to her suggesting she join. To this I received a tart reply that I must have a warped memory if I thought she would want to live in a crazy place like this.

Sometimes we ask ourselves how soon we will be able to take care of our parents when they are too old to take care of themselves. Most of us cannot stand the idea of their living out their lives in old-age institutions, and we believe that the commune is a natural and sensible solution to the whole problem of caring for them. Most of them would have Social Security checks and Medicare, which would offset their living expenses better in a commune than any place else in the world. But we are some years from being able to consider this as a serious plan. Right now we do not have any kind of proper facilities. We are short of bathrooms, and our cafeteria-style meals and casual habits in dozens of ways would not be suitable to age and weakness. As soon as possible we want to have people of all ages here. We do not want to be a young people's commune. We want to be a Good Society. Absorbing older people is not going to be an easy step, but it is a necessary one if we are to reach our goals.

XX

The Recurrent Debates

Robert Houriet, in his *Getting Back Together,* tells us that the major ideological battles he observed during his trips around to the different communes were: (1) whether a community should be open or closed; and (2) how much a commune can morally depend on the Outside for its resources (e.g., inheritances, food stamps). Those are perfectly good questions, but as I read his account I could not help feeling that they were essentially the questions of an outsider. For all Houriet's love of participation, he could not both write the book he wanted to write and become a real member of the communes he visited. If he had (or when he does) become a member of a group with a commitment to survival, he may discover that these two questions are simple to answer, and that there are a lot of other questions that will loom much larger as time goes on. Before I go into them, I might as well deal briefly with the two that Houriet brings up.

We never even thought of being an "open" group—a perpetual crash pad with no restrictions. It is obvious on the face of it that such an arrangement is not viable. As to living off the civilization that we disapprove of, we haven't many qualms about it. We don't have food stamps in this county, but if we did, we might have tried to qualify for them in our earlier, poorer days. Why not? For every boost we can get from the State, that's one more place we don't have to put our scarce resources and energy. It would leave us just that much more time free to devote to making the Community a better place. We are very glad indeed that there are free medical services in Richmond. It doesn't hurt our pride to use them. As to Hal's money, we are not ashamed that we had that donation to start off with. Without it we would have had to struggle with mortgage payments from the beginning, and we wouldn't be as far ahead as we are. True, we haven't "proved" that we can make it on our own. But who does? Not the State. Not Hal.

Those aren't the issues we argue about, as I said. We do argue, though.

Expansion versus the quality of life is probably the most enduring argument we have. I told about the beginnings of this debate in the chapter on food—Simon wanted meat on the table, and Dwight wanted to tighten our belts for the revolution. As I look back on it, it seems odd to me that this subject didn't come up until 1969. We have never ceased talking about it since. Dwight, Brian, and I shared the vision of the large community. *Walden Two* suggests a thousand as a reasonable number to shoot for (and after you get to a thousand, you divide your group; half of you go to a new location and start another community; the other half to stay where they are and accept new members to fill the vacated spaces; and so on, ad infinitum). Implicit in the expansion idea is the assumption that we have a task to perform for the world's population, and that we will not be living up to our responsibilities unless and until a good part of the population can make community living (Walden Two style) one of its choices. Simon was the first to give us any argument. He held that nobody had any moral obligation to anybody but himself. He lived up to this philosophy pretty well, as I have recounted in previous chapters. His blatant selfishness kept us from taking his point of view seriously, so we didn't meet "quality of life" as an issue until it came up again in later years, this time presented by people who quite seriously meant that they preferred a smaller community, that we should use our money and labor to improve our surroundings, rather than building for more members, and that though we might have a responsibility toward people who had not yet had a chance to join, we have a greater responsibility to ourselves to make our own lives more rewarding. I am not really capable of presenting the quality-of-life argument very well, since I am a very heavy partisan for the other side. No matter how it is argued, I can always hear the ring of "me first" in it, and I cannot help answering "Why you?" And yet I am no altruist. As an opponent once scornfully pointed out to me, I am as selfish as anybody else. It's just that I get my "reinforcement" from a different source. I want to see the big Walden Two scheme worked out. This bit of self-knowledge, however, changes nothing. I grant that we proponents of expansion deserve no praise for our attitudes. We are making no sacrifices. But that is beside the point. Motives aside, the fact is that a high material quality of life for insiders means that fewer can be included.

But I get carried away. I suppose I could divide Twin Oaks's membership into two categories—the quality-of-life people and the Expansion people. But it would be a false distinction. In truth, none of us are such fanatics that we can't work out the differences and find compromises. The expansionists would like to take a few more visitors and more members, and live a little more crowded, in order to use the surplus labor to build the Community faster. But we aren't in favor of throwing open the doors for today's drifting youth population to pour through, nor do we want to take serious health risks with an overloaded septic system. The quality-of-life people want us to cut down on short-term visitors, give private rooms for members a high priority in our spending, and put money and energy into basic improvements like a bigger dining room, more office and craft space, perhaps a paved driveway, before we take more members. But they are not arguing for a heated swimming pool or wall-to-wall carpeting. This means that all large budget decisions are a tug-of-war, but each side gives in gracefully and makes the best of it when the other side wins a point.

The last year has been won largely by the quality-of-life people. The cost of living per capita has doubled. All of our construction money went into improved eating (walk-in freezer $3,000, food processing room $500); and we took our summer hammock sales income (about $4,000) and used it for a vacation from outside work. Perhaps the next big expenditures will swing back the other direction—a new building that may allow us to admit a few new members. Fortunately, most of the large purchases on our priority list please everybody. A bigger septic system means both expansion and quality of life. So do expanded kitchen facilities, and shop space.

Another recurring argument is over something we sometimes call the "hard line." The individual issues vary a great deal, but in general the hard line is Determined Egalitarianism, and the soft line Individual Liberty. I have always been a fence-straddler on this question, so maybe I can be more objective this time.

This is the kind of thing that comes up: Felix has a yearning for the spiritual, and he wants to go to Richmond once a week for a course in Transcendental Meditation. Officially the Community has no use for Transcendental Meditation, but that is not the issue. The problem is that the course costs money. Felix knows that the Community will not pay for it, nor does he expect it to. He believes that his parents will send him the necessary thirty-five dollars if he writes home and asks. *But* (here's where the hard line comes in) we have a rule against that. When people join Twin Oaks, they are expected to share in such wealth and opportunities as the Community can provide, and leave it at that. We do not all have parents to whom we can write for goodies. The hard line says it is bad precedent to allow those with indulgent parents to get more than those without them. The soft line doesn't have much of an argument. It just says, "What the hell. Who cares?"

Or again: We have a member who has left the Community, then changed his mind and wants to get back in. He has been gone perhaps a month. Hard line says he either has to make up the labor he would have done had he been here during that month or enter as a new member, running the gauntlet of an entrance poll. Soft line says that since he wasn't here lying in a hammock, none of us actually *saw* him goofing off, and the inequality is academic and unimportant. Making up a month's work would be a terrible burden. Going through a poll like a stranger is dangerous (he may not make it). The member in question says that it isn't fair to charge him vacation credits for the time he was gone from the Community, because he did not, after all, enjoy himself, and it wasn't any vacation. Soft line says, "What difference does the rule make? This is a real human being with a human problem." Hard liners are sometimes looked upon as hard-hearted, rigid, even sadistic. The hard liner says he is not unsympathetic. It's just that the overall equality of the members is a more important consideration than this particular member's feelings at this particular time. In *fact* we had to do more work while this member was gone. We may not have noticed it, but we did do it—or else it went undone. Why should this member be given a free month's vacation, when the rest of us have to work for ours by saving up labor credits? It is true that we can do him a favor and absorb the cost without doing ourselves much economic damage. But why him? If we can afford a month's less labor, let's divide it up among all of us and each do less. Let's each take one day's free vacation.

Another case: We have decided to run a country grocery store, and the members who work in it find that they are unable to resist the temptation to eat potato chips and drink Cokes. Should we allow store workers to eat a certain minimal amount of junk for free? Or does it all come out of their allowances? Hard line says they take it out of their allowance. Resisting temptation or paying for it is part of the job, and if you can't make it, you don't sign up for it. Everybody is entitled to the same number of goodies, and there is no reason to favor store workers. Soft line says that store workers are subject to more temptation than any human can be expected to resist. It argues that a hard and fast rule will simply drive members to cheat (nobody has that much allowance), and we had better recognize it from the beginning and be realistic. Hard line says that that is disgusting, and that giving in is hardly a utopian approach to morality.

The hard-line–soft-line argument is never over, because there is no way we can make a rule that will cover all cases. Or rather, we have plenty of rules (they are hard-line rules), and the soft-line people are always saying we should make an exception in this case or that. So we are forced to argue anew each time a member asks for anything that might be construed as a special privilege.

Another frequently recurring dispute is the question of our obligation to bring about social change in America—more specifically, what are we doing for the "Revolution." The Walden Two line is clear here. It says that a Walden Two community is not political, and that we will be doing all we can do simply by being a successful community, providing an alternative, and being an example. But on this point both Dwight and Brian departed from Skinner.

At first we all agreed on the futility of trying to work on the outside to bring about any change. Brian, in particular, had come here after participating in demonstrations and seeing nothing concrete come of it. Criticism at first came to the Community from outsiders. Visitors would take us to task for not being part of the larger scene. Why did we not do local organizing? Were there not exploited people, black and white, in our immediate neighborhood? Why did we cut ourselves off from them and pursue our escapist paths when

there was work to be done? As long as the criticism came
from the outside, it made no impact on us. We disliked the
critical visitor, perhaps, but that was all the emotion we felt.

Eventually the questions began coming from insiders.
Dwight had hoped to make a big movement out of Walden
Two, but he saw that the progress of change through community would be very slow. For one thing, money problems
stood in the way of rapid expansion. For another, members
like Simon and Fred and even Pete threw him into despair.
He was not interested in making a comfortable community
for the bourgeoisie. As his frustration with the slowness of
our progress grew, he conceived the conviction that the Establishment would never let a Walden Two society survive
anyway. As soon as it became a threat to capitalism (as it
would, by removing both the exploitable labor force and a
vast number of over-consumers), the Establishment would
swoop down on it and make it illegal. Or it would plant
dope on our premises and jail our leaders, or it would simply
plant ugly rumors in the local neighborhood and let patriotic
vigilantes wipe us out. Reasoning from the war in Vietnam,
Dwight argued that the Establishment is ruthless when
threatened. As he saw it, the community movement is
doomed. Either we become large enough to have an effect
on society—in which case the Establishment will get us—or
else we will never get large enough to have any impact. In
either case, Dwight was not going to stick around and devote his life to a lost cause.

I have already recounted how Dwight left the Community
over the issue of internal government. I should explain that
he was gone for a few months and then returned for another
try. But the second try was never any good. His high hopes
would not come back. Outside revolutionary activity in the
interim had grown remarkably, and Dwight began to believe
that the direct approach was after all valid. He decided that
his place was on the Outside, working in the factories and
educating the workers.

Dwight was never a popular person. He was too critical, too fond of engaging in argument just for the pleasure of annihilating his opponent. He had a small group of friends who cared a great deal for him, and they were the leadership group—the "planner clique," as Hal and Simon called them. Therefore when Dwight changed his directions away from community and toward outside organizing activities, his opinions did not shake the group. They seriously affected only one person. But that person was Brian.

Dwight left the Community in November, 1969. Brian never recovered. For a while Brian, too, left Twin Oaks and wandered about in the big cities, letting his hair and beard grow long and taking part once again in demonstrations. He returned with a quiet decision to plug away a while longer on the community idea. We were low on members and morale at the time and needed him badly. His new radical hair style seemed to symbolize the change in him. He read vast quantities of radical literature. He kept in touch with Dwight. He was very well loved, and his influence was great. Over half the Community gathered to listen to public readings of books about the revolutions in China and Cuba. He tried to persuade us to turn our grocery into a cooperative in which the local farmers of both races would eventually take the lead and run it themselves; and we would then bow out. Nobody here is opposed to cooperatives, and we talked a lot about the plan. We ran into difficulty because there was no way we could get groceries, even wholesale, cheaper than the local chain store was selling them retail. So we had no argument on which to base a cooperative. At one point Brian wanted to start an underground newspaper aimed at high school people, to try to turn them on to radical life styles and explain the rationale of communal living to them before they got caught up in the System. The planners vetoed the plan as dangerous for the Community. Just before he left, Brian hit upon the idea of having a Community-sponsored house in Richmond which would serve as a radical education center in the city, as well as a convenient spot for our outside workers to spend the night from time to time. Again we turned him down.

Before he left, Brian saw that we were strong as a community and could survive without his help. Little by little over the last year he dropped out of active Community life, whether by deliberate plan or just lack of interest I do not know.

I am not so naïve as to assume that we have heard the last of the debate on involvement with national affairs. I have come to believe that all disputes are destined to be repeated in one form or another over and over again. Without even stopping to think, I can count five hard-line versus soft-line arguments we have had over the past four years. The revolution argument we have been through twice. I hope we don't lose a fine member every time we go through that one. Expansion versus Quality of Life comes up every time we spend over five hundred dollars.

And then there's the government question. We have rumbles of this one regularly every six months when we appoint a new planner—sometimes oftener. But this is a big one, and deserves a chapter by itself.

XXI

Overthrowing the Government

Like most Twin Oaks members, I have thought of myself as a rebel all my life. I have little respect for the Establishment. I view with pleasure and approval people who engage in passive resistance or civil disobedience in an effort to topple bad government.

So it feels odd to me to find myself at Twin Oaks a bulwark of our little Establishment, and an ironic echo rings through my mind when I hear myself saying of dissidents, "If they don't like it, why don't they go somewhere else?" (Love it or leave it.)

For there are disagreements about government from time to time. As I write, things are quiet on this front. We are united in our general aims, content with our channels of influence, optimistic about the progress we are making. Our last battle over government ended six months ago—the dissidents left. Was that the last one? I hope so, but I cannot say for sure. It is hard to know the difference between finding a solution and just enjoying a breathing space between conflicts.

The arguments over government—there have been several of them—have been remarkably alike: similar complaints, similar justifications, polarization of opinion, and eventual departure of the rebels.

We took our governmental patterns from *Walden Two*. I have already told how we elected our first board of planners. In a group of eight, it is perhaps not remarkable that the election of three did not leave many disgruntled office-seekers. Not everyone, after all, wants to be a group officer. Certainly Jenny and Carrie did not. Sandy had confidence in the three elected, and Quincy satisfied himself that proper form had been used. Fred, always a loner, did as he pleased with or without the approval of the planners. That was the entire membership. We had a legitimately elected government, and the elected officers did their best to make good decisions when things came up, which wasn't very often.

There was, however, one resident of the Community who, though not a member, had a great deal of influence. That was Hal. Hal was with us a great deal, almost from the beginning. He drove his own car and manipulated his own income, both for the benefit of the Community. Financially we leaned on him heavily. It was he who bought the cub tractor and paid for drilling the well, as well as putting up the money for our first building. He said at first that he could not join the Community, and he did not join it until we had been in existence for six months. By then Hal had spent all his available money. He told us ruefully that he would either have to join the Community or go back to work—either college teaching or working for industry (he was an engineer). He chose to join the Community.

But living in the Community without money to spend was not at all the same thing as it had been before Hal ran out of cash. The building was finished. The Community's work consisted mostly of routine farm and maintenance work, cooking and dishwashing, weaving hammocks. Hal was bored. He had not donated all his cash resources to us in order to live a humdrum existence. He wanted to see the Community grow, and grow rapidly. We had no argument with him on that score, but we were out of money. We, too, had donated all the resources we had. At this time we realized that the hammock business was not going to pick up fast enough to keep us out of city jobs, and we began going on outside work. Hal, as I have recounted elsewhere, did not go.

Those of us who worked in the city were not enjoying community life much at this period. We got up early, spent the day at useless and demeaning tasks, and returned to a dirty house, an ill-prepared meal, and complaining residents. Physical progress was nonexistent. We spent our weekends trying to think up industries that did not require capital, or ways to attract new members. That situation soon changed, however, and we had to spend all of our time thinking how to keep the Community from going under. For it was under attack from the inside.

Evidently, those who stayed on the farm during the day were not enjoying life, either. Hal and Fred, accustomed to such jobs as building, farming, and mechanical work, suddenly had to do household tasks. The population on the farm consisted of Hal and Fred, plus two temporary members, teen-agers without either skills or much interest in the Community. To us outside workers, it seemed that we were doing the best we could with the situation. We had to have money. Hal and Fred did not extend themselves making the best of it, however. What they did instead was discuss the Community's prospects with each other, and they had remarkably similar opinions on one subject—namely, that the Community was being disastrously run, and that we needed a different board of planners.

In defense of Hal, I must say that the board of planners (Brian, Dwight and I) had no idea what to do about our financial problems. The only skill we knew was working for a living, and that was what we were doing. We had formulated no plans for getting the Community on its feet. Furthermore, it is true that we had admitted the useless teen-age members, who were considered all around to be a deficit. And it is also true that in our adherence to the prin-

ciples of equality we had insisted that the teen-agers be
allowed to use the power tools, run the tractors, and otherwise subject the Community's property to possible abuse. All
these things together Hal and Fred considered gross admin-
istrative incompetence.

In defense of the planners, it might also be said that neither
Hal nor Fred ever came up with specific proposals for rem-
edying the situation, beyond such vague grumbles as "not
taking in lazy bums." Hal had schemes that involved borrowing money and setting the Community up in some industry, but we were leery of trusting Hal's enthusiasms.
He had gone on several hammock-selling trips, almost entirely without results, and had done an about-face about the
possible future of the hammock industry, at first saying that
it would make us rich, then saying that it had no market and
that we should try something else. We figured that our problem with hammocks was our inability to sell, and that we
would have exactly the same problem with any other manu-
facturing scheme. Hal was enthusiastic about making children's toys. To us, the toy industry looked remarkably like
the hammock industry, only with a higher capital investment.
Where was the money to come from? There was only one
place left: mortgage the land. Hal owned it; we held a lease
on it. It could not be mortgaged without cooperation between
us. The land was our security. Rich or poor, we could somehow survive as a community as long as we had the land. Hal
and Fred wanted us to take the risk "and either make it or
give up" as Fred once said. The planners never considered
giving up. We could not risk the land.

One day the workers came home to find a note from Hal.
It said that he would like to be a planner.

Being a planner wasn't supposed to be a very big deal.
Our idea was that decision-making, like milking a cow or
sweeping a floor or teaching a class, was a job, deserving no
more or less honor than other jobs. We had been placed in
the job by legitimate election. We didn't pretend to special

qualifications, other than our shared ideals and commitment. Hal's request to join the board had overtones that didn't jibe with our theories of leadership. If Hal had ideas, why didn't he come to the board and present them? What was stopping him? If we agreed with him, we would implement the ideas. If we didn't agree, we would outvote him, whether he was on the board or not. So why did he want to be on the board? What would he gain? As far as we could see, it was a simple question of prestige. Hal said to himself, "I belong on the board of planners." It grated on him that he was subject to the ultimate decision-making power of people he considered his inferiors.

We certainly were inferior to Hal in many ways. He had had more money, and had an air of being accustomed to money. He spoke about investments and interest rates and bank loans in a knowledgeable way that made the rest of us feel very naïve. Furthermore, he was older than we were, and had done more things. He had had four to six more years of schooling than we had, had taught college, had traveled in Europe, had read a lot. His engineering skill was considerable, and very useful to the Community. More than that, he was a good, thorough, skilled worker. When he picked up a saw or a hammer, he knew how to handle it. He even washed dishes with finesse. We respected Hal for all of these things, but our respect was limited. We did not assume that these obvious and admitted talents necessarily implied the possession of other unrelated talents, like the ability to make good judgments about matters of importance to the Community. In that area, his experience was no greater than ours, and his talent, we thought, somewhat less.

So we didn't put Hal on the board of planners. What we did was admit (in a memo on the bulletin board) that the current board of planners had been in office long enough to have made up a definite form of government beyond just using its discretion, and that the board ought to provide a reasonable means for its own replacement. We said we would set a new election. If Hal was to be a planner, we told each other, let him get there the same way we did—by the approval of the group. We were not about to lift him on our shoulders.

Hal considered the proposed election a ruse and a fraud, and said so. Perhaps it was. It was obvious to everyone concerned that there was no way he could win an election. The three planners were against him, and the other members, Hal pointed out angrily, were either wives or lovers of the planners. The only exceptions were the teen-agers that he had such contempt for, both of whom said obligingly that they didn't care who was on the board.

Much ugliness followed. Hal called us the "planner faction" and publicly deplored factionalism. At one point of extreme anger he threatened to end the Community by destroying the lease and kicking us off the land. Things grew so bad that we decided to do away with our government entirely. We dissolved the board of planners and lived without government other than the managerships, which fortunately kept our organization going and got the work out. The labor credit system remained intact.

Eventually we reinstituted the government over Hal's protest, reelected the same planners, and continued on our shaky way into the grim summer of 1968.

I am omitting reams of detail in the story of this battle. Unfortunately, prolonged conflict leads to bitterness. I find it difficult to write about the details of the political battle without being very negative about Hal. He did some bad things and said worse. I see that almost everything I write about him paints him as being a community villain. The fact is that Hal was and is a good person, cheerful, generous, and high-minded, and he meant nothing but good toward the Community. He probably showed us his worst sides. But probably it is true, as he often said, that his back was against the wall, that he felt frustrated beyond his power to tolerate, and he struck out with any weapon he could lay his hands on. Sometimes they were ugly weapons, and we tended to make moral judgments about his use of them. It is easier to understand him when I remind myself that he gave us everything he had, and then discovered that he had lost the power to control our direction. His experience had in no way prepared him for the surprise of finding that his influence ended when his cash did. He had never been poor before and had never had to depend purely on his social skills. He did not know how to gain control of a group, and he did not know how to be happy without it.

Anyway, what I wanted to talk about in this chapter is not the dirty little things that happened between Hal and the planner faction, but the accusations and criticisms of our governmental system that were first made by Hal, but were to be echoed and reechoed for the next four years.

It was Hal who first said, "I want to know what is going on." With hindsight I can readily see that he, like any other active mind, would be interested in the details of the decision-making process. He wanted to know not only what decisions we had reached, but the reasoning that was behind them. He wanted to participate in the discussion. And we very stupidly didn't allow him to.

Partly, I suppose, we had some theoretical commitment to professional government. The arguments for it aren't bad, and I will get to them in a minute. But partly we just didn't want to be bothered arguing with anyone who didn't think precisely the way we did. And in those early days the planners thought virtually in unison. Much of the time we spent in our private meetings was not in talk but in thinking of what we ought to do. One of us would say, for example, that we should perhaps discuss what to do about Fred's habit of spending his own money without going through the central treasury. Another of us would say that it was doubtful if anything could be done without alienating Fred to an unacceptable degree. The third would comment that it was exasperating and frustrating to have a member who wasn't with us on basic equality theory. And we would all sigh and sit there and think about it, partly in dismay at the stumbling block that Fred was becoming, partly in rather smug satisfaction at our own level of moral commitment. Then we would go on to the next topic, all of us understanding that we had reached a temporary decision to put up with Fred's conduct a while longer until we were strong enough to take a stand without endangering the Community's existence. That kind of communication would not have been possible with Hal on the board. We had no confidence that Hal shared our moral indignation at selfish behavior. For all we knew, Hal might think Fred perfectly justified, might balance Fred's technical competence against his lack of principles and decide that principles were expendable. The fact that we reached pretty much the same decision was beside the point. We reached it with regret. Hal, we suspected, would have been quite cheerful about it.

Were we self-righteous? Unquestionably. We were, furthermore, self-indulgent in our pleasure in each other's company and our exclusion of people who might argue irrelevantly and boringly. But what was worse, far worse, was that we were wrong.

Why shouldn't Hal have been in on the discussions in which we agreed, for example, to accept new members without skills, commitment, or assets? In truth, there were no such discussions. Accepting everyone who applied was a fundamental part of what the three of us believed in, and it never occurred to us that there was anything to discuss. If Hal had been there, we would have argued the matter out with him. Perhaps he would have been persuaded, or perhaps we would have. At least we would have heard each other's feelings about the importance of an open membership, and he might have understood our fears that the Community would fail in its first year out of sheer attrition. Furthermore, it would have been good for the three of us to verbalize those unspoken assumptions. Also, it would have been good for Jenny and Carrie to participate in such discussions. They would have begun to learn about the kind of thinking that had gone into forming the Community and might sooner have become active and interested in its basic aims. It is obvious, with the glorious wisdom of hindsight, that our snobbishness was self-defeating. We had a problem with government and a problem with educating new members. We could have solved both at once if we had given up our private planners' meetings.

We did give them up after that. Public planners' meetings have long been the norm. For all their annoyances and clumsiness, they serve us better than private ones did. But there is a difference between group discussion and group decision.

There are things that can reasonably be decided by groups and things that cannot. At Twin Oaks we are painfully trying to find out which is which. At the beginning we put virtually all the decision-making onto the planners. I still think that most of the actual decisions made were good ones, but the sense of being left out that was experienced by Hal and later by others was not at all desirable nor even necessary. Our experiences have taught us to bring up almost all issues for public discussion and to take the time to hear all sides and try to convince, rather than just overrule. This is still not the same thing as either waiting for group consensus or taking a vote.

The basic argument against placing decisions directly and simply in the hands of the group is that a group may decide at any time to go in directions not intended by the founders. Twin Oaks is a group with a specific purpose—the formation of an experimental community along the general lines of Walden Two. This goal, though broad, does exclude many possible directions. The planner system is deliberately self-perpetuating in order to protect its original goals.

Another thing that Hal said and implied over and over, and which we have heard again and again from other members since that time, was that the board of planners was grossly incompetent. We have, of course, replaced the officers on the board of planners many times since then, but the accusation was as prevalent last year as it was in 1968. Both Hal and his counterparts since have sensed that planners are chosen for some elusive quality that for some reason was found lacking in them, the accusers, but they cannot put their finger on what that quality is. In exasperation they hit on incompetence as the characteristic of all our appointments.

But this time they are wrong, and in their assumption of the kinds of competence a board of planners ought to have, they reveal a concept of leadership very foreign to the low-key kind of management we are aiming for. It is perfectly true that our boards of planners have typically been less competent than many nonplanners in such areas as economic planning, engineering, mechanics, architectural planning and building skills, product development, etc. Hal, and later Simon and others, saw the Community as a hierarchy—the general membership at the bottom, the managers over them, and the planners over the managers. Seen in that light, it is incongruous that the people on top of the pyramid should know less than the people below them. It seems like a classic case of misplacement, and the obvious thing to do is to reverse those positions, putting the most knowledgeable people on top.

But a Walden Two community is not a hierarchy. Nobody is on top of anybody. The job of decision-making requires decision-making skills, just as the job of salesman requires selling skills. The plannership is not a position to be awarded to the manager who rates promotion, any more than a managership is a promotion for a regular member with good behavior. Managerships are positions of responsibility and trust. A dairy manager needs skill in dairying, or at the very least a willingness and interest in learning it. Planners are just managers of miscellaneous decisions that don't come under other managerships. The job requires agility of mind, reasonableness of judgment, commitment to the goals of the Community, and sharp self-awareness. Except in necessary decisions that commit the Community's cash and labor resources, it does not in any real sense have power over the membership. It does not give orders. It has no power to legislate anything that the group as a whole does not want, no means of enforcement except persuasion. It does not deserve, expect, or want prestige. Planners are in every sense regular members of the Community, subject to their own regulations and serving without compensation. We have never had a board of planners that failed to discharge its duties with conscientious care. The charge of incompetence falls wide of its mark, because it imputes to the job what the job was never intended to have. Furthermore, the accuser invariably marks himself, by his accusation, as misunderstanding the purpose of the plannership. This in turn makes us fearful that such a person would abuse the position if he had it, so he never gets it. The biggest reason that Hal never became a planner is that he revealed his intense desire for the job. We couldn't help asking ourselves, "What does he want it for?"

At the bottom of the anger on this subject is the assumption that the person who can do intellectual work like decision-making is somehow better than one who has difficulty thinking straight, and that an appointment to a job that requires thinking therefore merits and gets prestige based on that evaluation. We come from a society that values brain above brawn. Recognizing this as a prejudice which is detrimental to an egalitarian society, we are determined to do away with it, if possible in one generation. Brain may at times be more needed than brawn is, in which case intelligence is a useful thing. If some people are more useful than others, then let them serve more. We want a society that rejoices in the useful and enjoyable talents of its members without according to anyone prestige or honor on account of them.

One thing that gets us into trouble is the word "planner." It readily lends itself to phrases like "If you're a planner, why don't you do some planning?" We thought about changing the name to something like "coordinator," but our sentimental attachment to *Walden Two* won out over this inconvenience, so we still use the term. Planning, however, is and should be done by all those capable of doing it, and that will vary according to what is being planned. Hal certainly did his share of planning. It was he who decided (by supplying the money) that we would drill a new well and buy a cub tractor, that we would build a large frame workshop, and what it would look like. Fred, for his part, decided that we would invest our money and labor heavily into farming, and particularly into pigs and ducks. As to the planners, we never in those early days had a word to say about our buildings or industries. We contented ourselves with planning our social institutions—the labor credit system, the behavioral code, the planner-manager system. These things, like Hal's well and shop building, are still with us.

XXII

What Do You Do for Recreation?

If the foregoing chapters make it sound as if Twin Oaks is
in constant turmoil and tension, it is probably because I am
trying to make this book interesting. Peace and happiness
are great to live but nothing to write about. So for interest's
sake I have concentrated on the conflict, and the resulting
presentation of Twin Oaks is badly unbalanced. At the risk
of dullness, therefore, I am devoting this chapter to cheerful
things and hope that the message comes across—conflict notwithstanding, we have a very good life here. If we aren't
Utopia, we are still happier than most people.

Take the physical environment. I used to think that communes ought to be rural rather than urban primarily because
it costs too much to live in the city, whereas in the country
the group can grow its own food and work toward self-
sufficiency. I am less sanguine about self-sufficiency now.
But I still think communes are better off in the country,
mostly because of the sheer pleasure of being there. Clean
air and clean water offer a good argument, but what I value
most is the pleasure of taking long, solitary walks. Though
there are forty people on the premises most of the time at
Twin Oaks, any of us can be alone in a minute just by going
for a walk. The woods are beautiful. Even the roads are
quiet. Some members do jogging regularly. Others go on

camping trips or just overnight sleep-outs. We are all out-of-doors for large portions of every day.

Being indoors isn't bad, either. Our buildings are not beautiful (architectural planning is still ahead of us; we put up the cheapest, fastest structures we could make), and there are gross faults in them, but they cover the basics. They are sturdy, heated, ventilated, screened. Half of the members have small private rooms. The rest of us have roommates, but even so can often find privacy in our rooms.

The electrical wiring is adequate; the plumbing works most of the time, and if it doesn't, our maintenance people are working on it full-time until it is fixed. The laundry and mending services the Community provides for the individual are pretty good. Meals are usually tasty, and there is always enough to eat. Cleanliness is a problem, but we do enough cleaning so that chaos doesn't ever quite overtake us. In short, our physical environment, if not luxurious, is generally satisfactory. It is not up to the American standard, but it is well above the worldwide average.

I admitted that our buildings are ugly. I say that because the newer members assure me that it is true. As one who was here when they were built, though, I don't feel that ugliness. I did a lot of construction work on our first structure in 1967, and I certainly was not thinking I was contributing to a blemish on the landscape when I pounded nails into roof shingles or put together an interior wall. I was thinking that pretty soon we would have good, solid shelter and get our members out of the barns. That was beautiful to me.

Construction is usually cheerful work, anyway. Members used to climb up on the rafters of our latest building during its construction and examine the view, deciding whether or not they wanted to live on the second floor. An unblemished slab is fun, too. We have a photograph of Jenny doing an Israeli dance on the slab before anything was constructed on it. It was a magnificent dance floor. I look forward to the time when we can afford to construct a floor and leave it open for dancing.

Lack of a dance floor hasn't kept us from dancing, though. We just use the lawn. It isn't a great dance floor, but it will do until something better comes along.

It was a little difficult overcoming prejudices against square dancing. There were people who felt it was just too square, and others who objected to its cultural content, especially its message of male chauvinism. "Why do we always have to promenade to the *gent's* home," the women wanted to know. In their determination to take the sting out of the sexual roles that square dance calls imply, the dancers did away with the distinctions altogether. The women would on occasion take the gents' places, and some of the ladies were men. This was probably good for our culture, but it made a mess of the dance. Nobody could remember who was what, and the calls didn't make much sense. A better approach would be to change the calls themselves, easily done if someone just takes the time and trouble.

In folk dancing it was easier to erase sex distinctions. The dancers just became "innies" and "outies," and left the dances themselves intact. Sometimes the teacher would comment, "It's better in this dance for the taller person to be the innie," but in most dances it made remarkably little difference.

Dancing is typical of the organized activity patterns at Twin Oaks. We will start something, keep it up for several weeks, then let it drop as we get bored with it, or the teacher does, or some competing activity comes along. Besides the various encounter group activities I have already mentioned, which follow this same pattern of initial enthusiasm and gradual death, we have had a good variety of activities. Life drawing has been a popular one. We have no lack of models. Almost anyone in the Community will pose for the class. The woman who leads this group makes a point of inviting people to join the class, even if they don't think of themselves as talented. It is difficult to overcome our feelings of inadequacy (I never could draw anything), but it is well understood at Twin Oaks that drawing and the other arts are pursued for the fun of doing it, and that we are not competing with each other in technical excellence or anything else. In the same spirit we have had classes in copper enameling and pottery.

The choir lasted a long time—almost a year with hardly a session missed. We sang traditional hymns in four parts. To sing in the choir, you had to be able to carry a part and have a little skill in reading music. We started a class to teach people these elementary skills. It turned out to be a class on How to Carry a Tune. This skill definitely can be taught, and it was going well for a while. Like everything else, it petered out after a few sessions.

You will recall that Fred used to grumble because he could not have five dollars a week for his private allowance spending. This was during a period when our total expenditure per person per year was less than seven hundred dollars. Two years later our financial condition had improved sufficiently that we decided to institute a recreation budget to buy things like art materials and sports equipment. To this purpose we allotted five dollars a month. The fund has bought a rod and reel, bought oars for the rowboat, rented two films, and paid transportation for the group to attend a music festival. These were all worthwhile uses of the recreation money. But the most fun we ever got for our money was the purchase of a volleyball.

We had some doubts about volleyball. Brian worried about its competitive spirit. I didn't. "Look at it this way," I said. "Each team is having the fun of meeting a challenge, and each team provides a challenge for the other team to meet. You're trying to see if you can pick the ball up from any place on the court and get it to the other side. The other side tries to make it difficult for you." Brian said that sounded all right, but why keep score?

We bought the volleyball and set up the net. During the

first game two traditions were set: no score-keeping, and full-court rotation. The game started, and someone started to call the score, but Jenny shouted out, "Oh, we aren't going to keep score, are we?" The other players, not knowing on what philosophical grounds to defend their desire to compete, followed her lead. Someone else suggested that it might be fun to have no set teams, but rotate entirely around the court on both sides of the net, so that your opponents one minute are your teammates the next. Competition still survives in the form of individuals showing off for each other, but even that is tempered by group pressure to pass the ball around. We have been playing volleyball almost daily for nearly a year now, and it is not a competitive game any more. It is by far the most popular group activity we have ever had, and the most enduring. It is played by men and women together, and it also serves as one of the better ways for members and visitors to get acquainted. Visitors, incidentally, quickly conform to the Community social norms in the game. Extreme show-offs and ball-hogs are not common, and their activities are met by silence when they occur. It doesn't take long to catch on. Other activities are sometimes stopped by weather, but people play volleyball right after a rain, the ball spattering mud in their faces as they hit it. Only darkness stops the games, and that only when it is literally too dark to see the ball. Some people have tried to play by sound, but it is difficult.

Might it be possible to make other traditional games non-competitive? Would they still be fun? How about tennis? Baseball? Monopoly? Maybe it would be easier to invent our own games.

The one recreational activity that has sustained itself without ever losing the group's interest is swimming. We are fortunate to have a farm that borders a small river. Sometimes the river disappoints visitors, because it is not clear but the muddy brown of the agricultural land through which it winds. Color notwithstanding, it provides excellent swimming. During the hot summers all the members use the river just to cool off. A swim twice a day makes the temperature just bearable in June and July. There are several trees that grow on the river's banks, most of them leaning far out over the water. These make good diving towers for the adventurous, and we have also rigged up ropes from which to swing into the water.

Many of the academic subjects which the outside world calls "education" are judged at Twin Oaks to be "recreation." I cannot exaggerate how this fact offends lecture audiences in the colleges I have visited. They ask questions like, "Would you pay for the education of one of your members who wanted to go to college?" and the reply is, "It depends on what was being studied. We might decide to pay for someone learning medicine or law or accounting, but not liberal arts—our recreation budget isn't big enough." The words "recreation budget" are fighting words to the students who are investing large chunks of their lives in those very subjects that our Community classifies as nonessential. What they don't understand is that we have a very high opinion of recreation. Most of what we put in that classification is what the Good Life is all about—art and music, love and friendship, literature and history, camping and flower-gardening, sports and games. We value all of those things and we want to have time for all of them. We have declined to value some of them higher than others. Therefore we do not give either money or labor credits to someone who spends his time, for example, studying the dialogues of Plato, any more than to the person who spends his time making love. Each is doing what he wants to do. Both are contributing to the cultural richness of Twin Oaks. The things we pay money or labor credits for are the things that we must have to survive—the things that bring us money or that are judged necessary (like dishwashing) for our physical comfort.

We have not as a group always agreed on this subject, and I personally once thought that the study of traditional academic subjects (the ones that require a lot of work) should be encouraged at the expense of activities like taking walks or reading a novel. But years of community living have changed my mind. I see my former attachment to the traditionally valued academic subjects as very arbitrary and heavily influenced by prestige considerations that no longer have any power to influence me. As time passes and I more and more believe that Twin Oaks will survive for a long time, I am more and more ready to find out and pursue just those activities that really are good, i.e., fun, stimulating, rewarding. The decision here is not in favor of short-term over deferred gratification; it is in favor of intrinsic rather than prestige-related satisfaction.

Under these conditions, it is interesting to see which intellectual and artistic pursuits do indeed attract and hold Community members. We have had classes (keep in mind that classes are always requested by the student; the teachers are paid labor credits for teaching) in the following subjects: plane geometry, world history, history of the Renaissance, shorthand, typing, guitar, recorder, flute, singing, folk dancing, square dancing, yoga, chemistry, advanced French, beginning and intermediate Spanish, and English composition.

Simon once got angry because Naomi was claiming credits for teaching Jenny to play the guitar, and Jenny was claiming credits for teaching Naomi to play the recorder. As Simon saw it, it was an abuse of the system, and he thought the planners were letting them get away with it because the girls were our personal favorites. He demanded that under the same theory, he be given labor credits for teaching classes in lovemaking. This demand reached me (as Education Manager) through the Bitch Box. I wrote back, "I think your demand is perfectly reasonable. If you can find a student who wants to take lovemaking lessons from you, the Community will give you labor credits." I heard nothing more about it.

Getting back to the classes we do find students for, our

experience to date is that most of them survive no more than five or six sessions, and many of them not that long. Longest lived have been choir and folk dance. Our data are not precise, but my observation is that classes tend to last longest when the teacher is enthusiastic about the subject and wants to teach it. Classes are so small here (from one to six persons) that the students quite often feel diffident about asking for a teacher's time, even if the teacher is "paid," unless the teacher himself is enthusiastic. In the case of chemistry, for example, it was Pete, the teacher, and not Jenny, the pupil, who put a stop to the classes. He was very busy with the cattle and did not like to take the time out for what he sensed was basically irrelevant to Jenny's life, his own, and (at that point) the Community's.

We have some members who have successfully engaged in independent study, as well as a lot who have tried it and failed to keep at it. Certainly both Dwight and Brian pursued reading courses (in their case, revolution) without any encouragement from anybody else. A similar reading program in Women's Liberation material was followed by Sheila and Katherine for several weeks—with similar results, i.e., they left the Community. But there are other, less dismal cases of independent study. Leif, already a trained ornithologist, became interested in the study of trees after coming here. He and another member have collected specimens of leaves, flowers, and seed pods, and have made exhibits for the rest of the Community to see. At least three members have taught themselves to play musical instruments and now play them well.

A project that has given pleasure to the whole Community is our "radio" station, which a group of members have installed in our buildings. It is not radio at all, but a one-way wired intercom system, which broadcasts the news, both Community and outside (national and international) every night at ten. A lot of members like to listen to the broadcast, even if they can find out the same information by check-ing the bulletin board.

In contrast with much of the communal movement, Twin Oaks has been to date somewhat anti-ritual. We have spurned the traditional holidays. Christmas is simply a season during which half the members have to go home and see their parents. Thanksgiving we have transformed into Harvest Festival. Like the rest of the nation, we celebrate it by stuff-ing ourselves. We also have Anniversary Day—the sixteenth of June. But once again, all we can think of to do on this memorable day is eat a lot of good things and take off from some of our regular work. What else is there to do? Give speeches about our glorious founders? Hardly. Someone once suggested that we start a tradition of taking a hike around the perimeter of the premises once a year on Anniversary Day. It's a good idea, but we haven't done it yet. Someone is bound to ask, "Why today? If it was a fun thing to do, we would have done it."

Nevertheless, ritual has its advocates. This year there is a small group that likes the atmosphere of religious ritual, and they have organized an institution called "the sweat." For a sweat, you need a sweat hut, and these members built one on their own time with materials on hand. It is a small round structure, partly dug into the ground and partly covered with saplings, burlap, and polyethylene. The polyethylene is to keep the steam in the hut. The burlap is to cover up the plastic, because it is considered ugly. In a small pit in the center of the hut are placed stones heated in a fire outside. Water poured onto the stones fills the hut with steam. That, together with eight or a dozen people huddled around in-side, raises the temperature. The sweat-hut people dislike having their device called a sauna. "Sounds like a damned hotel," they say. After the sweat, the overheated participants jump into the river (located handily a few feet away) and cool off.

One day I saw a note on the bulletin board announcing a

sweat and specifying "ritual atmosphere desired." I asked whether this was not discriminatory. What if somebody wanted to get all hot and then all cold but didn't care for ritual? The answer satisfied me. "It's a matter of work," I was told. "The sweat hut is there all the time, and anybody can use it. So if a group wants to get together and have a folk-singing sweat, or a poetry-reading sweat, or a punching each other and giggling sweat, all they have to do is organize it, and build the fire and get the stones hot, and prepare the hut. So far they haven't done that. What we like is a ritual atmosphere, a little chanting, and silence. If we do the work, we don't want anybody coming to our sweat and throwing water on their would-be girlfriends or whatever. It spoils it for us." Fair enough.

Part of Twin Oaks's intellectual life is centered on Community policy itself. There is always a minority of members who spend most of their waking hours thinking about the future of the Community and debating with each other about what steps ought to be taken next. The most used vehicle for discussion is the Opinion and Idea Board, on which members post papers containing their arguments on subjects relevant to the Community. It is there that we place our best arguments in favor of Selection or Nonselection, Standard of Living or Expansion, the necessity of private rooms, or the need for more positive reinforcement. I recall a paper entitled "Positive Reinforcement Is a Fraud," and another on the "Contradiction between Communism and Behaviorism." I have known people to laugh and shake their heads when I tell them that a popular intellectual recreation at Twin Oaks is the debate via the bulletin board, people writing papers to each other. But those who find it amusing are probably comparing it to similar activity on the outside, letters to Congressmen or the Editor, or suchlike. It must be kept in mind that people's opinions matter here. When we post a paper, it is because we hope and expect people to be influenced by the arguments in it. Policies are being made every day; our government is very much within our control. In other words, it is not just an intellectual game we are playing; the decisions that come out of those debates really do affect our lives.

XXIII

Experiments–Big and Little

"Hey, if you're an experimental community, where're your experiments?"

In one form or another we have heard this question over and over. We used to hear it more than we do now, probably because the cultural differences between Twin Oaks and the rest of the country are becoming more obvious as time goes on. I used to be exasperated by the question. Was not the whole community a grand experiment? What of the labor system? What about our whole determination to live as real equals, to do away with authority, hierarchies, and classes? What about the tremendous educational experiment that is going on here every day?

But I have come to understand that the question is simply a journalistic one. The questioner is saying, "Give me something simple and unusual that I can write about in my paper, something that catches the attention, remains in the memory, perhaps something that is easy to make fun of." In other words, it is not the real experiments that interest the journalist, but the trivia that catch the reader's eye.

Well, Twin Oaks has its share of cultural trivia. Twin Oaks Time, for instance. Back in 1967 when we were working on our first building, we found that we had difficulty making ourselves get up in the morning for an eight o'clock shift, and that by five in the afternoon it was beginning to get dark and cold and difficult to work. What we needed, obviously, was either some self-discipline or daylight saving time. We found the latter easier to come by. It was November, so the rest of the country was on standard time. We set our clocks ahead to see how we liked the effect. We liked it very well. It caused us to go to bed earlier and thus be able to rise earlier. We got more use out of the daylight hours. When spring came and the rest of the state went on daylight saving time, we set our clocks ahead still another hour, giving us a super-daylight time. We have continued the custom ever since, but it has nothing to do with construction any more. The biggest advantage turned out to be for outside workers. It takes an hour or more to drive to work, plus another hour for the van to drop off the individual members at their jobs. This would force them to get up at five in the morning if we were on the same time as Richmond. Since we are an hour ahead, our workers get to Richmond in no time at all— leaving at seven fifteen and arriving at seven fifteen. It takes two hours for them to get home, of course, but that gives them a realistic feeling about needing to get to bed on time. Meetings, which would otherwise be far too late for them, are at an hour such that they can reasonably attend them.

The system confuses us occasionally, especially when we have to meet buses. ("Did he mean he would be in at two o'clock outside time or Twin Oaks time?"—this makes a lot of difference if it happens to be two in the morning.) The Community uses the term "outside time," just as we say "outside jobs" or "the outside world." Anybody who slips and says "real time" is usually shouted down. An occasional visitor is shocked by our presumption in creating our own time zone. But most of them are pleased. It gives them something to tell their friends about.

A similar attention-getter, though less useful, was the air crib. I say "less useful" because we used it pretty much as any other crib would be used, and it was a lot more expensive. An air crib is a device invented by the author of *Walden Two*. Its purpose is to provide the baby with filtered, relatively germ-free air, and temperature control. It is basically a glass case with a thermostatically controlled heating unit. The baby should be able to sleep in it perfectly comfortably without any clothing but a diaper. An active baby should enjoy the freedom from clothing. The walls of the air crib are supposed to cut down somewhat on sound, also, keeping it quiet enough for baby to sleep while noisy things are happening around it.

We had a long planners' meeting about whether or not to buy one of these devices when we were expecting our first baby. The cost was about $250. It seemed an absurd expense, considering the marginal conditions the rest of us were living in. But we finally decided to go ahead with it, admittedly for symbolic reasons. As well as I can remember, I believe we said to ourselves something like, "We will feel more Waldon Twoish if we have an air crib." So we sent away for it, and it was ready for little Bonnie when she came home from the hospital.

But an air crib made by a commercial company is not at all the same thing Skinner invented. He did not have to consider how much it could be marketed for, and he used good materials. The commercial one was far inferior to the one pictured in *Cumulative Record*. The walls were made of flexible vinyl and snapped together. No child could have leaned against it to stand, nor is it likely that a child could have stood up on the stretched saran mattress, good though it was for taking care of the urine problems of the newborn. The "humidifier" turned out to be a dish of water and a fan, and the thermostat identical to the $5.95 one we could buy in our local hardware store. To top it off, the thermostat didn't work. We decided to send the commercial air crib back and build our own. It cost us nearly $100 for materials because of the use of expensive Plexiglas, but it was a nice, showy gadget when we finished. We, too, used a dish of water for a humidifier, and heated it with the unit from a radiant heater. An ordinary crib mattress served as the floor. We built plywood shelves underneath it for diapers and supplies. It had an intercom hookup to the mother's bedroom, so that she could be sure to hear if Bonnie cried at night. The Plexiglas did cut down on sound (the vinyl hadn't at all). Bonnie was warm, comfortable, and apparently perfectly happy in her goldfish bowl. And she was fully visible from all parts of the room. But the biggest plus by far was being able to take visitors into the nursery room and point to it. "And this is our air crib. You see this opaque Plexiglas window at this end is really a slide projection screen. The baby can make the slides change by pulling on this rattle." Visitors were impressed, but we had to disappoint them with the next line. "Unfortunately, Bonnie doesn't seem to be old enough yet to be interested. She hasn't pulled it yet."

We still have the air crib. It has been taken apart and stored in one of our barns waiting for our next newborn. Bonnie never did pull on the rattle to change the slide show. She and her mother left the Community before she got old enough.

Another petty cultural difference that I can think of is the Twin Oaks custom of name-changing. Actually this habit has a theoretical base. We are not interested in the nuclear family. When couples join the Community, we treat each of the parties to the marriage as individuals. We never say "John and his wife," for instance. We don't believe in private property much, anyway, and one person's owning another is the grossest kind of ownership there is. So we have entirely dropped the use of last names. We are just Bill and Joe and Joann and Mary. So what happens when we have a Mary in the Community and another Mary wants to join? We don't have any rules about it, but we generally expect the second Mary to change her name. Most people are delighted. "I have always wanted to change my name," they say.

This is one of the few places in the world where one can change one's name and get cooperation from others in making it stick. Of the forty members on the farm as I write this, ten of them are known by names they chose themselves when they got here. Some of them changed for no reason except their own taste. John became Matthew, Sandra became Rosemary, and Margaret became Maggie just out of personal whim. Others change because of the duplication problem. Once we had three Dicks on the farm, and they all changed their names. We got a Gideon and a Cross and a Zeke out of it, and left the name Dick free for some member-to-be who might be attached to it.

The only trouble with name-changing is distributing the mail and relaying telephone messages. A member will pick up the phone and tell a puzzled and frustrated parent that "we don't have anybody here named Irving Feinstein." And indeed we don't. He changed his name to Chaucer.

The major important area for scientific experiment is, of course, the behavior of the members. The first attempt to interest the group in self-improvement came from Brian in 1967. He wrote a paper on self-control and called the group together to read it aloud. I found the paper in the files the other day and read it. It is excellent. In it Brian went briefly over all the known techniques for changing behavior, with short examples and comments on their applicability to group problems. But at the time Brian lacked the ability to translate what he was saying into practical programs, and the rest of us didn't really understand him. Nothing happened at all.

The second thing that happened was Psychology Class. This was in 1969. Brian, admitting that he didn't know a great deal, offered to share what he did know about psychology with the rest of us if we cared to form a class. We thought it sufficiently important to award labor credits for attending, and the class was very successful. "Do you understand classical conditioning?" asked Brian's review after the second class. "Then you should be able to: (1) remove a child's fear of the dark; (2) remember things at the appropriate time; (3) eliminate stagefright; (4) cure stuttering; (5) cure impotency or frigidity; (6) cure bedwetting; (7) eliminate your fears of certain objects or situations; (8) break or make habits that seem involuntary; (9) reduce pain that is related to tense muscles, such as childbirth; (10) control whether you like or dislike such things as books, certain music, certain people, certain topics of conversation, certain kinds of art, work, or recreation. . . . Next week: Operant Conditioning, or How to Rule the World."

Both Jenny and I, who were among Brian's students in this class, felt tremendous excitement about what we were learning. I remember that we looked at each other with wonder and awe and said, "We can do anything, anything."

One of our couples did put classical conditioning to work in an attempt to cure an old problem of sexual impotence, with complete and immediate success. And Sheila made great strides in curing her fear of the dark. But most of us did very little with the information. Using it requires time and work, and there was much else to do.

Behavior graphs became a Twin Oaks fad for a while, and there are still spurts of it now and then. It is sufficiently popular that we found it economical to print up our own graph paper, because it is marked off in seven square blocks for seven days in a week, instead of the usual five.

Suppose I were trying to control my temper. My first task would be to define what I meant by temper. I might decide that I mean popping off with sarcastic comments or nasty put-downs or impatient, exasperated outbursts. The first week or so of my campaign, I would not try to change my behavior at all. I would just simply count the number of times in a day that I caught myself saying nasty things. Each night I would mark the number on a piece of graph paper. A week or two of just counting gives me a baseline from which to work. The third week I would start trying to control the behavior and watch what happened to the graph.

At one time there were about eight of us graphing various behaviors at one time. Some of the things we were graphing were difficult to keep track of because they occurred many times in a day. Brian once kept track of the number of drinking glasses he used and the number that he returned to the kitchen to be washed. This was in response to a criticism that he left dirty glasses all over the Community. This counting required some device for keeping track during the day. A psychologist friend, interested in what we were doing, sent us some expensive golf counters that can be worn on the wrist. You just push a button and it keeps track of the number of pushes. We have also used knitting stitch counters. But the simplest and cheapest thing has been simple beads on a string. People who are counting various behaviors at the same time developed pieces of jewelry involving several strings with different colored beads.

The reward for this kind of project is largely contained in the new behavior itself. That is, if I really learn to control my temper, I will probably find I have more friends, and if Brian brings all his drinking glasses back to the kitchen, he will stop feeling guilty for contributing to Community chaos. But most of us found that the graph itself was a reward. Watching the rate go down in response to our efforts was definitely reinforcing. We tried to increase the rewarding capacity of the graphs by getting together as a group and comparing graphs, patting each other on the back for improvement. But this was not successful. The meetings were too boring.

In fact, graphing itself has proved successful only for a very few people. Almost everyone has tried it, but most people do not care enough about it to be reinforced by it.

Self-control projects are more interesting when several

people are involved in them. We once did a project which we officially called SeMan (for self-management) but which rapidly became known as the M&M Project. We started by agreeing (just a few of us) that we wanted to help keep the house cleaner and we did not want to contribute to messiness. We wanted to learn to pick up after ourselves. It is difficult to remind yourself to clean up, but it is easy to notice sloppy behavior in other people. So we agreed to serve as monitors on each other's behavior. If, for example, I got up from the lunch table and left my pudding dish behind, another member would say to me, "Hey, give me an M&M for your pudding dish." Then I would return to the table, pick up my pudding dish and put it away, and give my reminding friend an M&M candy. Of course this involved all participants buying M&M's out of their tiny allowances, and it also encouraged more candy-eating than we could afford, but it worked for a while. This project, like all others we have done, has been for volunteers only, which insures cooperation but doesn't always hit the mark. (What if the sloppiest people won't play?)

Another behavior-change game was called BITS (which stood for Behavior Improvement Token System). Little cardboard tokens were made up, and Community members were requested to award them to certain members who were trying to modify some behavior. One wanted us to give him a token every time he smiled. Another wanted the tokens as a silent reminder each time we heard him bitch in public. Both members kept graphs of the number of tokens they received. The tokens were not exchangeable for anything.

Do we take all this seriously? We do and we don't. We know very well that the games we make up are dealing very simplistically with complicated behavior and that we do not really control the genuine reinforcers at all. I suspect that what really goes on behind these projects is the desire to be liked and approved of. If we succeed in changing an undesirable behavior, splendid. If we don't, at least the group knows that we are not defending the behavior but are making an attempt to change it. It makes a difference in the way we feel about each other.

XXIV

Breakthrough

This has been mostly the story of the first two years of Twin Oaks's life. Hal and Dwight and Brian and Fred have all been gone a long time. The people who have taken their places are hardly mentioned in this narrative. These are my friends now, and they hear me tell these stories of the beginning with a certain amount of puzzlement. There is a contrast between what I write about and what we live. Things somehow run more smoothly now. No one withholds paychecks or refuses to do outside work. We are not likely to forget to tell incoming members the rules about communal housing. We wouldn't even consider accepting a child without working out first a plan for the child's care. Planners do not closet themselves and try to bear the Community's ideological problems alone.

And money isn't so tight. Cars don't get grounded for lack of parts; meat is served almost every day; there is paint on the walls; the new building we are planning is graceful as well as useful.

What happened? At what point did we become successful? Do we get a better kind of people now than we used to? Have we succeeded through selection? Through a shift in philosophy? Through compromise with our values? When did the breakthrough occur? And who was responsible?

Part of this seemingly dramatic change is just a literary problem. If I were to wait a few more years and then write the story of this year's events, the problems and conflicts we are now going through would be telescoped into major events, and the present members would become, like Brian and Dwight, characters in my narrative.

Just the same, there *was* a breakthrough. The date was December, 1969. It started with a change in our policy for accepting new members. Our membership was once again down to ten after being as high as twenty-two, and we were worried about it. The only thing we could think of to do was to take away the entrance-fee barrier. It was a worrisome step. It meant opening the door to people I was still referring to as hippies, people who might or might not have any interest in community. Anybody who said he wanted to stay could stay. We had to build up the membership.

"Let them come through," we said. I called a meeting of the members—I recall we all fitted easily around a small dining room table—and shared my worries with the others. "It means we might get just about anybody. People will come through just to stay a day, a week. They will live here and leave just before their outside work shift comes up. We will get people who can't or won't keep up their share of the work. It will be necessary for us to watch the newcomers, and to expel them swiftly if they won't earn their labor credits." The membership all nodded and said they understood and agreed that it was the only thing to do. We passed the new regulation, and sent out announcements with our newsletter telling people that lack of money need no longer stand in the way. Then we waited. For several weeks nothing happened, except that Dwight left, leaving us even lower than before.

Then Jere and Katherine came hitchhiking into our lives. A week later Joanne and Larry arrived, equally unexpectedly, then Ned, Leif, Barbara, Gideon, Arnie. We filled up our spare rooms rapidly. The labor quota went down. Morale went up.

As to their being irresponsible drifters, I have never made a worse prediction. None of these people fulfilled my dismal expectations. Almost all of them stayed at least a year. Several of them are still here. They, in their turn, provided a very cheerful atmosphere and outlook for the prospective members who came after them. What the newcomers saw was that we had been in existence for two and a half years and that we had a lot of good people. It looked like success. They wanted to join.

How much did lowering the fee barrier have to do with it? "I would have gone out and worked for it," says Jere. "I really wanted to join." Nevertheless, not having to impose that delay must have helped us build our membership in a hurry.

Something was happening on the Outside, too. Discontent among the young at their opportunities was causing more and more of them to seek a communal way of life. Publicity for and against communes also started being prevalent at this time.

These new members who joined Twin Oaks at this critical time did not feel, however, that they were saving Twin Oaks. I was probably the only member to sense that we were experiencing a breakthrough. I went around saying to myself, "We're going to make it; we're really going to make it at last." But the new people didn't know they were saviors. They fitted into community patterns and norms that were already well established. Labor systems, government, outside work rotation, Bitch Box and Criticism sessions all gave a distinct form to their new communal life. What had been established with struggle became natural with the new crowd.

It was a combination of new enthusiasm and old forms that made 1970 and 1971 so much smoother than the preceding years. It is not a question of the new people being better. (Better than Dwight? Pete? Brian? There are no better people.) It is simply a matter of being new and not worn down by the initial battles that were required in order to establish the unique equalitarian institutions of this community.

It isn't easy to build a community. You have to want it a whole lot, and you have to be prepared to end up with different people from the ones you started with. But it is possible. All we really had to offer in 1967 was a piece of lovely rural land and a share of the Big Dream. Four years later we can offer a good-sized slice of the Good Life, if you're not hung up on material things. In a few years more, we will probably have a fair material standard as well.

Maybe four years isn't long enough for us to say confidently that we are succeeding as a community, but most Twin Oaks members feel that we are. Sometimes we ask ourselves why. We had a lot going against us.

We didn't have any money to start with; we were heavily dependent on the skills of one member; we had our heads full of autocratic notions of government; half of our original members weren't dedicated to our principles; most of us didn't know each other before we started, and a lot of us didn't trust each other; we knew nothing about techniques for solving interpersonal problems; there wasn't a truly charismatic leader among us, a situation that naturally led to leadership struggles; we knew nothing of farming or business or any other way of making a living; we believed in sexual freedom and therefore opened ourselves to mating competition and bitter jealousies; we never had a common religion, common community experience, or even a common enemy.

Any one of those things could have killed us. The combination was almost certain to. How is it that we have survived?

I am not sure, but I think the answer to that question is just that we didn't give up. Every time we lost a valuable member, the people who were left kept on working, hoping for better times. That work eventually accumulated a little capital, tools, buildings. New members built on the unfinished projects of those who left, and after a while we had enough tools to work with, some space to work in, some experience to solve our problems with. The people who came in 1970 and 1971 built on the skeletons, so to speak, of the earlier members. Life isn't as grim for them as it was for their predecessors.

Jenny and I are the only ones left of the original eight. Jenny has been in and out three times, so in a way I am the only one left. But no particular credit is due me for sticking it out. I stayed because I cannot imagine myself doing anything else. If there's any credit to be given, it goes to the people who drained themselves trying to make Twin Oaks work for them, and finally didn't make it—but left behind the fruit of their expended energy. I mean Dwight, Fred, Pete, Hal, and Brian, as well as a number of other people whom I remember less but who nevertheless also worked and contributed to Twin Oaks and who also left without ever cashing in on the Good Life.

Experience is certainly a valuable thing, but sometimes lack of experience can be an asset. The people who have joined in the last two years do not, for example, experience an automatic sinking feeling when a prospective member suggests bringing a house trailer, or see visions of Hal behind every Carolina accent. Hard-line versus soft-line decisions are fresh for them to decide, not poisoned by memories of Simon spending Community money on beer and justifying it as a special need. Issues are issues to them, not Fred-problems or Gwen-isms.

It would be an exaggeration to say that Twin Oaks has succeeded as a commune. After all, we still have to send members on outside work detail in the city, and we still lose members to the outside world. Our apparent success is only in comparison with communes that have folded, and with our apparent chances those first two doubtful years. We are succeeding as a local institution, our neighbors accepting us with very little hostility. We are on our way to being successful as a culture, though it will take a children's program to establish that beyond doubt. The state of our finances gets steadily better, and our turnover is slowing down.

Where do we go from here?

We are back to the grow-split-grow-split theory. As long as we can continue to attract members, we expect to keep growing in size. What the optimal size is we do not know and maybe won't know until we reach it. When we get there, we'll send a core cadre from our community to form a new one, this time with the security of Twin Oaks behind it, as well as our accumulated experience and skills.

Or if such security seems to lack adventure, there is nothing to stop a splinter group from breaking off sooner and establishing a sister commune, perhaps with slightly different ideas. We might have a hard-line commune and a soft-line commune, an expansionist group and an exclusivist one. Maybe the next group can take consensus procedure seriously as a form of government. They will have their own set of problems, but they will avoid the ones we had.

There is no end to where we can go from here. Dwight used to say that if the commune movement ever got big, the Government would close it down. That's his guess. Mine is that it won't. My guess is that we can keep growing until we run out of people who would be better off than they are now if they went communal. That time is a long way off.